# Investigating Audiences

*Andy Ruddock*

SAGE Publications

Los Angeles • London • New Delhi • Singapore

First published 2007

Apart from any fair dealing for the purposes of research or
private study, or criticism or review, as permitted under the
Copyright, Designs and Patents Act, 1988, this publication
may be reproduced, stored or transmitted in any form, or by
any means, only with the prior permission in writing of the
publishers, or in the case of reprographic reproduction, in
accordance with the terms of licences issued by the Copyright
Licensing Agency. Enquiries concerning reproduction outside
those terms should be sent to the publishers.

SAGE Publications Ltd
1 Oliver's Yard
55 City Road
London EC1Y 1SP

SAGE Publications Inc.
2455 Teller Road
Thousand Oaks, California 91320

SAGE Publications India Pvt Ltd
B 1/I 1 Mohan Cooperative Industrial Area
Mathura Road
New Delhi 110 044

SAGE Publications Asia-Pacific Pte Ltd
33 Pekin Street #02-01
Far East Square
Singapore 048763

**British Library Cataloguing in Publication data**

A catalogue record for this book is available from the British
Library

ISBN 978-1-4129-2269-2
ISBN 978-1-4129-2270-8 (pbk)

**Library of Congress Control Number: 2006937886**

Typeset by Cepha Imaging Pvt. Ltd., Bangalore, India
Printed in Great Britain by Cromwell Press
Printed on paper from sustainable resources

*For Christine Ruddock*

# Contents

# Acknowledgements

Thanks go to Martin Barker, Sarah Edwards, Kristyn Gorton, Julia Hall, Jenny Kitzinger, Alan McKee, Dianne Railton & Helen Wood for their help in guiding the direction of this book. I'm also grateful to Alan, Thomas Austin, Matt Hills and Cornel Sandvoss for giving me access to much of their important work before it was generally available in public.

Christine Ruddock, Jo, Colin, Alec & Jason Stratton, Jessica Asato & Gareth Butler, Tim Dunn, Michael Higgins, Keith Marley, Krista Puranen and Ben Watkins provided less formal help, which was of course far more important. *Nice one.*

# Introduction

In the winter of 2005/6, the UK news was awash with stories detailing the social havoc wreaked by media; teenager Luke Mitchell was jailed for the inhuman slaughter of 14-year-old Jodi Jones, a murder that the police felt may have been inspired by a Marilyn Manson video. Fighting erupted between Everton and Manchester United supporters, following a late afternoon football match that had left plenty of space for all day drinking. The reason for the 5.30 p.m. kick off? Television scheduling. Across the Atlantic, saturation coverage of the Michael Jackson child molestation case led many to question if justice was possible in a trial enveloped in celebrity frenzy. Anecdotally, the signs of media influence are ubiquitous to the point of redundancy: Querying *if* media have impact is a bit like asking if cars are faster than they used to be. Of course the answer is yes. The question is not 'do', but 'how', 'where' and 'for whom'?

However, these puzzles are just as difficult to answer empirically, and demand the monumental leap from what we think we know about effects to what we can research and demonstrate as scholars. Media power is hard to find mostly since it is hard to define. Do we find it in thoughts or behaviours? Does it happen instantly, or over a long period of time? Is it possible to distinguish media from other sorts of social influence? If not, how are we to account for their cultural importance? Crucially, what sort of evidence do we need, and what sort of information are we in a position to gather? In practice, these questions are so convoluted that once we explore them academically rather than instinctively, each becomes a sub-discipline.

As some readers might know, I have raised these subjects before in 2001's *Understanding Audiences*. Only the names have changed in some of the introductory anecdotes; Michael Jackson has replaced OJ Simpson, but the principle remains. This book is *not* a revised edition; but neither can it be an entirely different project. A critical revision of the earlier volume's thesis helps to locate the rationale for the present work. Additionally, this introduction will map the flow of the book, explaining the particular course of its journey through a field of audience research traversable via numerous paths.

Academic writing in any discipline is a matter of pragmatism and strategy. First year undergraduate and university professor alike must constantly bridge the gap between the quantity of work that has been written on a topic, and the amount of time available to ingest it. In my own situation, I have decided to concentrate *Investigating Audiences* on a review of largely (but not exclusively) post-1999 research. I have chosen to do this since the last decade has seen many fine surveys of audience studies (Abercrombie & Longhurst, 1999; Brooker & Jermyn, 2002; Nightingale, 1996; Schroder et al., 2002). Given this state of affairs, it seemed the best course of action was to try to write a different sort of book. So, the contemporary focus I offer is intended as a contrast, but not a conflict, that draws on the reception and reconsideration of my earlier work.

And, I must acknowledge, this tactic bears dangers. Audience studies did not drop out of the sky at some time toward the end of the last century. So it is necessary to reprise the main arguments of *Understanding Audiences* to give a sense of why this project takes its present shape. In particular, this relates to the way that the nexus between media and social power is conceptualized, which in turn informs how this book deals with matters of method.

If I were forced to explain the earlier work with recourse to only two scholars, Stuart Hall and George Gerbner would be my selections. The major methodological argument made in *Understanding Audiences* was that quantitative methods had a role to play in the critical analysis of relations between culture, popular culture and social power. To illustrate, I argued that similarities in the way that Gerbner and Hall theorized the mass communication process manifested the error of equating the qualitative/quantitative distinction with that made by Lemert (1989) between critical and administrative research. That is, *Understanding Audiences* was researched and written at a time where many assumed that statistics based devices, such as surveys and experiments, were mostly used by scholars who accepted the existing distribution of political, economic and social power. Harold Lasswell, an early pioneer in North American Mass communication research which institutionalized the experiment and survey as the tools par excellence for understanding media and audience power, had written: 'among all who share the traditions of America, the problem is not whether democracy ought to live, but how' (1953: 1975: 469). To critical scholars like Stuart Hall (1982) and Todd Gitlin (1978) statements like this avoided more important questions such as what and who defined democracy, and what happened to the people living without its limits so established. This, in their eyes, reduced the study of media and audiences to the question of how an assumed democracy could be sold via the strategic manipulation of discrete messages, or how 'bad' media could upset society's balance. As a result, a systemic analysis of how media functioned as ideological vehicles was avoided.

Gerbner's cultivation analysis had been painted as part of the problem. Originating in a series of content analyses of primetime US television in the 1960s and 1970s, cultivation analysis pointed to survey-identified correlations between the prevalence of media violence and the tendency for heavy television viewers to believe that the real world was far rougher than was truly the case. That its numbers asserted danger perception increased with the hours a person spent in front of 'the box' led some to accuse Gerbner of resurrecting the 'hypodermic' effects theory, where audiences are powerless to resist incontrovertible media messages (Gauntlett, 1998; Wober, 1998). That it was initially funded by the US Surgeon General's Office who was eager to find a scapegoat for escalating social unrest in late 1960s America (Ball-Rokeach, 2001) coloured Gerbner's work in administrative hues.

Entering postgraduate education to explore cultural studies, which favours qualitative methods of explaining culture in action, I would probably have been happy to follow along with this critique, had I not enrolled in a PhD programme at the University of Massachusetts whose core requirements insisted that I should read the mass communications dinosaurs, Gerbner included. Grudgingly doing so, I was struck by similarities between cultivation theory and Hall's encoding/decoding model (1980), which was then commonly selected as the cornerstone for empirical audience research within British Cultural Studies. To begin, in their studies of the effects of television violence, Gerbner and his colleagues had reached the conclusion that the consequences of media representation had more to do with the stabilization of existing political power structures than the production of aberrant behaviours. Violence was:

A dramatic demonstration of the power of certain individuals (which led to) a tendency to assume high levels of violence; to acquiesce to the use of violence by others (and) ... a sense of fear and need for protection (Gerbner et al., 1978: 184).

This shifted the question of media influence toward the matter of how structural media relations tended to produce politically loaded visions of reality; time and time again:

Any message is a socially and historically determined expression of concrete physical and social relationships. Messages imply propositions, assumptions and points of view that are understandable only in terms of the social relationships and contexts in which they are produced. Yet they also reconstitute those relationships and contexts. Messages thus sustain the structures and practices that produce them (Morgan & Shanahan, 1996: 4).

Because media messages, as agents of already existent structures and beliefs, had the primary function of maintaining what is, rather than the production of change, so too it was necessary to revisit the logic of statistical interpretation. Faced with the criticism that cultivation analysis was founded on the location of relatively small differences between 'heavy' and 'light' television viewers, Gerbner and his team offered the following retort:

> The observable independent contributions of television can only be relatively small. But just as an average shift of a few degrees can lead to an ice age ... so too can a relatively small but pervasive influence make a crucial difference. The size of an effect is far less critical than the direction of its steady influence (Gerbner et al., 1980: 14).

The reason why this attracted my attention was that the arguments being made appeared entirely compatible with a cultural studies position. In the US, the move from mass communication to interpretive approaches to culture was signalled by James Carey's distinction between researching the ritual as against the informational function of communication. By the above quotes, cultivation clearly strode into the latter camp. However, in articulating this position within a concern for structural media relations, Gerbner & co also connected with Hall's interest in hegemony. The argument in both camps was that media power came in the form of winning consent for particular political arrangements via the social and economic relations of message production and circulation.

I felt that this was an important argument to make since the common-sense relations between quantitative methods and administrative questions appeared to ignore the historical context of mass communication during and after the Second World War. If scholars had been led by the interests of government and media industries, this was hardly surprising given the realities of research funding and the fact that many of them had been drafted into the US military to seek out the propaganda 'magic bullet' that would persuade GI s to fight (for an interesting account of this period, see Peters, 1996a; 1996b). Nor was Gerbner's failure to explore theoretical compatibility with European neo-Marxist scholarship especially shocking given his teaching position in a major US university in the 1950s and 1960s. This being the case, cultivation analysis played a major role in *Understanding Audiences* as a vehicle for arguing that quantitative methods were not inherently hostile to the idea and analysis of culture.

Several years on, that argument is accepted in both principle and practice (although I am not the only person who was making it; see for example Lewis, 1997). As we shall see, many important figures in the development of critical qualitative audience research have turned to the survey as a means of addressing the media's social relevance. Additionally, it is also worth noting that qualitative methods have become influential within the 'administrative'. Anthropologist Greg McCracken has built a lucrative career using ethnographic methods to tell corporations like Coca-Cola how consumers attach meaning to their product (2006). He argues that industry has become methodologically agnostic; it seems that media studies has adopted the same attitude.

However, there is another reason why I felt a new book rather than a second edition was in order. In the new empirical research I have been doing, I have found many of the ideas that emanated from the integration of Gerbner and Hall either unhelpful or inappropriate. In part, this is due to a certain contradiction in the way that power was conceived. Addressing the perceived clash between Hall's deployment of ideology, and Foucault's development of the idea of discourse, I had attempted a rapprochement in arguing that the latter encouraged the analysis of power through close empirical analysis of small case studies. However, as the book was largely a review of other people's research, in writing *Understanding Audiences* I was never forced to engage with what, pragmatically, this might mean. Recently, I have been involved in a number of studies on the phenomenon of anti-social behaviour and the way that it is publicly understood and discussed in the UK. This has involved working with many 'institutional' forces. In one meeting, the fear was expressed that media coverage of Asb was worsening the problem by creating a 'moral panic' around youth. The words did not come from my mouth, but were uttered by a high-ranking member of the local Fire Service. In this event, situating critical theory as something that exists outside of governmental institutions, or assuming a symbiosis of interest between media and state, would not have helped the project.

Of course, it is hardly reasonable to expect 30-year-old scholarship to map contemporary cultural geography. Gerbner was very explicit in stating that his work was tied to a US televisual context, where the medium was the vastly dominant game in town, tied to the relatively narrow range of production sites characterizing the broadcast era. This environment also complimented an encoding/decoding model heavily influenced by Louis Althusser's work on 'ideological state apparatus', which assumed goodness-of-fit between media and various forms of governance. So, the decision to centre *Understanding Audiences* on these ideas exacted a price. The book tended to cast power as a function of meaning in an explicitly ideological sense which detracted from the consideration of cultural relevance. It also tended to ignore other academic trajectories. In particular, the decision to argue for a certain symbiosis between mass communication and cultural studies diluted the space given to exploring issues in critical audience studies.

Matt Hills (2004) has written that scholarship often rests on matters of faith; rather like religious zealots, media academics have a belief in certain theorists and theories that, in practice, remain beyond analysis. In his exceptionally well written book on media and gender, David Gauntlett (2002) offers proof in stating that given the choice between believing that people are essentially good and want to do the right thing versus the reverse proposition, he prefers the former option. In the same spirit, my grounding in Gerbner and Hall means that I find it difficult not to be a 'glass is half empty' sort of researcher. However, by situating this book in the ideas and practical problems of current scholarship that appears less marked by 'grand narratives' of media influence, my goal is to present a study that challenges assumptions about audiences/media relations. The task is to unravel what we know. Loose ends are good things.

This book begins and ends with me. Or, to be more precise, with the sort of research I do, how I do it and why I do it *as an operator within an academic discipline.* That is, although the fact that I am writing this book influences the things that it says, at the same time what I study and what I say is affected by external forces; what are my colleagues interested in? How can I get into the conversation? What does society care about? How can I attract research funding by connecting with these concerns? And over and above this, how is it possible to say something meaningful about culture that someone, somewhere will find useful?

The following chapters make of scholarly conversations about media and audiences within the context of my own empirical studies. Readers may be struck by the attention I have paid to my own experiences in a book that is supposed to be about ways of doing research. Chapter one legitimates this decision by showing the importance of remembering that research is always conducted by a specific person in a particular place and time, while simultaneously establishing core questions that audience researchers are obliged to consider. Chapters two and three explore 'information' and 'meaning' as both central and problematic cornerstones in audience research. Although the former is often related to unhelpful 'transmission' communication models, I argue that recent developments in narrative based research return to normative questions about learning. This signals opportunities to re-engage with traditional questions about how media can edify, or rather enable inclusive public cultures; a question that is fundamental to all that follows. Chapter three develops this theme by exploring the political dimensions of entertainment. Here, politics is conceived as a broad reference to the processes through which audiences become social, even in apparently meaningless media experiences. To close the 'mapping' section of the book, the chapter on fan scholarship develops the idea of the political by framing fan discourses within the issue of democratic speech.

I then move on to more topic centred considerations, inspired by major subjects in the field and also my experiences of the sorts of questions that tend to get asked about the social impact of media. The intention is both to summarize these areas and suggest avenues for different approaches to the same topics, illustrated by some of my own projects. No audience scholar can avoid the topics of sex and violence. Critical scholars have usually taken the position that their primary role in these discussions is to look at the poverty of evidence claiming to show how pornography and violent media have negative behavioural consequences. Looking at relations between media use and perceptions of alcohol abuse in the UK, I argue that it is possible to draw connections between media violence and the development of unhelpful social attitudes without succumbing to behaviourist thinking. That is, one can accept that, for the reasons explored in chapters one to four, media influence is an uneven and often unobservable process, without concluding that it is impossible to engage with practical questions. Here, a critique of direct effects thinking is used to inform research on how drinkers use media to make sense of alcohol-related violence.

The chapter on celebrity and reality media draws on a project on public readings of 'star' politicians to show how the ideas developed on information, narrative, pleasure and citizen/fan parallels can be applied to the sphere of politics proper. Additionally, I argue that these topics are indicative of deeper issues in media theory relating to the shift toward a multimedia environment where distinctions between media and interpersonal communication are no longer as clear as they once were. This is important as it explains why the theoretical basis of *Understanding Audiences* is no longer adequate, given the fluidity of relations between the public and institutions, media and other.

What emerges from this is a decentred notion of media power grounded in the work of Nick Couldry. Couldry's idea that life should be seen as media related rather than media centred creates a challenge for the sorts of things that audience researchers should study. To explain, in the final chapter I show how this shift has influenced my work on young people and media. A current projects uses survey data, qualitative interviewing, participant observation and creative research techniques to study youth outreach programmes staged by an English regional fire service. One of the goals of these programmes is to reduce fire offending by improving lines of communication between firefighters and young people. The initial idea of the project was to examine how face-to-face contact could overcome problematic media representations of both groups. However, it has rapidly become clear that 'media' cannot be defined in opposition to other sorts of communication, not least because a) images of firefighting from television and film do not seem very important to the young people and b) media are used *in* the programme as a means of changing public perceptions of *both* the Fire Service *and* young people. This is important as the fire service's work is happening in the context of general public distrust of young people sparked by fears over anti-social behaviour. I end with this topic as an illustration of how the general themes identified in audience research feed into an actual research project, and how a multimethod approach is vital as any techniques that look good on paper can prove a spectacular disaster in the field. In this sense, *Investigating Audiences* takes an 'embedded' approach to method, dealing with practical issues as they arise from conceptual applications.

The path I have chosen reflects the fact that my training in mass communication has left an enduring interest in normative questions about communication and problem solving, particularly in the areas of electoral politics and public health. That is, I tend to study questions falling under the broad rubric of how media can be used as a basis for healthier, more inclusive public cultures. However, one cannot explore these issues without accounting for popular culture; areas of media that common sense would place beyond the bounds of learning and rational debate. So another way to think about the book's organization is to consider how the chapters on news and information, pleasure, fans and celebrity/reality expand the bounds of learning and what we understand to be the political, and the way that audiences engage with public debates. What these chapters do is establish the argument that although we should still expect media to function as learning resources, we need to understand that learning involves pleasure and emotion, and as such apparently trivial aspects of media culture, for good or ill, have an important impact on how we understand and participate in social life. In this, the intention is to direct some of the issues that scholars of the popular have pursued back toward the study of relations between media and democracy. As an example, from my perspective fan studies are useful as they allow us to reflect on the sorts of citizenship one can expect within today's media cultures. The point if asking these questions is to create a platform from which critical audience research can be seen to engage with matters of media and public policy.

# 1    Can I Write 'I' in an Essay?

## WHERE TO BEGIN?

**1.1** In a content analysis of major mass communication journals spanning the years 1956–2000, Bryant and Miron (2004) discovered that of the 1806 analyses of media matters sampled, 576 included 1393 references to a staggering 604 theories. Given this complexity, it is easy to see how audience research can appear a haphazard affair. Alternatively, we can appreciate the variety of conceptual and methodological opportunities in the field. But what we do have to recognize, pragmatically, is that the multiplicity of gateways to audience research means that circumstance and serendipity influence the questions that a researcher will ask, and the techniques that he or she will use to find answers. Think of this in terms of the 'Five Ws' often defined as the basic elements of a good news story: 'what' researchers study and 'why' they do so is influenced by 'who' they are, 'where' they are, and 'when' they are working. Yet this is a not particularly radical claim to make; it simply describes the reality of any 'expert' field. The 'Five Ws' indicate three questions that can be generally used as a starting point. What is it that we do not know about relations between audience and media? How do social, cultural, political and educational experiences influence the things we want to study? Where do the answers to these queries intersect?

The first question is inspired by Helen Nowotny's take on the fragility of expertise (2003). Referencing science, Nowotny argues that the contemporary world confronts the expert with a number of challenges. Now more than ever, he or she is publicly accountable; that is, he or she must communicate with audiences beyond the circle of fellow experts, and as such faces challenges from other sorts of authority. In the instance of genetics, by way of illustration, we recognize that moral and ethical issues often rank aside technical ones. For Nowotny, being an expert thus involves a certain abdication, where we publicly confess that we cannot provide quick, clear solutions to social enigmas. This has a direct relevance to a media studies discipline that addresses a number of sharp public concerns. What are video games doing to kids? Why are we so obsessed with celebrities? Have the media killed politics by talking about personalities rather than policies?

Under interrogation, the best and most useful responses can focus on what we *don't* know about public/media interactions.

In a sense, our task as scholars is to complicate understanding of what the media 'do'. Largely, this is due to the way that a number of contestable conclusions about media effects have passed unchallenged into the common sense of public opinion and media policy. Accordingly, this chapter will review a number of traditions within communications research that have set out to unravel not only what we apparently 'know' about audiences, but also the very act of scholarship. The term 'communications', rather than media, mass communications or cultural studies, is used for two reasons. First, it will become clear that mediated and non-mediated communications overlap; it is often difficult to tell where media end and everyday life begins. Second, many of the methods that have become popular in audience studies are rooted in other social research forms. Issues arising in these areas help media scholars to understand their own activities.

Appreciating the context of expertise is a vital part of 'unlearning'. It is easy to conceive scholarship as an anonymous process. Straying beyond the theories and methods to the *history* of communications scholarship, we discover that time, place and resources influence how we arrive at scholarly 'conclusions'. This chapter will consider what this means for the audience 'expert' by examining a question that undergraduates often direct at lecturers: 'Can I use "I" in an essay?' The answer is 'yes', as long as one understands that the 'I' here refers to the scholarly self, as a recognition of the responsibilities entailed in working within a certain academic parameters. However, while cultural studies has formed the vanguard for the foregrounding of academic subjectivity, I will also argue that in paying insufficient attention to the context of mass communications research, it has generated a number of erroneous conclusions about what scholars who use quantitative experimental and survey research are trying to do and say. Overcoming this prejudice by understanding the historical genesis of mass communications research expands the methodological opportunities open to critical audience researchers. Davison's theory of the 'third person effect' (1983) will be used in elucidation, as an example of a numerically based paradigm that sets out to further knowledge by deconstructing its own facts.

## AN OBVIOUS PLACE TO START: MEDIA AND BAD BEHAVIOUR

**1.2** Consider the following quote:

I'm 16, I love modern music and freedom of expression, but having listened to Eminem, I must say I was deeply disturbed, not by the language but the content.

He seems to be becoming an idol for those younger than me, a fact which I am not comfortable with. Should Eminem be banned? No. But stronger controls on the music that young children are allowed to buy need to be introduced. (Nigel, 2001) (news.bbc.co.uk/1/hi/talking_point/1158016.stm. Accessed 9 February 2005.)

Nigel's comments were a reaction to Sheffield University Student Union's decision to ban US rapper Eminem from their facilities during his 2001 UK tour. At the time, many had expressed concerns over his homophobic and violent lyrics. The BBC asked audiences how they felt about this decision, prompting Nigel's comments.

What would a cultural studies audience expert say to Nigel? How can we use his words as evidence in debates on media effects? With regard to the first question, Richard Butsch offers the following:

[cultural studies] focuses on actual audiences in natural settings rather than theoretically or laboratory constructed audiences. In situating audiences in their social and historical context, we may understand media use as well as contemporary interpretations of media use. This helps to highlight audience practices rather than media effects. It also helps to recognize that audience–medium interactions are embedded in other social relations and cultural practices (2003: 16)

Butsch's definition grounds the cultural studies critique of the idea that media have negative behavioural effects on certain sorts of 'weak' people. In its first edition, *Particip@tions* (the first academic journal to focus exclusively on audiences) published a review of the media violence controversy. Signed by a number of leading media scholars, the article contended that most quantitative experimental audience studies show no behavioural or causal relations between media and real world violence, and those that do are conceptually and/or methodologically flawed. Consequently:

researchers' attempts to reduce the myriad effects of art and entertainment to numerical measurements and artificial laboratory experiments are not likely to yield useful insights about the way that viewers actually use popular culture. Likewise, in a field as complex as human aggression, it is questionable whether quantitative studies can ever provide an adequately nuanced description of the interacting influences that cause some people to become violent. (*Particip@tions*, 1. www.participations.org/volume%201/issue%201/1_01_amici_contents.htm St. Louis Court Brief, 2003.)

Taken in combination, Butsch and the St. Louis collaborators cast audience research as a qualitative, interpretive exercise, involving the study of human subjects who are irreducible to sequences of objectively observable causes and effects. Applied to the Eminem comment, we might say that Nigel failed to consider the context in which younger listeners might have encountered the rapper. His lyrical focus assumed that children, or anyone, for that matter, were paying attention and, if so, comprehended what they heard.

Both assumptions are problematic. When Dr. Dre states: 'if I got my niner you know I'm straight trippin" on 1993's *Nuthin but a 'G' Thang*, I understand the words, but I have no idea what he is talking about.

Nigel's comments have significance, then, as part of the familiar tendency to displace effects onto other people, based on a number of unsubstantiated conclusions about how certain sorts of audiences relate to the media. It is, to use Karl Schoenbach's (2001) work, 'mythic'. Nigel accepted a number of contestable hypotheses about media effects as matters of fact. Reviewing centuries of apocalyptic predications on everything from the book to the internet, Schoenbach identifies a number of recurrent themes which are:

- A desire to discern clear cause and effect sequences.
- A focus on *negative* influence, from Plato's fears that reading would destroy memory, to 17th century Dutch concerns about newspapers and the erosion of respect for authority, to Wertham's study (1955) of links between comic books and teen delinquency in the 1950s.
- A focus on psychological factors; the role that media can play in provoking aggression, fear etc.
- Physiological concerns. In the 1970s it was widely feared that television damaged eyesight.

All are based on a fundamental fear about the anonymous mass. People out there, apparently, cannot help but embrace any new media temptation on offer, and have no power to influence what these experiences do to them. The trouble is, the myths are harmful, as they invert the research process. According to their logic, we already know what the media do and who they do it to; the researcher's task is simply to labour the point. Using Schoenbach's ideas, a cultural studies audience researcher would confront Nigel by dismantling many of the facts that he accepted. The expert would point out that:

- It is NOT obvious that children are more susceptible to media influence than adults. This assumption makes all sorts of ham-fisted conflations between different sorts of texts, media and influences.
- It is NOT obvious that the most pressing audience questions surround violence.
- It is NOT obvious that the primary impact of media violence is real world violent behaviour.
- It is NOT obvious that media influence, if it happens at all, will declare itself in material behaviours that are observable, hence measurable. For this same reason
- It is NOT obvious that we should be able to reproduce and thus analyze connections between media and behaviour in controlled academic settings.
- In the notion of effects, it is NOT obvious what effects are or where we should find them.

## THE INTERPRETIVE TURN

**1.3** There is another way to look at Nigel's comments. They are cultural artefacts. Even if they are ill-informed, they have become part of the historical record of how society makes sense of the media. In this sense, Nigel's words are a 'fact' that social researchers can use. But to do this, we must be clear what 'fact' means.

The definition used here comes from Paul Ten Have's work on ethnomethodology (2004). Ethnomethodology examines how society works through the creation and circulation of meaning among its actors. The focus on meaning, communication and everyday life has made ethnomethodology influential in research on the media's relevance. Ten Have makes it clear that this tradition views research as a constitutive action. What this means is that social research involves interpreting and creating rather than finding reality. This is not to say that ethnomethodology is an entirely fictive activity, but it is to say that it lives in a world of fluid meanings and interpretations that rarely condense to matters of incontrovertible truth. Ten Have explains this by contrasting sociological and ethnomethodological definitions and uses of the fact. For the former, facts are building blocks for explanation of how society works. The latter case is more interested in the process of how such things come to be constituted and recognized as social facts in the first place.

Hopefully we can see a relationship between these ideas and Butsch's earlier definition of critical audience research that illuminates another way of viewing Nigel's comments. Why would a UK-based 16-year-old in the year 2000 use rap music as a vehicle to express concerns for younger children? What were his motivations for doing so? We might hypothesize that his words reflect typical adolescent concerns; namely the desire to distance oneself from the cultural category of childhood. Even if we think Nigel's judgements were wrong, they are still interesting for what they say about issues beyond media violence.

Note the shifted research emphasis; instead of talking about what the media might be doing to children, we are looking at Nigel himself as the influenced object. A switch from what he said to why he said it is in line with understanding audience research as an interpretive activity. However, it is also in keeping with a tradition using quantitative research procedures. In 1983, W.P. Davison identified the so-called 'third person effect' which stated that:

> individuals who are members of an audience that is exposed to a persuasive communication ... will expect the communication to have a greater effect on others than on themselves ... the impact that they expect this communication to have may lead them to take some action. Any effect that the communication achieves may thus be due not to the ostensible audience, but rather the behavior of those who anticipate, or think they perceive, some reaction on the part of others (Davison, 1983: 3)

This is a 'post-mythic' hypothesis, inasmuch as it recognizes that media influence evolves in unexpected places. This is relevant to a review of what audience research is and does, as it suggests that qualitative scholars have their own 'myths' about the concepts and methods deployed in other traditions. The next section of this chapter will define critical audience research in greater detail by outlining the role played by two key terms, reflexivity and subjectivity. It will also, however, argue that quantitative mass communications research has always been a reflexive enterprise, exemplified by the genesis and evolution of third person research. This is worth noting as it expands the conceptual and methodological range of critical audience research.

## THERE'S NO 'I' IN RESEARCH?

**1.4** In an influential review of ethnographic methods, Lincoln and Denzin (1994) characterize the post-1986 period as a time of crisis. Ethnography emerged in the late 19th and early 20th centuries as the study of everyday life. In its original inception, the ethnographer was understood as a sort of living camera, producing detailed snapshots of human interactions in social settings. Early ethnography thus accepted traditional objective scientific values. By ensuring meticulous attention to the recording of detail, the ethnographer could effectively remove him or herself from the picture that he or she created. By the late eighties, this goal had been dismissed. Ethnography inevitably involves decision making. Certain things are recorded, others are not. Some details are deemed worthier of analysis than others. Moreover, Hallet and Fine's review of the ethnographic research published in *The American Journal of Sociology* from 1895–1900 reveals that many early ethnographers had political motivations. Themes of conflict and dispossession irrigated studies of urban poverty. Far from neutral, these 'snapshots' had an openly reformist agenda (Hallet & Fine, 2000). Clearly, then, ethnographic analysis is produced by an active subject with feelings and opinions. So, the post-1986 period has witnessed a growing scrutiny of the ethnographer (Denzin & Lincoln, 1994).

This has a direct relevance to the evolution of critical audience research. John Tulloch (2000), who pioneered the 'ethnographic turn' in media research in his study of science fiction fans, locates his work firmly within Denzin and Lincoln's 'reflexive' phase. He explains his interest in this area as the product of two sorts of biographies, one personal, and one professional. In the former, he references his love of the BBC's science fiction series *Dr Who* and his left-leaning conflicts with a conservative father. In the latter, he cites a seminal encounter with Marxist scholarship. These biographies met during the UK miners' strike of 1973. *Dr Who* featured a story set in a

Welsh coalmine. The narrative subsequently became a site of tension between Tullochs junior and senior. This personal conflict alerted Tulloch junior's professional sensibilities, graphically illustrating the political relevance of popular culture. Fan research, a major branch of audience study, thus rises from a particular nexus of academic and social experience. What does this say about the sort of knowledge that interpretive social research can produce, and who can produce it?

## AUTOETHNOGRAPHY: USES AND ABUSES

**1.5** According to Anderson and Baym (2004), the disparate field addressed by Bryant and Miron's meta-analysis is united by one thing; the need to acknowledge and use the subjective aspects of social research. Mapping the field, Anderson and Baym outline a territory bounded by two sets of opposed poles; foundationalism versus reflexivity, and empiricism versus analysis. This offers a more sophisticated version of old controversies on objective versus subjective views of research. Some communication scholars lean toward viewing reality as an objectively describable thing 'out there' (a foundational and empirical preference). Others see many aspects of the real as the product of human sense making, thus viewing 'the researcher as an instrument advancing claims from a cultural and sociological subjectivity' (2004: 593). The second position errs toward the reflexive and the analytic. For Anderson and Baym, the problem with foundational/empirical orientations is that they render the concept of communication as a secondary category. Foundationalism conceives language as descriptive rather than constitutive. As a consequence, it implies abandoning the study of communication as a phenomenon in its own right (as herein we are interested in reality, not the way that the interpretation and communication of reality functions as a relatively independent force).

Autoethnography emerges as a part of the turn toward reflexive/analytic scholarship. Like Tulloch, many communication scholars are as interested in academic performance as they are in media audiences. For others, this interest is merely an alibi for theoreticians who do not wish to soil their hands with empirical matters. Autoethnography is thus a useful means of discussing relations between theory and method in the larger issue of what interpretive audience research can say, and who can speak its language.

To illustrate, I would direct your attention to a spat that broke out over the publication of an article called *The Critical Life* by R.J. Pelias (2000) in the journal *Communication Education*. Pelias is a professor of communication at a US university. In this piece, he rather unusually described a day in his life in the third person. We discover how he brushes his teeth, how he likes his coffee.

We listen in as he comforts a colleague who latest piece has been rejected by a journal, consoles prospective graduate students whose applications for further study have been rejected, congratulates another who has been admitted and is elated/disappointed by a range of engaged/unenthusiastic student presentations. Pelias' avowed purpose was to point to the way that 'criticism', the evaluation of other people and what they do, pervades every aspect of life. In doing this, Pelias claimed a deconstruction of scholar/non-scholar boundaries, revealing critique as the art of living. In the process he risked his own professional status by adopting a writing style that colleagues might condemn.

His essay was welcomed in certain circles. Despite being one of the reviewers who had initially rejected it, Susan Ragan (2000) was glad that her decision had been overturned. Her judgment had been based on the view that Pelias' essay was unassessable by the journal's definition of scholarship. On reflection, she concluded that it was the criteria rather than the essay that needed to be revised:

> we should focus on non-methodological evaluative criteria: Is this piece interesting and accurately written? Is its fundamental issue important? Will readers learn anything by reading it? Does it (potentially) make a contribution to the discipline and to scholarly inquiry in general? (Ragan, 2000: 230)

Banks and Banks were similarly congratulatory. The Pelias piece offers 'autoethnography [as] a method for circumventing the colonizing and exoticizing action of the ethnographer upon the cultural other' (2000: 234). In drawing attention to the everyday mechanics of the academy, Pelias took a step toward democratizing knowledge by both diminishing the social distance between the professional scholar and lay audiences, and investing the research process with a relevance-bearing emotional charge. Academic work is about feeling as well as thinking, and to pretend otherwise is to misrepresent its nature. It is also to avoid the social duty of the academy to communicate, share and develop public knowledge. A part of doing this is creating the awareness that learning is not an elite preserve. Laying bare the idiosyncracies of academic life, in Pelias' case by pointing to the everyday aspects of criticism, communicates this idea. Given that media studies debates questions of major public concern, the anti-elitist position expressed here had clear relevance for the audience researcher.

But not everyone welcomed *The Critical Life*. In counter-attack, Shields (2000) painted autoethnography as one of the great twentieth-century oxymorons, alongside 'Cold War' and 'United Nations'. Autoethnography, as it has come to be practised in communication research, perverts the notion of reflexivity. The reflexive ethnographic account considers how the researcher has applied theories and methods to the study *of other people* . Even if we consider 'private' records such as diaries, great diarists constructed their work as quasi-public records, reflecting on matters of public substance rather than tooth brushing and coffee drinking. Shields sarcastically described 'sipping a beer and eating a donut' while cogitating on these matters.

If autoethnography were truly reflexive, he continued, it would realize that it has established undeliverable goals. Designed to emancipate the dispossessed by unveiling academic power structures, autoethnography has made the very people for whom it claims to speak invisible by not bothering to research them anymore. Banks and Banks feared that 'readers might interpret *The Critical Life* as a narcissistic display of self absorbtion' (2000: 234). In likening reading the piece to watching a newscaster interviewing him/herself, Shields concurred.

The lesson is that we must be very careful in positioning the 'I' in research. Returning to Nigel, we might say that one of the problems with his words is that the object of his concerns, younger children, are completely absent from the debate. As audience researchers inspired by reflexive methods we might, then, want to know what these younger children made of Eminem. It is not entirely clear how this would be achieved by reflecting on our own roles as researchers, and why it is we are interested in pursuing the questions that we do in the way that we do. Shield's offered as damning a critique of 'subjective' research as it is possible to find. In many ways, his ideas complement Martin Barker's complaint that critical audience research suffers from the absence of clear criteria for what counts as good work (2003). How are we to deal with this?

A minor, but important step lies in looking at the structure of Shields's argument. While claiming to have exhaustively reviewed communication scholarship for autoethnographic works, most of his attacks were directed at the unfortunate R. Boyd's *Compromising positions: or the unhappy transformations of a 'transformative intellectual'* (1999), referenced *twenty-four times*. It seems that Shields had built an identikit vision of what autoethnography is and does, and had found a study fitting the bill. Where Boyd's piece was displayed as representative, it could be that it was simply a poor application of subjective research.

Another way of confronting the Shields critique is to consider the communicative aspects of social research outlined by Korth (2002). Korth defined good research as a 'dialogic' process of 'consciousness raising'. Her thoughts were framed within the recognition that ethnographic research is grounded in the analysis of social power relationships, with the goal of expanding the ranges of voices heard in public deliberations. This is done by researchers who recognize that their encounters with 'real people' represent neither the discovery of a 'natural' setting (something that would have existed in the researcher's absence) nor a piece of fiction (where the researcher uses real people as raw materials to build pretty much any vision of 'reality' that pleases him/her) but rather a 'third space' created by the inter-action between both parties. Good research constantly asks 'why did I/they say that'? The goal is the production of a 'text of difference'; a record that alerts us to the conflicts and alternative rationalities at work in social settings. Accordingly, we should judge this sort of research not by its ability to get things right or wrong, but rather by the degree to which it pays attention to the dialogic aspects of the venture, and its ability to provoke contemplation on social difference. This presents the 'I' as important, but not central.

So, what does the application of this criterion to a piece of media autoethnography look like? Consider Grant Farrad's *Long Distance Love: growing up a Liverpool football club fan* (2002). Farrad is a Black South African Professor of English Literature, working at Duke University in the USA. He is then, a gifted scholar, one who has applied his abilities within accepted academic traditions, to the point where he as earned tenure at one of the world's leading institutions. *Long Distance Love* is, as a consequence, a bizarre read. Why would a Professor of English publish his reasons for being a Liverpool fan? Why did he feel the need to explain his attachment to a particular player, John Barnes? What does this have to do with scholarly audience research?

The last question is relatively easy to answer. Farrad's 'fandom' is an entirely mediated phenomenon. He was a Liverpool fan for thirty years before ever seeing them play live, subsisting on newspaper and magazine arti-cles, radio broadcasts and, just occasionally, live television transmissions. Moreover, Farrad used his fan experience as a way of reflecting upon different aspects of the 'I'. By the 1980s, the already avid Liverpool fan was confronted with a cultural dilemma. While a generation of black footballers had moved to the fore of the English game, none had done so at Liverpool. This was an obvious affront to Farrad's Black South African self, creating an internal apartheid with the fan side of his personality. The rift was only resolved when Jamaican born Barnes claimed his place in Liverpool's midfield.

*Long Distance Love*, then, speaks to interesting dynamics wherein media create possibilities and problems in processes of identification. However, Farrad's essay begs the question; what sort of 'I' can produce this sort of work? His is an unusual life story. If his reflections on media 'fandom' are grounded in personal experience, does audience research depend on the possession, or the ability to manufacture an exotic back story? If so, is it narcissistic in nature?

Autoethnographically inspired work might even be dangerous. Barbara Jago's *Chronicling an Academic Depression* presents us with:

> [a] layered account... [that] reflexively explores the multiplicity of experiences, voices and emotions that inform my depression and recovery experiences in the

context of a role shift from graduate student to assistant professor, in hopes that my story can shed light on the emotional, relational, biological, cultural and historical forces shaping my experiences (2002: 753)

which in practice translates into a tale of her descent into mental illness. We learn more than we might want or need to know about the author's fear of teaching, family history, sex life and booze battles. As Jago struggles to come to terms with the death of an ex-partner's partner, we are presented with the following vignette:

Yet for some reason, maybe a desire to turn this tragedy into something positive ... I walk into the class with a sense of purpose ... 'I want to tell you a story', I begin, and the words just come ... recounting details of my relationship with Thom, our ability to forge a lasting friendship out of a lost romance, his heartbreaking loss, the grief ... 'we have a visceral need to connect with others, to feel not so alone, so doomed. And this is what this class is all about', I pause for effect 'we are here to learn how to make stronger and more satisfying connections'. I stop speaking and glance around the room. The air feels transformed. My students are silent, a few wiping tears on shirtsleeves. (2002: 736)

Two things strike me as fundamentally false in this account. The first is the implication that autoethnography is premised on the willingness to relay intimate details of one's private life to the reader, which in turn assumes that the research is ultimately about you. This level of disclosure is just plain unsafe, personally and professionally.

The other striking thing about this account, and perhaps the thing that is more problematic, is the complete absence of reflection it contains. Jago admits that much of the story comes from memory. This is all she can draw upon, with her real task being to convey a sense of what these experiences were like for the people who were there. But I would argue that evidence is not the problem here. As someone with several years of university teaching, I find Jago's account unpersuasive. My hunch is that if I devoted lesson times to extensive, tragic, personal anecdotes, some students would be touched, but others would be bemused, amused, appalled and bored. Some might even want their tuition fees back. My objections, however, are not based on the absence of evidence; they are based on Jago's failure to interrogate the evidence that she *does* have. Were those students wiping their eyes moved, or bored to tears? Did she even bother asking them? The problem with Jago's piece then, is not that it uses personal experience and casual methods of gathering data, but that it exclusively places the researcher at the centre of the method with little regard for the data. Returning to Tulloch's use of different biographies, this approach reminds us that the 'I' is subordinate to questions of theory and method that structure audience research as a discipline. At this point, then, we can formulate a tentative definition of what 'good' research that does not dismiss subjectivity looks like. I would suggest that Ragan's definition is largely correct; the task of the audience researcher is to be interesting in a persuasive and rigorous way. Applying this criterion to Jago, we might say that the weakness of her piece lies not so much in its method and style, more in the lack of reflection on what such an approach can and cannot say. It could easily evade Shields's concerns using the same methods by restructuring itself around key questions identified by Martin Barker (2003):

- Research design. What is the 'degree of fit' between research question, method, evidence gathered and conclusions drawn? Has the researcher looked for evidence that confronts the conclusions that he or she wishes to reach (e.g. did Jago consider the 'bored to tears' possibility?).
- Elaboration. To what extent does the research inform wider disciplinary concerns? Is it likely to inspire other projects? Which audiences are likely to find this research useful?

Under these terms, we can defend Farrad and Tulloch against Shields's narcissistic charge. In positioning the 'I' as the space between different parts of the self (football fan versus Black South African, scholar versus son), these writers demonstrated Ann Gray's (2003) point that something is always at stake in audience research. Ultimately media matter because they deal with macropolitical issues that have deeply personal consequences, in that they influence how real people experience their lives.

We can also argue that if anything, cultural studies audience research has not paid enough attention to subjectivity issues in one crucial area. The St. Louis Brief's dismissal of quantitative research methods demonstrates a tendency to dismiss mass communication research, especially that carried out in the 1940s and 1950s. However, an alternative reading of this history, using the third person effect as a case study, reveals that within quantitative work it has always been 'post-1986'. This is worth noting as it extends the range of methods on offer to critical researchers.

## QUANTITATIVE AUDIENCE RESEARCH: IT'S BEEN 1986 SINCE 1929

**1.6** Let us pause to summarize and define what critical social research is. It is an interpretive exercise where the researcher's activity produces not only description and analysis, but possibly change (this is what is at stake in Korth's notion of consciousness raising). For example, the

St. Louis Brief's signatories were not simply interested in outlining the history of effects research; their goal was to influence public debate and hence policy on the issue. All audience research is activist, if for no other reason than it persuades us to take media culture seriously. The trick in handling this role lies in understanding and communicating why you are doing it and how it influences your methods and conclusions.

This is part of the reason why quantitative methods and mass communication research are viewed with suspicion by cultural studies. In a piece that in many ways grounds critical audience research, Todd Gitlin (1978) attacked the mid-20th century North American mass communication tradition, embodied in the figure of Paul Lazarsfeld. Mass communication scholars had developed a hopelessly limited view of communication and its social influence serving no-one save the media industry that, not coincidentally, funded much of this work. Lazarsfeld was an Austrian Jewish émigré who founded the Bureau of Applied Social Research at Columbia University during the World War Two. His main contribution to media theory, according to received wisdom, is the development of the theory of 'limited effects'. Searching for the media's power to change opinions and thus behaviours in voting and consuming, Lazarsfeld found that people tended to use media messages to reinforce decisions or opinions that they had already made. Media messages were used 'selectively'; either people sought out content that they knew would marry with their understandings of the way things were, or else they interpreted texts according to the same structures, regardless of what they actually said. For Gitlin, this made two fatal errors. First, it assumed that media power provoked change, when it is perfectly possible to argue that the reverse might be true; that the media stabilize traditional beliefs. Second, it assumed that a range of very different sorts of decision based human activities worked according to the same cognitive and social processes. As such, the experimental and survey protocols that Lazarsfeld and the like had developed were incapable of dealing with variations between different social settings. Recalling the St. Louis Brief, we can see how these ideas remain influential almost thirty years later.

I want to argue that this position has itself become mythic. It has become a story that qualitative researchers tell themselves to avoid the complexities and, indeed, interpretative aspects of quantitative work. To begin, it is interesting to note recent critical re-evaluations of Lazarsfeld's life and work provided by Elihu Katz (2001) and Elisabeth Noelle-Neumann (2001). Katz's was the more formal piece, taking issue with Gitlin's accusation that Lazarsfeld was responsible for 'whitewashing the true effects of the media' (2001: 271). Looking at Lazarsfeld's early conceptual work, he found a range of research interests shattering the image of the industrial lackey that Gitlin painted. Lazarsfeld was hugely concerned that the US media were structured by commercial concerns. This depoliticized the public; people were beginning to feel that activism began and ended with watching the news rather than 'making politics', all the more problematic given the growing amount of trivia being offered. But why were these curiously modern questions never pursued? Simply, Lazarsfeld could never afford it. Despite the relative wealth of the Columbia project, Lazarsfeld was unable to secure funding for studying long-term consequences of media use going beyond the snapshot of the survey or the experiment. He knew that effects, if such things existed, evolved over a long period of time involving all sorts of interacting variables. He was simply never allowed to put these theories to the test.

Elisabeth Noelle-Neumann sketched a more evocative personal picture. Lazarsfeld had begun life as a methodological maverick. As a young postgraduate in Vienna, he had been involved in a project that recorded the effects of economic depression in the weaving town of Marienthal. In the study, he hypothesized that depression could be felt and thus seen in every aspect of life. At one point, Lazarsfeld took to hiding behind curtains in town houses, measuring the cadence of passing walkers. As the depression deepened, so the pace slowed. Lazarsfeld was, then, open to a range of indicators of social meaning that were not tied to traditional social science methods. Noelle-Neumann pointed out that few realize this, as the Nazis burned most copies of the Marienthal study.

Gitlin's view was therefore reconfigured as a one-dimensional caricature that did justice to neither Lazarsfeld the man nor researcher. It, therefore, served as a shaky foundation for the dismissal of mass communication research. This becomes even shakier if we look at third person effect research. The origins and development of this tradition show a great deal of reflexivity; an unravelling process that shows how quantitative methods are capable of embracing subjectivity.

## THE THIRD PERSON EFFECT

**1.7** Opening a piece of contemporary third person effect research, such as Tewkesbury, Moy and Weis's study of how it worked in concerns over the Y2K bug (2004), one finds a dizzying array of statistical procedures that try to quantify an intricate set of relations between interacting social variables, both in terms of direction and size of effect. This belies the relatively humble origins of the discipline. As he tells the story himself, in the late 1940s a fledgling sociologist called W.P. Davison had a chance encounter with a historian with an interesting tale to tell. The historian was researching United States Marine Corps actions in the Pacific theatre during World War Two. He had discovered that the Japanese had dropped propaganda leaflets on a group of black marines, decrying the war as racist. A white officer had found one of the leaflets. Despite the absence of a single act of mutiny or insubordination, the unit was immediately withdrawn from the field. The main effect of the propaganda, the historian pointed out, was on the officer, not the men. This chance encounter eventually led to the definition of the third person effect found earlier, a conceptualization which is, then, clearly grounded in everyday observation and the social position of the researcher. Davison began gathering evidence for his hunch in a series of surveys and experiments using small numbers of students. In this early work, he found that in around fifty per cent of cases, the main effect of being exposed to persuasive messages was the belief that other people were likely to be influenced by them. Remarkably, Paul, Salwen and Dupagne's meta-analysis of third person research 1983–2000 show that this fifty per cent figure recurs in many more substantial projects (2000).

As third person effect research developed, much of it focussed around the issue of violence. To what extent, researchers asked, did media violence cause viewers to fear the effect that such content was having on other people? Did this lead toward censorious views (Gunther & Storey, 2003)? Cultural studies researchers might offer this as an explanation of the real significance of Nigel's quote. However, is it not strange that Davison's early results tend to be reproduced again and again? In critique of scientific culture, Thomas Kuhn (1974) developed the idea of normal science. The scientist is a flesh and blood figure, with hopes and fears, mortgages to pay and children to feed. There is therefore a risk in following Nowotny's advice by looking at the flaws in one's work. Careers are better served by applying the same methods to the same problems, finding the same results.

But this is not the way that third person effect studies progressed. Perloff (2003) cast the third person effect as a 'social fact' in an almost ethnomethodological style. That is, there has, in his view, been enough research to show that fear about what the media do to other people can be cast as a significant factor of media culture. This, however, creates more questions than solutions. First, even if we believe the fifty per cent variance figure, this still leaves fifty per cent of the audience unexplained. Second, when the third person effect does happen, researchers have yet to explore why it happens, or what it means when it does.

Some have explained third person effects in terms of self–other power relations. Earlier, we posited that Nigel's words may have represented a strategy to distance himself from childhood by displaying a greater knowledge and vocabulary of how media work. Perhaps, then, they said more about how he wished to be seen by others as a knowledgeable social actor. So, is the third person effect a measure of self-esteem (Banning, 2001; Paul, Salwen and Dupagne, 2000)?

All of this is premised, however, on the belief that people see being influenced by the media as a bad thing. But does this depend on the sort of message that we are dealing with? For example, Perloff hypothesized that if the purpose of the third person effect is to create a knowledge gap between the self and the mass audience, then in the case of materials such as AIDS commercials the individual might wish to describe him/herself as *more* open to media influence than the average person. McLeod, Detenber and Evalans (2001), in a study of music violence, claimed that the extent of third person positions will also be moderated by one's familiarity with the text in question. This argument would explain why Nigel's concerns about Eminem did not translate into censorious sentiments.

Lo and Paddon (2000) pointed out that the connection between third person perceptions and behavioural consequences in most research has been weak. People often say that they favour censorship in reaction to what they see as objectionable content, but there is little evidence to show that they ever act on this. And what about other sorts of actions? In their work on responses to news stories about the Y2K bug, Tewkesbury, Moy and Weis (2004) identified two opposing behaviours explicable by the third person hypothesis. There were two rational reactions to the belief that other people would be panicked by warnings of systemic social failure: either *not* panic buying, based on the belief that the media were scaremongering, or hoarding, based on the belief that even if this was a scare the shops would be stripped bare by media dopes.

And above and beyond all of this is the concern that the whole idea might be an artefact of sample design. So much third person research uses student samples that we do not know how useful it is in explaining media relationships outside the young middle classes, which now desperately need to be investigated.

What this says is that if qualitative researchers take the time to consider where their mass communications counterparts come from, and how they view the application of numbers to fluid cultural realities, they will find that certain quantitative procedures are used to recognize that fluidity. Perfloff's comments on the fifty per cent variance found in most third person work suggest the view that figures lend shape without concretizing social reality. This conclusion is confirmed in that many of Davison's followers have spent their time unravelling the simplicity of his early statement on media power. This is good news for the critical audience researcher, as it widens the range of methods open to him or her. This means that he or she can produce more interesting, although never complete, pictures of the relationships between media and audiences.

To summarize, we have learned that regardless of method or theory, subjectivity, or to be more precise the social, historical and cultural context of the researcher, inevitably plays a part in the formulation and operationalization of research questions. Whether in words or numbers, we are involved in describing and explaining meaningful cultures; efforts to remove subjectivity from the equation simply deny the ontology of the task at hand.

But this does not mean that research is arbitrary. Recognizing that there is an 'I' in research makes us more responsible. We have to be clear about what we are doing, why we are doing it, and how our actions contribute toward the wider study of media. To this end, while we can begin from a variety of positions within communication studies, I would suggest a number of key concepts and antagonisms that should be considered by all audience researchers.

## POWER

**1.8** Arguably, audience research has always revolved around issues of power. Either we want to know what the media do to people, what people do to media, or perhaps, what people do to themselves and others *with* media.

James Curran gives a very useful overview of how mass communications research differs from British cultural studies in its understandings of power (2002; 108–113). In essence, this turns on the former making language and the symbolic a central research issue. As an illustrative point, consider how we might conceive 'persuasion'. Lazarsfeld et al.'s (1948) study of the 1941 presidential election, which looked at how media could change voting preferences, assumed that language worked in a fairly neutral way. That is, if a candidate gave a speech, it was assumed that he had a clear persuasive intent that was obviously 'there' in the message. The only question was whether the audience recognized it and moved in accordance.

For Curran, this 'liberal pluralist' position defines language as a natural phenomenon, inasmuch as the meaning of a message is unambiguous, and assumes that society works as a harmonious whole. We all understand each other, and have common social goals. Yet we have already seen the problems of such assumptions in our consideration of the 'Nigel'quote. If we unravel Nigel's logic, the focus on the negative lyrical content of Eminem raps asserts that that content is unambiguously there for all listeners to hear. Accent, lexicon and radio/television editing mean that this may not be the case.

Curran located the origins of critical media analysis in the moment where, via Marxist and post-Marxist scholarship, language and the symbolic are reconceived as central to the formation and understanding of society. This was first expressed through the concept of 'ideology', succeeded by the less deterministic 'discourse'. The former idea conceived media power as the ability to promote the values of powerful groups in society across a range of texts, over a long period of time. The latter adopted a less fatalistic sheen, in that it saw power struggles happening in every area where humans communicate. Think of Nigel again to illustrate the difference. If we were to argue that Nigel was the victim of ideology, was persuaded more by the way that certain groups would like childhood to be understood, rather than the way it functions in a material sense, we would have a problem relating this to media power. Although he clearly believed that young audiences are weak, there is no evidence to suggest that this belief came exclusively from the media. Second, the passive position suggested by the ideological critique does not explain Nigel's actions. The idea that his was a rhetorical strategy creating a distance between himself and childhood makes Nigel powerful. It is easy to see how this power might find its way into everyday life. If Nigel had siblings, nieces, nephews, they may have found themselves at the receiving end of his censorious impulses.

This explains why studies of everyday human interactions are relevant to media studies. It also explains the St. Louis Brief's take on media influence. The signatories agree that the media obviously have some power on some level. But the complexities of the relationships between audiences and media (witnessed by third person effect researchers' ever complicated view of how a simple idea might work in practice) are such that it is too early to reach conclusions on media power.

Nick Couldry offers a compromise between ideological and discursive positions.

> The ritual space of the media is highly uneven. It is formed around one central inequality (the historic concentration of symbolic power in media institutions) but it is shaped locally through many detailed patterns, particularly the categories (such as those of media and ordinary person, or liveness and so on...) through which we understand our actions and orientations in relation to media. (2003: 13)

In this view, media power relates to the fact that everyday life is media related rather than media centred. What this means is while the media offer us a ranges of images and ideas that we can ignore or reject, at the same time they create a common cultural archive on which we all draw in making sense of the world, ourselves, and other people. In this view, when Nigel wished to articulate his emergence into the adult world, he did so by referencing the global phenomenon of rap music.

## MEANING OR PLEASURE?

**1.9** Critical audience research has been defined as the exploration of why media matter to viewers, readers and listeners (Gray, 2003). Meaning is thus important, but less clear is the idea that we have to ask what meaning means.

At its most obvious level, meaning based audience research asks how the media influence, or are used in forming a sense of social reality, self and other. Ang (1985) and Katz and Liebes (1990) explored this topic in studying the reception of the television soap *Dallas*. Both works began from the premise that an ideological critique might position the internationally successful show as an imperialist tool. At face value, the story of a Texan oil family celebrated the values of a consumer society. In the Netherlands and Israel respectively, however, the researchers found audiences who read the show in a variety of ways, related to how viewers understood their own gendered and ethnic identities.

But media texts are more than simple vehicles for ideology. In his influential study of pleasure, Roland Barthes (1975) identified the goal of reading as achieving *jouissance*, a state of pleasure where the self escapes culture (and, consequently, the need to define oneself in terms of gender, ethnicity or class). We might say, then, that the problem with the *Dallas* work is that it paid too much attention to the rational aspects of the mind. An emerging interest in emotional literacy suggest that the media's ability to prompt *feelings* of anxiety, anger or joy are a precondition for activities such as identification (Richards, 2004). As a result, media researchers need to pay attention to the physical and emotional aspects of the audience experience. This leads into our next point.

## TEXT OR TECHNOLOGY?

**1.10** As a closely related question, we should ask if the social relevance of media cultures lies not only in the texts that they make available, but the contexts in which we receive them. This question has a technological dimension. For example, Sonia Livingstone has recently asked if the shift to a multimedia era means that audience research needs a complete conceptual makeover:

> For the past half century, we have not so much researched 'the television audience' as researched national, often public service, mass broadcast, non-interactive television along with the nationally conceived, consensus oriented, sit back on the couch, family audience in the living room. (2004: 76)

A cultural phenomenon such as *Big Brother*, for instance, raises interesting questions over how we define the audience in the first place, l*et al*one how we study them. This has long been a concern in audience research (Allor, 1988; Lull, 1988; Bird, 1992). One of the reasons why third person effect research is interesting is that it is also based on the idea that it isn't entirely obvious who the audience is. If we consider the controversy that surrounds rappers such as Eminem and 50 Cent, it is clear that in a way the audience includes many people who would like the entire genre to disappear. The point is that in a multimedia world, where the meanings, lexicon and style of rap passes into everyday interactions, rap is a part of our cultural environment.

The same can be said of *Big Brother*, which features a number of textual incarnations. When we speak of the show, what are we talking about? Edited highlights? Live feeds? Eviction shows? Websites? Print media? The show crosses all forms, meaning that it is speaking to many different audiences in many different places. These differences influence the sorts of questions that we ask about audiences.

## QUANTITATIVE OR QUALITATIVE?

**1.11** While the St. Louis Court Brief is unequivocal in its condemnation of quantitative research, one of its signatories has actually started using them (Barker, 2005b). As we shall see, the survey is becoming a popular way of asking critical questions. In part, this is based on a frustration with certain qualitative methods that are seen in some circles as just as artificial as the experiment. Early responses to the limitations of experiments and surveys included interviewing people about how they made sense and use of the media. Sometimes, this meant gathering groups of viewers to watch and respond to a specific text (e.g. Katz and Liebes, 1990). Others took a more 'naturalistic' approach, studying audiences in their natural viewing habitat (Morley, 1989). Both efforts have been criticized as artificial, in that they turn on the belief that audiences are able to translate feelings into words (Gauntlett & Holzwarth, 2006[AU234]) and that the idea of the natural habitat is naïve.

The lesson is that methodological choice is strategic. The question of what method you use is less important than that of why you are using it, and your consciousness of what you can and cannot say with the tools at your disposal.

## CONCLUSION

**1.12** This chapter has mapped out a possible view of the nature of critical audience research. It does not conform to the view of the researcher as neutral observer of the social world. Research is inevitably coloured by personal interest and social experience. The key, however, lies in understanding how you can convert this to legitimate academic currency. To do so, one must take cognizance of the questions, concepts and methods that frame audience research, and how 'gut' feelings about things that are interesting and/or important can be subordinated to the wider disciplinary question of why media matter.

As I have argued that method choice is a matter of strategy rather than orthodoxy, this book will embed 'how' questions within conceptual discussions of how to assess media influence. Each chapter will mention a variety of quantitative and qualitative studies, assessing the quality of fit between research question, method and conclusions on a case by case basis. This is appropriate as contemporary audience research no longer dismisses any one method on principle. Additionally, even if there are methods which one prefers not to use, the researcher still needs to have a reading knowledge of how different approaches work.

# 2 News and Public Information

## INTRODUCTION

**2.1** Thousands of studies have assessed the impact of news and public information on various audiences. This chapter will not provide a comprehensive overview of every issue to emerge from this massive literature. Instead, Jenny Kitzinger's work on news framing and public understanding of child sex abuse (2004) is used to focus a number of key questions. A landmark volume, *Framing Sex Abuse* conceives a clear relationship between news and public information. It also serves as a crossroads between informative and narrative issues in communicating the 'real world'. Much of the audience research described hereafter critiques news for its poor narrative structures. Kitzinger's study, self-identified as an example of 'new influence research', accepts relations between storytelling and knowing. But it does so in a way that reinvests factual information with a critical currency. Kitzinger therefore offers a vantage from which we can survey the history of how audiences for 'factual' media content have been understood. With the benefit of hindsight, I will argue that 'framing' emerges as a lingua franca in this area.

## SOME REASONS WHY IT IS STILL WORTH STUDYING NEWS AND PUBLIC INFORMATION

**2.2** Qualitatively inspired critical audience research directs *relatively* little attention to news. Part of the reason is the energy it has taken to establish the political importance of entertainment. Much effort has been required to convince other scholars and the public that popular culture is a potent bearer of information, meaning and power. Indeed, the frequent derisive attacks directed at media studies shows that for many the argument remains unpersuasive.

Audiences also seem to find news and information campaigns unappealing, uninformative and incomprehensible. In a recent radio debate, I was scolded by *The Times'* political columnist Andrew Pearce for suggesting that voters might yearn for more meaningful, less mediated connections with politicians.

His point was in many ways valid. People used to be able to see politicians in the flesh at public meetings. Such moments are now rare largely because voters do not want them (*Thinking Allowed*, BBC Radio 4, 12 October 2005). Pearce's thesis has scholarly support. Distinguished political scientist Doris Graber (2005) notes that the ignorant/apathetic voter is unquestioningly enshrined in her discipline as a symbol of how things are.

None of this invalidates news and information research. Recall the way that Chapter 1 approached the social fact. Even if it is true that audiences are largely uninterested in and unmoved by factual media programming, we still need to know how this state of affairs has come to pass. Peter Kellner's work on post-1996 UK voter apathy (2004) is a case in point. Kellner argues that it is common to see apathy as something that has steadily grown since World War Two as the almost inevitable by-product of dwindling party and union membership, social interaction, rising consumerism and therefore diminished public investment in political processes. This story cannot, however, explain the dramatic decline in voter turnout post-1996. In fact, when controlling for factors such as the lowering of the voting age from twenty-one to eighteen in 1968, it appears that 'apathy', in the form of low participation levels, is a new phenomenon. Kellner offers public distaste for 'spin' as one explanation, but does so as a spur for further research. His point is that there is much about voter/media relations to be explained. Apathy might be a social fact, but what it means and where it came from is open to question.

A second reason why news and public information remains important is, according to Graber, that so far we have defined 'political communication' in narrow terms.

> the field of political communication ... encompasses the construction, sending, receiving, and processing of messages that potentially have a significant direct or indirect impact on politics. The message senders or receivers may be politicians, journalists, members of interest groups, or private unorganized citizens (2005: 479)

What this means is that audiences might appear docile because researchers have a blinkered view of what political engagement is and where it happens.

This is tied to the third motivation for maintaining an interest in news and information, which is the possibility that audience apathy is a methodological artifact. Apathy's sibling, the ignorant voter, is summoned by knowledge surveys that ask audiences to recall information that may have a tangential relation to reasoning, and which often is not present in media coverage (Graber, 2005). Methodologically, audiences are treated like students presented with the wrong exam paper; the fault lies in the measure, not the examinee.

In complementary fashion, David Miller (2002) shows how the structure and interpretation of quantitative opinion surveys can produce startlingly different images of what people think. As the 'war against terror' rumbled into Afghanistan, UK media were universal in reporting overwhelming public support for military action. For Miller, this reading was selective to the point of deception. What the polls actually showed was that a majority of the public *opposed* the war *when* they were asked questions inviting them to contemplate civilian casualties. War support also became a minority position when respondents were offered diplomatic alternatives. Therefore, public backing for the intervention in Afghanistan was an illusory product of poor question wording and selective reporting. Can we assume the 'factual' status of apathy if it depends on such fragile research techniques?

What is more, Nina Eliasoph (2004) asks us to consider if it is clear who the public are and where they can be found. Eliasoph expands on Graber's doubts over traditional sender/receiver relations in political communication. Never mind the opinion they produce; the notion of 'public' can misleadingly depict who we are and what we think as a reflex of central political institutions. She asks us to replace the idea of 'public' with the plural 'publics', and the idea that different sorts of people and social groups are more than simply the receivers of information. Publics, whoever they might be, have a part to play in shaping the form and content of news and information. What Eliasoph criticizes here are 'transmission' views of communication (Carey, 1989), which posit the unidirectional flow of information from dominant centres of social power to those they control.

In 2005, Hurricane Katrina demonstrated the inadequacies of this model. Flood waters apparently swept the city of New Orleans into havoc. The media circulated stories of rape and murder in the Superdome, where thousands had sought shelter. Rescue services inexplicably became sniper targets. Crocodiles were rumoured to perambulate the streets; sharks of the piscine variety swam the French Quarter. Reviewing the evidence weeks later, David Usborne (2005) unsurprisingly found all of these stories to be without substance. Rumour and urban myths are hardly new phenomena, but what was surprising was their success in seducing the political elite. Mayor Ralph Nagin had vastly exaggerated casualty figures, presumably egged on by tales of murderous anarchy. Police Superintendent Eddie Compass repeated the Superdome allegations on television, despite later admitting he had no evidence of any rapes, and just one of the deaths in the stadium was regarded as suspicious. Earlier generations of media theorists outlined the gatekeeping powers of public figures such as policemen and women and government officials. Routinely identified as sources of authoritative information, such people have the power to determine the shape of public debate (Hall et al., 1978; Tuchman, 1978). Not so in New Orleans. Power failures hamstrung intelligence gathering (Usborne, 2005). This meant that, when asked to comment on the situation, public officials became reliant on rumour. In this case, it could be argued that public interpersonal communication set the news agenda.

The orthodoxies criticized by Graber and Eliasoph have no explanation for such events. They conceive news and information as sorts of shop window displays. However much the public presses its face against the glass to get a better look, it cannot touch the spectacle beyond the cool membrane. But in New Orleans, certain forms of public intercourse had dressed the scene. News, then, is not a 'given'. Its conventions may be tried and tested, but they remain disruptable.

Katrina lets us revisit 'old' questions about the social uses of the mass media. In the 1940s and 1950s, mass communications scholars in the USA spent huge amounts of time and money on elaborate experiments looking for the most efficient ways to communicate essential information to the public. Some of these studies looked for alternative methods of communication, to be used in the event of a collapse of mass media systems (Ruddock, 2001). The 2005 New Orleans disaster was an eerie reminder of the prescience of these questions. It thus reminds us of shifting emphases in understanding the form and function of news and information, or news *as* information. The sharks swimming down Canal Street signal that Katrina was memorable and compelling as a story; like 9/11 before it, a real life disaster movie, with elements of horror added for good measure. But this does not change the importance of factual communication. Issues of what really was happening were crucial as audiences sought advice on the best course of action to take in unprecedented circumstances. As the hurricane season continued, they remained vital to the evaluation of local, state and federal liability that would inform future disaster policy and public action.

This brings me to my summary of why news and information are still worth studying, and how Kitzinger focuses the connection between the two concepts. Qualitative audience research has tended to privilege narrative over information as a research focus. In doing so, it has valuably demonstrated the status of news as specific signifying practices, rather than a simple statement of how things are. Kitzinger's work is certainly related to this tradition.

Yet *Framing Sex Abuse* also allows us to draw a through line between important mass communication models of media influence (specifically diffusion studies, agenda setting research, the spiral of silence and cultivation analysis) and cultural studies. First, it reconnects news with issues of public information. Second, the concept of framing outlines a common interest in the way that the media actively shape the reality of social issues and problems. Third, while framing is described in narrative form, its significance is that inadequate framing causes all sorts of problems by cultivating beliefs about the real world that are just plain wrong. In Kitzinger's example, media and public stories built around the sexual abuse of children (what it is, where it happens and who does it) actively amplify the problem. So, framing is presented as a way of reconnecting with traditional yet important questions about how we use media to understand material reality. Here, information is linked to learning, understanding and experience.

Kitzinger also develops the previous discussion on the nature of audience research. As we have seen in Miller's work (2002), questions of method are important to the images of public knowledge and engagement that we make as researchers. His comments on how to ask questions and interpret answers are, however, germane to considering the qualitative data gathering methods that we will find in many of the studies discussed below. *Framing Sex Abuse* provides many compelling insights into how these concerns apply to interviewing protocols. It also allows us to assess the relative merits of 'surface' and 'depth' approaches to public knowledge/opinion. Finally, Kitzinger extends the 'research as consciousness raising' analogy in doing studies that are clearly extensions rather than studies of public awareness campaigns.

To understand why I have located this as a landmark work, it is necessary to review three broad areas: the history of diffusion research, which complicates the apparently simple ideas of information and learning; the genesis of what Stephen Chaffee (2001) calls 'post-limited effects effects research' and cultural studies' development of grounded theory on the social uses of news and information.

## THE DIFFUSION OF IDEAS AND INFORMATION

**2.3** Diffusion research studies how information flows through social settings. Meyer's review (2004) locates its origins in rural sociology. The first diffusion studies of the 1940s looked at how the media could be used to encourage farming communities to adopt new products and practices. Interest rapidly turned to the areas of health and electioneering (see Chaffee, 1975).

There are many reasons to argue that problems endemic in the idea of diffusion give it little current purchase. The concept seems too close to transmission ideas about communication, where powerful figures possessing the right knowledge discover how that knowledge can be transplanted into the minds of the less enlightened. Learning is conceptualized in a very narrow sense, with effects similarly measured as the adoption of new behaviours. That is, if we were researching the effectiveness of an anti-drinking campaign aimed at teenagers, and observed that the campaign produced no significant behavioural modifications in the target audience, we would conclude that the campaign had no effect. The problem with this, as we shall see, is that such messages can have other sorts of influences.

At this juncture, we may wish to ask how far we want to go in rejecting the idea of behavioural change. Of course, the idea that if the mass media had any power, we should be able to see it in rapid changes in thought and action within the audience, has been identified as the wrong turn that drove media research into the cul-de-sac of limited effects (Gitlin, 1978). However, critical qualitative research in the area of public health shows that there is an interest in relations between media use and changing cultural practices (Tulloch, 1999; Seale, 2003; Kitzinger, 2004).

Additionally, like Lazarsfeld, diffusion researchers are aware that their findings have been influenced by the limitations of their methods. Writing in 1975, Chaffee defined the 'classic' diffusion piece as a panel study. This entailed selecting a sample, and surveying their opinions and actions on a certain issue or practice at several times. This allowed scholars to describe both a pattern and process of change, typically taking the form of the so-called 's-curve'. Here, media campaigns would attract gradually increasing attention, leading to the adoption of new behaviours, until such time as a point of saturation was reached beyond which significant change could not be expected.

For Meyer, the reality of diffusion research was somewhat different. Panel studies were the exception rather than the rule among researchers who, largely for pragmatic reasons, tended to favour cheaper and quicker snapshot surveys. In reality, most studies build an ersatz process by surveying 'adopters' at the end of a diffusion cycle (e.g. one might research the effectiveness of a drink–driving campaign in the first week of January). These surveys measure how respondents recall their behavioural change, rather than observing it as it happens. This is not necessarily the wrong approach, but it does limit how diffusion can be understood; we don't know why people do *not become* adopters; we don't know how long people *remain* adopters; nor do we ask how adoption *can take on different forms beyond those intended*.

Meyer offers some interesting corrective measures relating diffusion to ethnographic explorations of relations between media, interpersonal communication, learning and practice. The problem with diffusion surveys does not lie in the qualitative/quantitative controversy, identified in Chapter 1 by the St. Louis Brief, but in the time issue. Meyer identifies a number of imaginative strategies for simulating a sense of 'time in the field'. These include using depth interviews to get a better, more 'grounded' feel for why people learn and change, or do not. Archival materials can create historical illusion. Prescription records, for example, can chart the rate at which a new drug is adopted. Additionally, communication researchers can use quasi-experimental techniques, working with health care professionals to see how different forms of interactions with target audiences can influence change. Many of Meyer's thoughts and strategies are echoed in Kitzinger's research.

The point is that critical audience research does not dispense with traditional ideas about learning and social change. It simply understands that the process cannot be straightforward. To begin, we cannot assume that all social actors *want* the 'right' information to flow through society (Ruddock, 2001). Also, diffusion research tells us that information meanders through both media and non-media communicative processes differing in form and function. Therefore, we must understand diffusion has a social context, where multiple sources of information and meaning produce different sorts of learning. To this end, the field of health communication has produced a number of studies using a combination of qualitative and quantitative methods to show how the idea of information and learning applies to social structures that are, in important ways, fractured.

In précis, the work that I discuss emphasizes learning as a matter of experience and relevance as well as information. Macias, Stavchansky-Lewis and Smith's work on health issue message boards (2005) unintentionally shows that 'information' works within wider questions of who wants who to know what for what reason. Their quantitative coding of 791 messages sent to twenty-four sites paints a largely positive picture of goal oriented web users who know what they want from the boards. Emotional support emerges as a key impetus; people seek encouragement and comfort as well as information and advice. Almost as an aside, Macias et al. mention the topic has become controversial in the US following the Surgeon General's decision to allow drug companies and health insurers to sponsor sites. Although these organizations are not allowed to influence the content of their sites beyond normal legal requirements, eyebrows must be raised by the fact that product advice and drug protocols are frequently asked questions. This tells us that 'diffusion' is often the site of conflict between interest groups with different and even opposing agendas.

However, the impact of information campaigns is also determined in large part by the needs of audiences, or potential adopters. Pillsbury and Mayer's research on women's anti-violence activism in Africa (2005) shows that well intentioned campaigns are easily ignored if they fail to understand or connect with the life and world of those they try to help.

Based on *Women Connect*, a five-year programme sponsored by Annenberg USC and the Pacific Institute for Women's Health to aid twenty-nine women's non-governmental organizations (NGOs) in Zimbabwe, Zambia and Uganda, this article alerts us to the importance of cultural factors in determining both the use of communications technologies and the nature of learning. To begin, the sorts of problems that the NGOs were trying to address – changing behaviours around women's rights, abuse of women, sexual health practices – extended beyond informational needs. As with Kitzinger's work on UK child abuse, the *Women Connect* projects had to deal with the fact that their target audience often did not understand abuse as abuse. Accordingly, some campaigns fell on deaf ears, serving mostly as a rallying cry for the already politicized. One poster campaign was so unsuccessful that its primary 'impact' was as a source of wrapping paper.

Nor did new communication technologies offer any simple solutions. While information and communication technology was the fulcrum for many of these projects, at the same time it has been widely pointed out that computers have little impact in settings where target audiences don't have electricity or do not know how to use them. To address this internet cafes were introduced, as such settings marry the need for information *and* the provision of training that makes that information accessible.

What this tells us is that campaigns cannot be top-down processes; they have to begin from where audiences 'are' in terms of what they know and what they do. Mohammed and Thombre's work on HIV/AIDS narratives show how this perspective can produce a new understanding of learning (2005). The authors used internet search engines to locate websites where people with HIV/AIDS share their experiences of the disease. This method delivered 164 testimonies, which were then quantitatively coded to discern any common themes in how the illness is understood.

Mohammed and Thombre's work is noteworthy in representing a transition from a transmission to a transformation approach to learning. This argues that the key to promoting 'adoption' or behavioural change is working with what people already know, rather than trying to force new information upon them. They identify technological and conceptual problems in transmission thinking. First, like Pillsbury and Mayer, they resist enlightenment narratives around the internet. The speed and spread of the medium hampers diffusion by proliferating false knowledge. In the health field, the internet has created a generation of 'cyberquacks' using erroneous facts to sell HIV 'cures' such as shark cartilage. Also like Pillsbury and Mayer, they argue that health communication has to connect with the culture of the target audience. In this case, the narratives that they found suggest that the focus on information inverts the learning process. The 164 stories tell us that what people with HIV/AIDS need are resources that allow them to make sense of their experiences so that they can make informed judgments about future treatments.

Having coded the stories, the authors noted that seventy-three per cent contained some sort of emotional content – much more space than was devoted to exchanging facts. Looking at the structure of these stories, they all centred on key stages in the process of the illness; diagnosis, post-diagnosis change, immersion in the world of HIV/AIDS, post-immersion change and finally the revealing of one's HIV status to others. The important thing to note here is that what people with HIV/AIDS seem to need is to give their illness a meaning by approaching it as a cultural as well as physical experience. The internet becomes key in this regard when the final stage of 'transformation' is reached; its anonymity makes revealing one's positivity a safer business.

Mohammed and Thombre conclude that this makes diffusion a matter of emotion as well as information. People become 'adopters' of health practices on the basis of how they understand what medical conditions mean; this is a matter of feeling as much as knowing. In this case, how one behaves around HIV/AIDS status is influenced as much by concerns about its social as its physical impact. Educators would be advised, then, to focus on what HIV/AIDS means as well as what it is.

Mohammed and Thombre's thoughts radically change how we think about one of the cornerstones of diffusion theory, the concept of cognitive dissonance. A psychological phenomenon explored by Leo Festinger (1963), cognitive dissonance posits that human beings experience mental discomfort when they perceive contradictions between the things that they do and the things that they know and believe. This was applied to health campaigns, in the sense that the idea was to induce such a state by getting people to recognize unhealthy habits. However, the focus on narrative learning opens the possibility that we need to understand what 'being healthy' means for people, as this definition will determine the strength of cognitive dissonance.

The narrative focus also suggests the relevance of qualitative methods. Mohammed and Thombre usefully outline the broad structure of health narratives, but we also need to know how they work within the intricacies of actual social experiences. DeSantis, in his 'Smoke Screen: an ethnographic study of a cigar shop's collectivity and collective rationalization' (2002), shows how the idea that language creates rather than describes reality applies to the apparently more mundane questions that would appear to owe more to objective truths; in this case how you persuade people to accept the blindingly obvious fact that cigar smoking is bad for you.

The point DeSantis makes is that the hazards of the cigar might *be* clearcut, but they are not *perceived* as such. One explanation for this is the ambiguity of the cigar's public image; athletes are frequently shown enjoying a Havana. Another is provided by data gathered during a detailed two-year ethnography of customers at a Kentuckian cigar shop. The shop was more like a bar, as customers smoked as well as bought there. Using interviews, focus groups and data collected during lengthy periods of 'hanging out' (participant observation), DeSantis comes to the conclusion that collective talk about cigar smoking provided a shield to deflect concerns over its hazards.

Looking at the data, DeSantis noticed that the health risks of cigar smoking were a regular discussion point. However, these conversations tended to follow a ritualistic form and function where discrete dialogues took on repetitive patterns. The spatial arrangement of the bar was noted, where the owner took a central physical and discursive vantage. All conversations flowed through him, and each turn taker affirmed the previous (pro-smoking) point made by the antecedent speaker. Over the two years, the smokers circled around the same six points. Cigar smoking is one of life's benign pleasures as long as it remains a moderate habit; medical research is flawed, partly because cigar smoking has yet to be studied with the same rigour as cigarette smoking; anti-smokers are anti-freedom; the cigar smokers were 'smart guys' who could decode the myths around their habits; society was unfairly trying to oppress them. Each conversation added new 'content' to these commitments. On one occasion, the idea that smoking is benign was linked to a sort of sub-myth that life is inherently hazardous, supported by a story about the dangers of fumes from petrol mowers. Peer pressure was replaced by the idea that groups collectively narrate and validate the cigar smoker as a 'smart guy' (there were no women in this study) who understands life as one long risk assessment exercise. Not everyone in the group had the same power, but there was the sense that everyone contributed to the creation and maintenance of their own culture. This 'peer cluster theory' was used to frame cognitive dissonance in a particular way, illustrating the take that cultural studies has on psychological processes. Some mental dispositions are not antecedent to reception. Anxiety, or lack thereof, can be a result of the meaning making process. Cognitive dissonance is only possible where someone *perceives*, constructs or interprets a dislocation between thought and behaviour. It is, in this sense, a matter of framing.

DeSantis also addressed the common research problem of relying on self-reporting. This in turn relates to critical ethnography and the technique of triangulation. Recall in the previous chapter we said that ethnography begins as the effort to describe cultures. This is an important aspect of DeSantis' study; the author tried to describe how people can ignore obviously risky behaviour. But he was also alert to the fact that culture involves a set of non-conscious behaviours, things which are either beyond the vocabulary or vision of respondents. DeSantis noted that the frames he witnessed are rolled out frequently and regularly, with different people taking turns to make the same point. Yet when directly questioned on the process, individuals claimed to be the authors of their own positions. Only painstaking note taking and looking for patterns, in this case quantitatively coded, allowed the author to demonstrate that the interviewees' accounts were wrong.

Learning is, then, about more than the transmission of facts. Clearly, media campaigning has to connect with everyday forms of intercourse and the needs of the audience. In this sense, learning is more of a conversation rather than a lecture. There is more to learning obstacles than simple misunderstanding. As modern diffusion studies show, consensus cannot be assumed between 'sender' and 'receiver'. Sometimes a conflict model is more appropriate in understanding why learning fails.

## DIFFUSION, NEWS AND MASS COMMUNICATION: AGENDA SETTING, CULTIVATION ANALYSIS, THE SPIRAL OF SILENCE AND FRAMING

**2.4** Esteemed mass communication scholar Everett Rogers (2000) notes the analysis of diffusion and learning was soon applied to the reception of news, and has since acknowledged social, cultural and technological conflict. In this, diffusion connects to three important paradigms which tried, via quantitative experiments and surveys, to articulate media power in terms of socialization rather than direct effects. Agenda setting, cultivation analysis and spiral of silence research shared a desire to explain how media generated general beliefs about how the world is and works, rather than specific beliefs on particular issues. Consider Hurricane Katrina. We might say that the most important questions to ask about the news coverage centre on general issues of class and race representations. The impact of these images is far more important than whether or not viewers really believed that sharks swam down Canal Street. Agenda setting is foundational to this shifted perspective, developing the 'framing' concept that Kitzinger powerfully uses.

In many ways, agenda setting inherited the diffusion mantle, addressing structural obstacles which, either by design or implication, impede information flow and knowledge development. By the 1960s, diffusion researchers had begun to ask if the main media effect was to accentuate the gap between information rich and poor. The wide publicity given to the established connection between smoking and lung cancer, for example, was found to have a wider reach and impact within the US middle as opposed to working classes (Tichenor, Donohue & Olien, 1970). More recently, researchers have begun to study how the interactions between media forms influence diffusion pathways. Singhal studied the spread of a story in India about deities drinking milk in Hindu places of worship. Here, the audience amplified media coverage. Many viewers and listeners immediately felt the need to pass the news on. Therefore, the telephone became as important as television and radio. But why? Singhal concluded that the story spread so widely and quickly as it resonated with the rise of a particular form of Hindu nationalism. In other words, it was politically salient (cited in Rogers, 2000).

Salience is a foundational idea in agenda setting research. The agenda setting idea is often pithily summarized in the phrase 'the media don't tell us what to think, but they do tell us what to think about'. This hardly seems a foundation for forty years of research. Like the 'third person effect', agenda setting began in what looked like a fairly simple idea; that public opinion tends to reflect media definitions of what is important. However, this became the basis for a much more complicated exploration of why this might be the case, how it comes about, and what it all means.

Maxwell McCombs, a founding figure in agenda setting research, summarizes its themes, methods and flaws (2005). The research itself has taken a variety of quantitative forms, not all of which are audience related. Given it begins in the argument that the media present a selection of public issues for our consideration, many have devoted time to content analyses that quantify the breadth and depth of media coverage. When the audience is studied, this can take the form of the survey or the experiment. The latter is suitable since agenda setting draws on the concepts of psychological needs. So it has been hypothesized that agenda setting effects are greatest when individuals have a high need for orientation on a topic. They have also been related to the idea of 'priming'. That is, media emphasis predisposes audiences to look out for certain themes or stories, or to recognize events as representative of particular classifications of political themes. Agenda setting works, then, through two processes; applicability and accessibility. Both explain how audiences recognize media definitions of importance. Applicability is a relevance construct. Accessibility is a priming issue, in that it references the audiences' ability to recognize the salience of an event as a representation of a theme or issue which they already feel is important (McCombs, 2005). In this regard, we might hypothesize that Hurricane Katrina sustained interest as it accessed issues around George Bush Jnr's presidential credentials raised during the elections of 2001 and 2004 and again over Iraq.

As with theories of cognitive dissonance, the question that critical audience research might ask is, where do these psychological needs come from? That is, the notion of the psychological might suggest that these needs are 'in our heads' by virtue of mental structures somehow existing prior to lived experience. The framing issue, and understanding how it develops over the forty years of agenda setting work, helps overcome this potential difficulty. The pithy version of agenda setting, Kitzinger points out, represents a weak notion of effects. The idea implied by 'what to think about, not what to think' is that agenda setting merely establishes the outer limits of public debate. So, everyone has to talk about Katrina, but not everyone has to agree why; George Bush Jnr, federal incompetence, local incompetence, police corruption, poverty in America, racism, global warming, the real-time generation of urban folklore.

All are possible. The frame implied here is analogous to a picture frame, which determines the size of the image, but not what it is.

Why then, in defining framing, does McCombs choose to cite Entman?

> to frame is to select some aspects of perceived reality and make them more salient in a communicating text, in such a way as to promote a particular problem definition, causal interpretation, moral evaluation and/or treatment recommendation for the item described above. (Entman, cited in McCombs, 2005: 546)

McCombs uses this definition as it fits the distinction he makes within and between objects and attributes. The 'picture frame' understanding of agenda setting is driven by focusing on agenda objects i.e. what the media and public represent and think about. However, as the model develops it places more emphasis on attributes, further defining the category in terms of aspects and central themes. An attribute is a characterizing feature of an object. Central themes are special cases of attributes that define what an object is about. What this means is that according to McCombs, modern agenda setting research would not ask only if news audiences recognized Hurricane Katrina as an important news story (the object of perception). Nor would it end in delineating the themes attached to the event (the aspects of perception). It would go on to identify which of these aspects became the central theme (the conclusion of perception). I will argue that these distinctions are important as they explain how Kitzinger replaces the idea of the picture frame with the metaphor of the cookie cutter. What McCombs is saying is that today, agenda setting does in fact mean telling people what to think about what they think about. Framing is a deterministic practice, as *Framing Sex Abuse* shows.

Before we explain this, it is worth exploring two other sorts of mass communication research which developed useful ideas that outline the political effects framing has. Agenda setting argues that the news media present inevitably selective images of the world influencing how we organize reality into the things that matter and the things that do not. Two other traditions have explored the ideological consequences of media related understanding on things that we do and say. Cultivation analysis quantifies the differences between the real and televisual worlds through content analysis, thereafter using surveys to show how the divergence influences light and heavy viewers. Romer, Hall Jamieson and Aday (2003) applied this idea to the study of news and crime. Cultivation analysis is appropriate in this area, as in early 1990s America, while real crime was falling, its profile on local news flourished. Dovetailing with agenda setting theory, Romer et al. hypothesized that the repetition of crime stories in the local news made it a readily accessible answer when viewers were asked about pressing social issues. The hypothesis was supported by survey data correlating opinions with exposure to television news. So crime, which was falling, became more important at the expense of other phenomena, such as poverty, which really were on the increase.

But how might this influence communication within the audience? As we know from diffusion research, talk affects the effects that media messages have. An early effort to examine this question came in the form of spiral of silence research. Originally developed by German scholar Elisabeth Noelle-Neuman, the theory asks if: 'an individual's willingness to express his or her opinion [is] a function of how he or she [perceives] public opinion' (Scheufle & Moy, 2000: 3). The theory posits a dysfunctional notion of public opinion. Here, the primary motivation beneath public discussions of political issues is the desire to fit in. Individuals 'scan' what others think before speaking. Relations with agenda setting are clear. The media are major scanning resources. Media coverage, the theory goes, can have a 'chilling effect', in creating the impression that some opinions are more popular and thus sayable than others (Scheufle & Moy, 2000).

Although some have objected to the theoretical, methodological and historical origins of the spiral of silence (Scheufle & Moy, 2000), scholars continue to find it conceptually fruitful. Experimental research has been used to augment the idea. McDevitt, Kiousis and Wahl-Jorgensen (2003) demonstrated that such methods can be used for hypothesis raising as well as testing. The researchers began by exploring the reasons why the spiral of silence might *not* be expected to work in new media environments. The original hypothesis assumed mass, face-to-face and verbal exchange. But what of computer mediated communication? Using a student sample, McDevitt et al. studied differences between face-to-face and 'chat room' opinion expression. The reason for this comparison was that reduced social cues (tone of voice, facial expression) and the relative absence of social sanctions ('tis better to be flamed than slapped) meant that perceived majority opinion might be expected to have less inhibitive power. Forty-eight students were split into groups asked to debate the abortion issue. Using 'confederates', planted subjects working to the researcher's agenda, each group was weighted in pro-abortion or anti-abortion directions. The groups were also evenly split to debate the issue as a group or via computer. Surprizingly, computer discussions revealed a 'spiral of moderation'. The minorities were less likely to virtually announce their view on abortion. But, when surveyed for how they would define other group members' views, computer users were likely to interpret others as far more moderate than they actually were. Equally, the perception of minority status did not stop participation in the discussions. This may be explained by the fact that the reduced social cues on the web, combined with the explosion of agendas on offer (McCombs, 2005) make it harder to figure what majority opinion is.

McDevitt et al. concluded that the spiral of silence idea is worth pursuing, recognizing that technological shifts necessitate further empirical work.

## APPLYING FRAMING AND ITS EFFECTS TO CRITICAL AUDIENCE RESEARCH

**2.5** Carragee and Roefs (2004) dismissed mass communication framing models as incapable of dealing with the nuances of media and political power. They argued that agenda setting equates frame with topic, and, therefore, cannot conceive media as places of struggle between agendas sponsored by competing power groups. As McCombs's recent work shows, this conclusion is quite wrong. Nevertheless, we might ask how 'top-down' thinking matches the reality of reception. Nick Couldry's definition of media power, used in Chapter 1, modern diffusion studies and the Hurricane Katrina example show that structural qualities of media environments offer power possibilities, but not guarantees. We must therefore consider how 'top-down' understandings of cultural power meet with 'bottom-up' studies of audience activity.

Addressing the former, Chaffee's 'second wave' of mass communication research placed the concept of structural disinhibition to dissemination on the agenda. James Stanyer (2002) argued that audiences' lack of interest in politics is the product of structural changes in the way that news is produced and disseminated. Broadly, a global economic recession which has cut advertising revenues pushes news corporations toward tabloidization. In the UK, election campaigns have become unappealing to television news. Angered by the stifling choreography of political briefings and events in the national election campaign of 2001, producers often chose to go with non-election items that were more real. Political news has increased in one key area, digital services. Banished to unknown channels, politics becomes the sound of one hand clapping.

When political issues are discussed, they can offer highly circumscribed versions of the world. Miller's poll analysis sources the spiral of silence; because journalists believed that the majority of the public favoured the war in Afghanistan, they felt less obliged to cover the anti-war position. Miller hypothesized that this could have had the result of silencing those opposing force, as they might have felt they were in a minority. At least those journalists that Miller interviewed were thinking about the audience. Others have found that while public opinion is frequently invoked in press and onscreen, journalists rarely bother to research what readers and viewers actually think (Wahl-Jorgensen, 2002, 2004; Lewis, Wahl-Jorgensen & Inthorn, 2004). Gillespie's study of reactions to news of the Iraq War (2002) showed how this disregard for the audience can produce anger and anxiety as well as apathy. British Muslim news viewers were dismayed by the limited range of topics and perspectives offered by the media. Blinkered reporting presented the Islamic world as irrational and homogenous, a message that ostracized Muslim audiences.

This research, however, tends to focus on 'hard' news about high profile events. Peter Dahlgren (2005) argued for an expanded notion of the political, which in turn changes how we understand audience apathy. If political engagement is defined not as knowing about facts, but engaging in discussions on matters of social importance, then politics happens in all sorts of places, using many kinds of languages. Dahlgren agreed with Stanyer that digital and computer-mediated communication fragmentation can have detrimental effects on this sort of engagement, as it makes it easy for audiences to ignore politics and each other. But it can also mean that engagement happens in surprising places and forms. It also creates enclaves where specific sorts of audiences can find a recognition and sense of community denied by mainstream media. For Gillespie's Muslim audiences, Al Jazeera, delivered by cable and satellite systems, became a vital cultural resource in reflecting the diversity of Islamic experiences. Eventually, these enclaves have to reconnect with a central political system. But Dahlgren suggests that rather than lamenting audiences' inability to live up to the golden mean of citizenship: 'a viable democracy must have an anchoring at the level of citizens' lived experiences, personal resources and subjective dispositions' (2005:158).

What this means is, as well as asking how news frames the world, we should understand how audiences frame news. And indeed this question leads to an important methodological question: how have audience researchers framed audiences, and what happens to these frameworks when applied to close studies of news in action?

## WHERE 'ARE' NEWS AUDIENCES?

**2.6** Thomas (2004) began to address this question in his research on readers of the UK tabloid the *Daily Mirror* in the 1940s. Thomas used letters written by ordinary people to the Mass Observation Archive at the University of Sussex. Mass observation began in the 1930s as an effort to map everyday life in Britain. Panels of 'observers' are asked for their thoughts on issues of the day, many of which are media related. Using this resource, Thomas argued that current pessimism about audiences is based on a sense of a 'golden age' of popular political engagement that might never have existed. The *Daily Mirror* has been seen as a catalyst in delivering the post-World War Two Labour government and the welfare state. In contrast, Thomas's research showed only three per cent of readers bought the paper for its political content, and over half could not identify its editorial position. So what attracted readers to the *Daily Mirror* in the 1940s? Comic strips and the letters page.

Of course, the idea that audiences have never been especially interested in politics is not a comforting one, and offers little to anyone who is interested in understanding engagement. To this end Hagan (1997) and Vettehen, Schaap and Schlosser (2004) provided evidence on why certain sorts of audiences are disenfranchised. Barry Richards (2004) complained that discussions of public apathy prioritize the wrong issues. Instead of asking what people know about politics, we should ask how they feel about it. Hagan's interviews with Norwegian news watchers illustrate the relevance of Richards' ideas. Asking viewers what they thought about television news, she found descriptions that were indeed based on feelings, namely duty, frustration, anxiety, disappointment and ambivalence. In a nation characterized by a relatively high rate of news consumption, while viewers indeed disliked television news, at least they knew why. Watching was regarded as something of a chore. It also clashed with domestic obligations, and most of the time failed to reward viewers. Foreign news was singled out for special criticism, seemingly consisting of an endless catalogue of fragmented, contextless cycles of violence with neither rhyme nor reason. Bourdon (2000) argues that what compels viewers to return to a medium which is largely repetitive and predictable is the knowledge that sometimes it is not. For example, the UK audience for the 1980 World Snooker Final became inadvertent witnesses to the Special Air Service storming of the Iranian Embassy in London as breaking news filled their screens. Similarly, much as they hate the news, Hagan's Norwegian sample continued to watch for fear of missing out.

Vettehen, Schaap and Schlosser examined the gender dimensions of disliking news in a way that questioned scholarly framing of 'disengagement'. Taking data that illustrated women's lack of interest in news, their study asked if this 'fact' depended more on how we understand what news and engagement are. The researchers used a quasi-experimental method. Real news items were edited to produce a 'masculine' programme, featuring mostly male presenters reporting stories where most of the central actors were also men. Nineteen male and female viewers were then asked to verbalize their responses to the show. These comments were sorted into six categories; opinion, empathy, interpreting actors' motives, distraction, dissatisfaction, lack of interest. While the results bear out what we already 'know' about differences between men and women, in that men express a greater interest in this sort of news, Vettehen, Schaap and Schlosser's thesis was that this 'fact' discusses different sorts of engagement. Women were more likely to admit to finding news confusing, but did so in a way that demonstrated an understanding of news as a cultural form. That is, where men tended to speak of content, the women in the study were more interested in discussing deeper questions about what news is, and what it should be. The point is that these women were not less interested in the world than the men, but they were frustrated that television news does not deliver an experience allowing them to connect with the political. Vettehen, Schaap and Schlosser were able to come to this conclusion because they asked people how they feel rather than what they know about news.

## USEFUL NEWS

**2.7** Is all research on news relentlessly pessimistic? Addressing news as a cultural form, Ekstrom (2002) dismissed a knowledge survey approach to audience research as misunderstanding what news is. Consider television. A story about, say, Britain's entry into a European single currency has to speak to a general audience encompassing professional economists to people who cannot balance their chequebooks. The 'one size fits all' task means that the best strategy for television news is to focus on the experience of what it might feel like to live with a single currency, rather than the mechanics of how the transition would work. That is, news can do little more than provide cultural resources that people can use to make sense of things for themselves.

Methodologically, this leads to the conclusion that it is important to spend time with audiences to examine how they understand what news is, and how this influences relations between news, information and everyday life. Practically, this raises time problems similar to those faced by diffusion researchers. The point has often been made that while qualitative audience research is inspired by ethnography, it rarely involves lengthy periods in the field. So, aside from asking what qualitative studies tell us about how people use news, we will also consider how a feel of immersion might be achieved.

Machin (2002) adopted an orthodox strategy, spending eighteen months working in factories and bars in Valencia to study Spanish newspaper readers. During this period three girls were abducted and murdered. Unusually, reporting took on sensationalistic aspects normally absent from the Spanish press. Superficially, this represented a capitulation to tabloidization as a global form. Yet Machin's ethnography provides evidence that this was an audience driven phenomenon. Tragically, events such as this are not rare in Spain. Therefore, the level of coverage devoted to the case was not a reflection of a pre-existing production agenda. Instead, the actions of the girls' fathers pushed the story onto the media agenda. Second, however, the story represented a sort of raw material that newsreaders cold use to articulate social concerns, and also to negotiate a social position.

Machin witnessed 'Ignacio', a bar patron and factory colleague, expressing very different views on the story. At times Ignacio cut a Bronsonesque figure, advocating rough justice for those who threaten decent society. At other times, he described the murders as a product of social deprivation rather than individual evil. These contradictory positions were in fact coherent, as they represented strategic responses motivated by a desire to achieve a certain sort of powerful position – either within decent society, or as someone media literate enough to see through populist rhetoric (as a way of condescending to those who cannot). Neither represented what Ignacio 'really' thought, but instead showed how news becomes a cultural resource used to achieve specific social aims – both of which can be real. They also influence the news itself. News gathering processes, which involved lengthy interviews with people like Ignacio to get the popular feel, reflected back on the way that journalists wrote the story.

Staying in Spain, Barnhurst (2000) approximated time by getting sixty-two students to write narratives describing how they had used news media since childhood. Contrasting with similar accounts written by US students, Barnhurst argued that the greater enthusiasm shown for news reading by the Spanish group was explained by ritual aspects of newspaper reading. A common theme in the Spanish accounts was the integration of newspapers and newspaper reading into family life. This led, according to Barnhurst, to a more sophisticated news reading culture driven by the fact that news became a part of everyday rhythms, rather than a disruptive force.

Using the same technique, Calavita (2003) disagrees, in showing that US students produce the same sorts of stories about their experiences with television news. Calavita critiques models of political socialization that treat the factors that influence how we think as discrete forces. For example, we might view mass and face-to-face communication as different and often contradictory entities. The television news narratives Calavita collected show that these are often related. One student, for example, spoke of the way that his father used television news as a means of establishing authority. During evening broadcasts, his father could induce silence in the family by turning the volume up during stories he deemed to be important. In this sense, mass and interpersonal communication worked in league.

Studying the minute processes of reception, then, suggests that news and information is partly framed by the cultural needs and practices found in the audience rather than the media. But what does this do to questions of power and normative views of what news should do?

## JUST THE FACTS? NEW INFLUENCE RESEARCH, WEAK FRAMES AND POOR PUBLIC UNDERSTANDING

**2.8** Machin, Barnhurst and Calavita all suggest that the cultural impact of news is determined as much by audience practices as media structures. But there are limits to this position. Elizabeth Bird outlines these in her study of US tabloid television viewers (2003). For Bird, there is little point in regarding news as a 'bitter pill' that audiences must be forced to swallow. Given that they are different forms, there is also nothing to suggest that tabloid television viewers would watch more 'proper' news if the former disappeared.

Having said this, narrative is not the ultimate panacea. Bird defines the tabloid as a narrative style high on personal experience and visual content. Driven by the need to widen profit margins by cutting costs, the tabloid style cannot improve news on foreign policy. This would take an expensive strategy of permanently deploying personnel in 'hotspots' so that news organizations could truly grasp the cultures they report on. Nor is it clear that this would improve public understanding. During the Gulf War, the extensive use of experience narratives from low-ranking troops on the ground was used to avoid broader discussions of what was happening, why it was happening and whether any of it should have happened at all.

What does this have to do with framing? Reviewing, a common theme in the work referenced is that a frame is a narratively organized map telling us what an event means. Where mass communication models tend to look at the media-driven aspects of framing, others focus on how audiences build the same sorts of structures. Ignacio, for example, selectively used media content to frame himself as different sorts of people as needs be. Bird, however, asks if we should view such actions positively.

Metzger's research (2000) similarly portrayed news audiences as 'meaning machines'. All narratives need resolution. When news fails to provide closure, the audience often infers it. When drought-induced famine fades from the screen, viewers assume that this is because the problem has been solved. They do this by placing 'drought' and 'famine' within a natural disaster frame. When nature has corrected the imbalance between resource and demand, things return to normal. Of course, this narrative prevents us from asking how drought and famine are caused and prolonged by human action; agricultural mismanagement; exploitative economic links or unsustained public attention. In other words, while narrative frames help us to engage with politics by telling us why we should care about something, the wrong frame can misrepresent the world in a way that exacerbates the problem. This is the argument made by Philo and Berry's research (2004) on reception of news on the Israeli occupation of Palestine.

Philo and Berry's work is an example of how one can lend a richer feel to 'snapshot' research by using multiple methods. They studied how viewers made sense of news from Palestine through focus group interviews and news writing exercises. Here, respondents were asked to write stories to accompany visual images drawn from actual news broadcasts. This technique is complementary to agenda setting ideas; the point is to assess the proximity between media and audience narratives, and to identify other frames that audiences draw upon. Accepting that absence of context is a key reason why UK audiences know and care little about Palestine, Philo and Berry also used experimental approaches. Groups were asked to watch news clips, given short histories of the conflict to read, then asked to view the same segments again to see if the reading exercise altered comprehension.

Moreover, the authors also intended to influence the direction of opinion on Palestine. Traditionally, media research has often tried to use 'naturally' occurring groups (e.g. Morley, 1980, 1989). Philo and Berry, however, placed media professionals among the public so that diverse perspectives on the news would emerge. Having reviewed the conflict's history and its media coverage, their clear conclusion was that British television news fails to signal the reality that the Israeli presence in Palestine is an illegal occupation denying the local Arab population of human and civic rights. This was not descriptive work. Nor did it accept what audiences have to say as legitimate. In one memorable section, a focus group interviewer harassed participants until they delivered a particular response. Content analysis concluded that most of the time Israeli Defence Force soldiers are depicted as reacting to Palestinian violence. This frames such actions as defensive, when in reality, in the authors' judgment, the very presence of Israeli troops is aggressive. However, when asked to view a clip of clashes between troops and Palestinian protestors, one respondent claimed that Israelis were identified as catalysts. The interviewer felt that this represented what the respondent thought about the conflict in general, not the clip in particular. The interviewee was then hounded into changing his mind, agreeing that the clip placed Palestinian protestors in the aggressive role.

Originating in the premise that UK news is wrong about Palestine, Philo and Berry stressed how narrative structures can invert social reality. Moreover, creative audience strategies become complicit in the process. Akin to Metzger's research, Berry and Philo were struck by the fact that while their respondents demonstrably knew little about the conflict, they were still able to produce literate stories about it in news writing exercises. Lacking knowledge of the historical and political specifics, the groups drew on more familiar narratives; the pity of war, the callous inefficiency of macropolitical processes. The problem with these frames is that they left little to say about the Palestinian conflict in particular, and therefore how political pressure should be brought to bear to effect change. Part of the problem was factual; the 'war is hell' theme meant that when respondents made guesses about causality, they were often wrong.

At the same time, cultural empathy emerged as a factor in determining who the audience sided with. For groups conducted in London, experiences with Irish Republican Army bombing made it easier to identify with Israelis as terrorist targets. For the same people, displays of Palestinian grief were articulated in an unknown language; it was hard to relate in concrete ways with mourning displays that seemed so alien. The solution is to contextualize why grief is expressed so; but here we again confront the problem Bird outlines. This would mean news organizations expanding their resource commitments. Aside from matters of profit margins, Philo and Berry discovered that journalistic ideas about balance refer to information but not cultural context.

Philo and Berry's *Bad News from Israel* (2004) demonstrates that narrative frames are important for engaging audiences. But in a real world where oppression exists regardless of how it is understood, the stories we tell must respect the material form of social problems. Enter Kitzinger's *Framing Sex Abuse*. Depressingly, this is not a study that anyone could do with just a solid grasp of audience research techniques. In it, Kitzinger draws on twenty years of working with sex abuse survivors as both volunteer and researcher. In the 1980s, significantly before the abuse of children had emerged as a media issue, Kitzinger began recording survivors' stories, at their behest. Thus started a two-decade interest in public understanding of the problem, which has increasingly come to rely on media representations. By 2004, Kitzinger was in a unique position to examine changes in the way media and audiences defined sexual abuse, and the impact that this had had on opinion and policy. In this project she united diffusion and framing research, reinvesting interests in media and learning with a critical edge acknowledging the complex, interactive origins and effects of framing.

The book develops an argument via a number of related case studies; early 1980s representations of sexual abuse; the impact of two high-profile sex abuse scandals in the UK; the media and 'moral panics' around paedophilia in the 1990s; Kitzinger's evaluation study of the 'zero tolerance' campaign designed to 'reframe' what abuse is and where it happens. The thrust of the argument is as follows; media representation matters. It is important for sex abuse survivors that their stories be told. It is also important, however, that the variety of stories presented to the public represent the full range of sexual abuse experiences. In framing sex abuse an action of obviously monstrous people that only happens in certain places, the media might actually have impeded efforts to combat the problem.

According to Kitzinger's data, in the early 1980s surviving sex abuse was made harder by its invisibility as an issue to be reckoned with. The law offered children little protection from domestic sexual abuse, a phenomenon rarely depicted in the media. Collecting narratives from survivors, Kitzinger found a common thread where the absence of public representation left no language to describe their experiences. The inclusion of a storyline in the UK television soap opera *Brookside*, featuring a mother and daughter both being abused by a husband/father, became of supreme cultural importance. Here was an acknowledgment that survivors were not alone, and that their suffering was the product of social forces, not bad luck or personal fault.

Sadly, this early representation was something of a high point in the history of how UK media have handled the issue. Unlike politics, the problem with media representations of child sex abuse is not that people cannot associate with them. The subject has become a matter of intense public concern. However, sexual abuse is framed in narratives that distort its material form. Kitzinger argued that media and audience alike have tended to define cases according to one of two 'templates'. The first relates to 'stranger danger'. Media campaigns to publicize the whereabouts of convicted paedophiles have developed an 'identikit' picture of the typical offender; he is a mentally-ill, gay stranger of visibly evil or monstrous appearance. Interviewing a variety of audiences about the paedophile issue, Kitzinger showed how his image creates a false sense of security about the places where most sexual abuse occurs; inside the home, perpetuated by apparently kind, trustworthy people.

The other template works in the opposite direction. In the 1980s and 1990s much coverage was given to two cases where social services placed a number of children in care following allegations that they were being abused by their parents. Studying reception of the Cleveland and Orkney cases, Kitzinger found that the former had been summarized as being essentially 'about' the incompetence of the social services, all children having been eventually returned to their parents. The case was, in fact, much more complicated, involving issues such as the difficulties of bringing alleged abusers to court. Nonetheless, this simplified version was used as a map to understand the meaning of an apparently similar case in the Scottish Orkney Islands. The latter story also drew on 'stranger danger' ideas; many audiences could not conceive that abuse could happen in such bucolic surroundings, performed by nice, ordinary parents.

The idea of the template, then, draws on the agenda setting technique of identifying central attributes. While media placed child sex abuse on the public agenda, the lesson it taught was that children were safe as long as they stayed away from certain people and places; or as long as certain people were kept away from them. The news media had been spectacularly successful in making news audiences care about the wrong things.

However, the idea of the template, and the methods that developed it, add new dimensions to the discussion on news and public information. The first element of note is that while the template is a powerful force, its roots lie within interactions between state, media and culture. Concerns over the whereabouts of paedophiles are not presented as simply a moral panic, where the media create and amplify public issues. First, in the mid-1990s there was something of a vacuum around the issue. State policy on registered sex offenders was developing in an ad hoc way. Second, media amplification of the issue was successful as it connected with organic public concerns. Suspected sex offenders at times became victims of apparent vigilantism, but Kitzinger understands this as more than simple mob rule. The paedophile scares were part of longer, logical complaints about deteriorating conditions in working class communities. Released sex offenders were much like landfills, power lines and nightmare neighbours, another environmental hazard foisted on the poor by 'not in my back yard' middle class muscle. This moral panic, and its stranger danger associations, drew energy as much from organic political unrest as media manipulation.

It is in the power of articulated self experience that Kitzinger founds hope in this deeply depressing subject. This relates, finally, to the way that research is conceptualized. Kitzinger's methods are largely akin to those used by Philo and Berry; focus group and individual interviews, writing exercises. What is novel is that these are places for disclosure, reflection and revelation, locating researcher as activist, not archivist. Developing the idea of research as consciousness raising, the protocols Kitzinger used allow respondents not just to state what they think and how they read the media, but to confront and change these same phenomena. In early research, the act of documenting their experiences gave survivors the space to reflect upon and reorganize how they understood their lives. Similarly, group sessions often contained revelations that confronted media frames. When people who had no first-hand experience of sexual abuse trotted out stranger danger frames, they were at times shocked by others' tales of abuse at the hands of the known and the trusted. This was particularly the case in 'zero tolerance' studies and, in this sense, Kitzinger's work became an extension of that campaign to change public understandings of sexual abuse.

## CONCLUSION

**2.9** What all of this teaches us is that a cultural studies orientation refuting 'transmission' views of communication is *not* antithetical to questions of how media function as public information tools. It does tend to focus on knowledge rather than information (exploring the distinction between facts and significance), and on the structural obstacles that prevent media cultures from working in a democratic, egalitarian fashion. However, as these issues have come to circulate around 'framing', asking how media explain rather than describe the world, so scholars have began to work back toward factual concerns that reconnect scholarship with normative concerns about how we would like the media to work.

# 3   Media, Pleasure and Identity: The Meaning of the Meaningless

## INTRODUCTION

**3.1** An early foray into audience research found me sitting in an American middle class living room asking a man and his teenage sons why they enjoyed *The Simpsons* (Ruddock, 1997). I had decided that the animated series was replete with politically subversive messages, including an opening sequence offering an Althusserian critique of American living. Louis Althusser's neo-Marxist analysis argued that social and cultural institutions worked in league with capital and the state to reproduce class divisions (1972). Paul Willis used these ideas in *Learning to Labour* (1977). His study characterized the UK educational system as an ambition suppressant. Far from maximizing potential, schools ensured that, as the book's subtitle declares, 'working class kids get working class jobs'. This, I was sure, was what *The Simpsons* was saying about Bart's education, where paranoid, alcoholic, inept teachers nurture his delinquency to guarantee that he morphs into his television watching, donut eating, beer swilling father.

My interviewees found this suggestion palpably insane. Much as he might have once told his boys there are no werewolves under the bed, the father reassured me that *The Simpsons* was an animated comedy, not a political diatribe. Watching it was about getting away from society and its everyday challenges, not dissecting them. Perhaps this is why I published the project under the title *It Just Doesn't Matter*.

This chapter will argue that popular culture and its reception do matter. My *Simpsons* experience represents a common problem in audience research. Implicit in the bemused reaction to my questions was the belief that media live in meaningless worlds of private pleasure expressing nothing but idiosyncratic tastes. Alternatively, I will assert that both the individual and the subsequent definitions of 'meaningless' media experience turn on cultural constructions that are neither casual nor insignificant.

Such an argument hinges on distinctions between cultural studies and uses and gratifications research (u&g hereafter). Despite its use of quantitative surveys and experiments, u&g is often understood as a cousin to cultural studies, since both paradigms insist on active audiences. However, u&g rests on psychological and biological essentials that largely ignore culture. Media are meaningless, in the respect that our use of them is determined by internal drives having little to do with representation and interpretation. Thus, a u&g perspective avoids a number of important questions about the media's social and symbolic relevance. In this chapter, I argue that media meanings have a material impact. Even the idea of the meaningless is strangely meaningful, as it relates to the common desire to express individuality.

Research on diasporic audiences will be used to combine the meaningful and the meaningless in illustrating the relationship between collective and individual experiences of identity. Diasporic studies explore how dispersed global audiences use media to maintain connections with distant racial, ethnic, religious or national homelands. Diaspora is our final destination for four reasons. First, diasporic audiences bespeak the inadequacy of biological and psychological factors in explaining the total process of subjectivity and media use. Second, they intimate how anti-essentialist models of cultural power work in practice. Third, in outlining the irregularity of power relationships and the impossibility of reducing sense-making to biological or geographic essentials, diasporic studies explain relations between the individual and culture. Finally, diaspora turns on a notion of social imaginary that clarifies why media matter politically.

## USES AND GRATIFICATIONS RESEARCH: THE ROAD TO BIOLOGICAL DETERMINISM

**3.2** Differences between u&g and cultural studies have been accentuated by recent work representing individuality in an unhelpfully asocial way. However, we need to understand how and why this has happened in order to show how we can speak of cultural patterns while respecting differences within and between audiences.

U&g research seeks to understand media culture from the point of view of the people who use it. Elihu Katz summarizes its ethos in the following way:

> Less attention should be paid to what media do to people and more to what people do to the media. Such an approach assumes that even the most potent of mass media content cannot ordinarily influence an individual who has no use for it in the social and psychological context in which he [sic] lives. The uses approach assumes that people's values, their interests, their associations, their social roles, are pre-potent, and that people selectively fashion what they see and hear to these interests (cited in McQuail, 1998: 152)

Although such statements are often taken to signal a similarity between u&g and cultural studies, in that both assume audience agency, appearances are deceiving. Carey and Kreiling (1974) denounced the former as descriptive, functionalist and insensitive to the idea of culture. The basic problem with u&g research, in its original formulation, is that it assumed that media use is always rational and directed toward maintaining positive social integration. The concentration on pre-existing social and psychological needs also impairs u&g as a means of analysing the specific role of the media as compared to other leisure forms (see Ruddock, 2002).

Recently, the gulf between u&g and cultural studies has grown, as the former heads deeper into not only psychological but also biological determinism. Carey and Kreiling criticized Katz for failing to acknowledge the symbolic aspects of the human experience. Influenced by American anthropologist Clifford Geertz (1973), their thesis was that human beings are as fundamentally cultural as they are psychological; that is, what we are depends greatly on the meanings we make from a world made of symbols. In conceiving gratifications as being predicated on needs that exist before media use, Katz made the mistake of assuming that motivations are pre-symbolic and hence acultural.

Presumably, then, Carey and Kreiling would be appalled by Henning and Vorderer's research (2001). Henning and Vorderer's central thesis, based on surveys correlating media use with personality traits and social context among US college students, is that a great deal of television watching is prompted by a need for escapism based on an aversion to thinking. The argument pivots on a distinction between sociological and psychological escapism. Sociological escapism is a misleading term, since it refers to the forensic use of media to dissect social impotence. That is, we turn to mediated fantasies, where we can cogitate what it would feel like to live in a world where we could be whatever we wanted to be, because we know that the real world debars autonomy. So, sociological escapism is predicated on thinking about society. Psychological escapism, on the other hand 'refers to aspects of the personality largely unaffected ... by the social setting' (2001: 102). It also refers to the need not just to escape society, but also to escape the self. In their surveys, Henning and Vorderer found that cognitive aversion was a stronger predictor of greater television viewing than 'sociological' explanations such as life satisfaction, loneliness, tensions or perceptions of personal efficacy. This conclusion does not marginalize the symbolic dimension of media use; it rejects it outright. The more television you watch, the less interest you have in what life means.

Sherry (2001) goes even further in locating motivations for media use in our DNA.

Behavioural genetic research has shown that, for a wide variety of traits, including measures of intelligence, specific cognitive abilities, personality, and psychopathology in north American and European population, the heritability of such traits is between 0.4 and 0.7 (Scarr, cited in Sherry, 2001: 274)

What this means, if it is correct, is that between forty and seventy per cent of what we are and what we do is determined not by our families, our schooling or our culture, but by our genes. In similar vein, Sherry asserts that differential patterns of media use depend on brain chemistry:

Attention and vigilance systems ... are heavily modulated by serotonin ... therefore, temperament traits that predict media use motivations ... offer a possible etiological explanation for media use ... low levels of serotonin (resulting in ... negative mood) ... will [teach] that television viewing can regulate ... neural drives, perhaps resulting in chronic, high amounts of television viewing. (2001: 285)

This being the case, media content can be medically managed.

If depressed, low task oriented, rigid individuals make up the primary chronic television audience, producers will design shows that attract these individuals (as evidenced by ... ratings). Such programming would need to counter negative mood (situation comedies), contain enough stimulation to continually attract and maintain low attention (low task orientation) and provide few narrative surprises (rigidity). These features are typical of most current television programs. (2001: 285)

Sherry reaches this conclusion based on surveys demonstrating that personality traits, understood as mental dispositions that are inherited and remain relatively stable throughout life, are the major predictors of motivations behind media selection.

If u&g has been criticized for a functionalist orientation (see Ruddock, 2002), then Sherry's work takes this to a new level. Here we have a case for social engineering eradicating questions of culture. In a nutshell, audiences don't need better media; they need better drugs. With the right serotonin levels, audiences will abandon formulaic programming, forcing media industries to come up with something more imaginative. Audiences also do not need media and cultural studies, now part of medical territory.

Even if we accept this argument, the rationale for qualitative research into the cultural dimensions of media use remains. By Sherry's own figures, up to sixty per cent of media applications are explained by non-biological factors. This being the case, it is worth attending to his simplistic handling of media habits. Sherry makes the common distinction between active and passive audience motivations, where the former relates to information seeking and the latter to the 'ritualistic' pursuit of physical pleasure: 'Ritualistic gratifications are intrinsic emotional responses to the media and are there-fore ... subconscious. These gratifications include central nervous system stimulation related to arousal and relaxation' (2001: 280).

By Sherry's calculations, this might only explain forty per cent of why people use the 'plug-in drug'. What about the other sixty per cent? Consider Barker and Brooks' (1999) study of audiences for the 1999 Sylvester Stallone blockbuster, *Judge Dredd*. The authors would agree that approaching this film as meaningful, in the sense that it provides access to the sort of sociological engagement I had looked for in my *Simpsons* study, misses the point. Many went to see the film to 'switch off'. However, disconnection is based on a knowing engagement with the cultural geography of the cinematic experience. *Judge Dredd's* audience had to work hard to relax: they had to read cinema reviews to pick the right film; they had to go to the right cinema, possessing the technology to allow a full appreciation of the movie's special effects; they had to build a sense of anticipation and excitement by discussing their expectations with friends; this of course meant that they had to pick the right viewing company. Indubitably, this sort of relaxation is anything but subconscious and passive. So, the other sixty per cent of media use is explained by film history (where does the blockbuster genre come from?), its economic and social structures (where do multiplexes come from and why do we like going to them?) and our understanding of these factors. A large part of the way that we use media as entertainment, then, is explained by spatial arrangements having little to do with biology or psychology. So what else does cultural studies offer on the nature and significance of media pleasure?

## CULTURAL STUDIES AND THE QUESTION OF POWER

**3.3** Barker and Brooks' work signals a number of important dualities in understanding media audiences. While people who went to see *Judge Dredd* were in many ways the authors of their own pleasure, at the same time this agency was exercised within social and historical parameters beyond their control. Where the goal was to achieve a physical euphoria (blockbusters thrill us, shock us, excite us and overwhelm our sense with sights and sounds), this was predicated on a good deal of mental effort. O'Connor and Klaus (2000) see these tensions as constitutive of the way that cultural studies explains how pleasure serves as a point of articulation between the individual and the social. Gratification is always personal and individual inasmuch as it is delivered on and to the body (Barthes, 1975).

Nevertheless, as this happens through culture, satisfaction remains social. Fantasy, for example, often relies on contrasting how the world is with how we would like to be. Janice Radway (1983) famously demonstrated this in her study of women romance novel readers. Radway's analysis depicted this escapist fare as a tool used by women to speak their frustration at the lack of nurturing they received in their marriages. So, while the motivation for reading romance novels was often physical and personal, in terms of making the body unavailable for domestic work, it was also cultural, in that it made a statement about matrimony as an unsatisfactory arrangement of romance and labour. Thus, physical, personal media pleasure provides audiences with a means of making sense of who and where they are, and relations between individual agency and wider forms of social power.

Radway's work represents the importance of feminist scholarship, which enabled media scholars to show why popular culture matters by decon-structing barriers between the public and the private, and entertainment versus information. Far from trivial, media entertainment was the place where opposing political agendas competed for public consent. Radway, along with scholars such as Ang (1985), Press (1991), Gray (1992) and Seiter (1999) put theories of encoding/decoding (Hall, 1980) and resistance (Fiske, 1987) to the empirical test. Both are models of media power that draw upon neo-Marxist and semiotic theory. Although different in impor-tant ways (see Ruddock, 2001), encoding/decoding and resistance theories share the idea that social power depends significantly on the ability to influence the meaning making process which Carey and Kreiling saw as a fundamental part of the human condition. The structure of media industries privileges some groups over others. However, since one can never completely fix the meaning of a sign, one cannot assume that audiences will accept 'preferred' media meanings.

As an example, in previous work I have described how the 1987 Tom Cruise film *Top Gun* was open to certain sorts of 'resistant' readings at the hands of gay audiences. *Top Gun* was made with the willing participation of the US Navy, which was refusing calls to lift its ban on recruiting openly lesbian and gay people. It featured an actor ready to sue anyone who suggests that he is not heterosexual. Nevertheless several factors in *Top Gun* were semiotically ambiguous enough to open a gay reading. Reconsidering this in 2005, the recreation of the movie's iconography and narrative in UK singer Will Young's *Switch It On* video suggests something more. Openly gay, Young's performance demonstrates that alternative readings of the Cruise vehicle have become so widespread that they are almost the norm. This is relevant as it shows how gay discourse, once all but invisible in the media (Gross, 1989), has now become an everyday part of media fare (Young having emerged as the winner of the hugely successful *Pop Idol*).

These ideas of power and struggle are an important corrective to Katz's u&g view. Audiences indeed 'do' things to and with media but not, to paraphrase Marx, under conditions of their own choosing. While we select and interpret, neither function is innocent of extrinsic factors. Consequently, while our media preferences and understandings may be idiosyncratic, they are never personal or private in the fullest sense of the word.

Vandebosch (2000) and Jewkes (2002a; 2002b) explore these ideas in studies of how media are deployed in prisons. This area is noteworthy is it demonstrates key differences between u&g and cultural studies. Succinctly, the argument is that the things being done to them hugely affect what prisoners do with media. Gaols are insightful settings for analyses of media power for three reasons. First, convicts' 'gratifications' have to be understood as part of a 'deprivation' model. That is, the question of prisoners' media habits has to take the absence of alternatives into account (Vandebosch, 2000). Additionally, one must reflect on television's use as a disciplinary agent of pacification, reward and punishment (Jewkes, 2002a). Therefore, the media's penal relevance lies in relations between prisons and prisoners, not the psychology of the latter. This leads to the second insight. Enmeshed in systems of punishment and rehabilitation, media use is a public affair. Prison geographies express this in refusing private space, hence rendering media use as a constant source of surveillance. Third, having said this, while there are intelligible power imbalances within the prison environment, authority is not an exclusively top-down affair. Prisoners have their own internal networks of influence. Even within these circles, no-one is entirely subjugated. In this regard, Jewkes speaks of how male prisoners use television to maintain distinctions between 'front' and 'back' behaviours. Prisons demand a hyper-masculine 'front' that can be destructive to a man's 'outside' personality. The outside self has to be protected for the moment when the prisoner returns to society. So, alongside the expected tastes for football and tabloid newspapers, Jewkes also found passions directed toward preserving mental sensitivities; a heavily tattooed biker expresses a penchant for home makeover shows featuring the foppish UK presenter Laurence Llewellyn-Bowen. Jewkes also described how the prison's disciplinary machinery had unexpected consequences. Radios are more accessible than newspapers. Radio news tends to be more analytical than newspaper reporting. Prisoners, therefore, often exhibited high levels of knowledge about public affairs.

## MEANINGFUL MEDIA

**3.4** Vandebosch's and Jewkes's work thereby argues that popular entertainment (the latter finds that the ITV soap opera *Emmerdale* is hugely popular among UK male prisoners, for reasons that no-one can quite explain) is of very real importance to 'serious' social relations. Moreover, the setting they choose does no more than exaggerate media/audience relations common beyond prison walls. Therefore, their work suggests the importance of looking for explanations of gratification in the meanings that people make from media as a way of understanding how the subject becomes social, and the way that this process is influenced by the shape and power of both text and society.

An initial strategy in this regard has often been to illustrate the permeability between media fact and fiction. Early cultivation analysis did this by highlighting similar representations of social groups that were common across television genres (Morgan, 1989). John Ellis (1999) displaces news sovereignty in his thesis that fictional media is the place where audiences solidify their understanding of the political world. Porto (2005) and Holbert et al. (2003) apply Ellis's assertion to Brazilian soap operas (telenovellas) and prime time drama. Porto's focus group interviews showed how *Terra Nostra*, a tale of life among Italian immigrant labour on a 19th-century coffee plantation, serves an 'orientation role' (2005: 342). He uses the concept of 'commutation' (explained by Livingstone, Allen and Reiner, 2001), whereby audience talk about media tends to slip between discussions of texts and everyday life. As a result, the often openly political content of *Terra Nostra*, which featured struggles between plantation owners and workers, encouraged conversations on contemporary politics. In particular, the appeal of *Terra Nostra* was partly based on its sourcing of a general Brazilian sentiment that politicians are inherently inept or corrupt.

Changing location and method, Holbert et al. use quantitative surveys and experimental techniques to scrutinize how American television series *The West Wing* shapes feelings toward real life politicians on the basis of fictional exemplars. It has been claimed that *The West Wing* 'has tapped into our nation's [America's] fantasies about how we want our president to behave' (Pergament, cited in Holbert et al., 2003: 431). To test this hypothesis, the researchers measured how watching the programme influenced opinions about real life presidents. A sample was asked to evaluate the fictional President Bartlett, played by Martin Sheen, in terms of his morality, charisma and skill with the common touch. The same questions were asked on former president Bill Clinton, and the incumbent George Bush Jnr. The survey was then readministered after respondents had been shown an episode from the series. Although the fictional president outscored his real life counterparts on almost every dimension, both pre-test and post-test, audiences were more positive about Clinton and Bush after watching the show. Holbert et al. hypothesize that this may be explained by the fact that television fiction can has a more powerful 'reality reach' than does news. Regarding the presidency, journalists are kept at arms length from day-to-day White House affairs. This 'domestic' focus is the core subject matter of

*The West Wing*, whose political content is subordinate to the interpersonal relations between Oval Office staff. This, Holbert et al. continue, imbues the presidency with a level of authenticity, passed on by osmosis to all who hold it.

These studies connect television fiction to the version of persuasion entailed in the encoding/decoding model. Despite its focus on short-term effects, in that it measures immediate reactions to a television programme, Holbert et al.'s research is conceptually bound to the idea that media power works to cement our commitment to the political substratum, if not to the exact players crossing its stage. Porto similarly intimates that *Terra Nostra* activates general beliefs about life that are so widespread that audiences are barely conscious of their presence.

The idea that media power happens behind audiences' backs, however, is often unhelpful. As many of the studies that we will encounter show, viewers, readers and listeners frequently know only too well how the media work. Therefore, some researchers have set out to dissect how media appeal exploits rather than overrides public media literacy. Andrew Skuse (2002) and Helen Wood (2005) both reveal how textual power can work even when audiences understand what the media are trying to 'do' to them, and fight back with their own interpretive strategies.

Skuse researched the reception of *New Life, New Home*, a BBC World Service radio soap opera set in and broadcast to Afghanistan. Located in a fictional rural community somewhere in the middle of the country, *New Life, New Home* has a dual role of entertaining audiences while at the same time disseminating agricultural and health information. The soap is meant to be persuasive, insofar as it makes a connection between media and the real world. But this persuasive function is housed in a textual vagueness which, on the face of things, encourages 'oppositional' readings that expose *New Life, New Home's* inauthentic depiction of life in Afghanistan.

On a denotative level, *New Life, New Home* makes a number of 'howlers'. Listeners point out that the dialects of many of the characters do not fit the soap's putative setting. A storyline surrounding poppy harvesting was laughed off; no-one grows the flowers in central Afghanistan. However, Skuse argues that these 'mistakes' are nothing of the sort. They are instead an example of 'semantic plasticity' (2002: 413) that reflects production processes. Tasked with speaking to an ethnically and linguistically diverse audience, the soap is necessarily vague, as a precise reproduction of life in central Afghanistan would alienate many listeners. Counterintuitively, *New Life, New Home's* veracity depends on building a placeless sense of place via 'the purposeful stripping away of the specificities of culture and society' (2002: 412). Didactic imperatives also demand 'inauthenticity'. If many listeners complain that the soap's farmers enjoy abundant resources that are rare in the real world, this simply reflects that the agricultural innovations depicted in the show have to be seen to work. Why would real farmers adopt bad practice?

Equally, focussing on the 'oppositional' rejection of the soap's denotative realism ignores *New Life, New Home's* emotional register which exploits the intimacy of radio communication (Ryfe, 2000). The inauthenticity of an actor's dialect might be offset by other factors in aural personality. The peculiar cough of one character, caused by incorrectly prescribed medicine, impelled this response from a listener: 'when I heard Jabbar Khan coughing and that he want some tablets to make him better I recalled my brother [killed by mispresecribed medicine] and wept ...'. So, Skuse concludes that focussing on textual anomalies misses how *New Life, New Home* is persuasive on different levels. The mistakes, in many ways, become part of the pleasure of the show, hence drawing listeners in. This exposes them to powerful emotional claims to veracity. Both are necessary strategies used to open 'artfully crafted spaces' (2002: 413) for listeners. In this sense, active interpretation is encouraged not by semiotic ambiguity, but conscious textual design.

Helen Wood continues this theme in her research of UK daytime talk show viewers. Drawing on the feminist scholarship previously referenced, Wood defines this work as informing general perspectives on how we become who we are as cultural beings via media:

> Leisure pursuits, lifestyling processes and therefore media consumption are becoming more central to the processes of constructing and negotiating identity than older, context bound social structures ... [achieving] a conceptualisation of the subject as a reflexive individual rather than as a part of the collective social organism (2005: 118)

However, while the 'reflexive individual' is more than the sum of his/her gender, race, class, sexuality and ethnicity, he or she does not enjoy complete cultural autonomy, with the media serving as a major extrinsic force.

To corroborate, Wood presents detailed transcripts of conversations held with viewers in the act of watching *Kilroy*, a BBC morning talk show. Mapping viewers' comments and actions against the synchronous onscreen actions, both collected in the real time of the broadcast, Wood echoes Skuse in showing how the apparent spontaneity of viewers' reactions follow textual structures. Much as *Kilroy's* domestic audience was wont to 'interrupt' the show, talking over host and guest to offer comments that frequently led to lengthy narratives where virtually no attention was being paid to the screen, this was hardly an independent act. Interruption and personal exposition are intrinsic parts of the talk show text. Additionally, the audience only speaks because they and the text are co-present:

> broadcasting phenomenologically engages in the real time and space of viewers, where they pragmatically take part in the reflexive production of the self. Subjectivity in these instances is therefore accomplished through a series of discursive acts while the broadcast text is alive (2005: 133)

What Wood argues, therefore, is that media sense making depends in large part on the structure and availability of the text as a cultural resource, which explains why 'individual reflexivity' is not an autonomous phenomenon.

None of this is to say, however, that audiences have to accept the symbolic world that television offers. Healey and Ross's (2002) exploration of older television viewers show how such audiences indeed 'use' media to articulate what it means to be venerable. However, this can be an unpleasant task. Healey and Ross begin with the gulf between television, which features few people over the age of fifty, and the real world, where by 2020 half of Europe will fall into this demographic. If daytime television is popularly described as a soporific aimed at the old and unemployed, the drugs don't work for those to whom Healey and Ross talk.

Overall, the interviewees felt insulted by television. They were depicted as defined by age; as poor, sick and senile. Older viewers are also insulted by television's structure. Daytime viewing, which they saw as being directed at them, was condemned not only for the poor programming, but also the advertising:

> [Advertisers] are commercially naïve because I have a much higher level of disposable income than many younger people, but I don't want to know about pension plans and conservatories, it's embarrassing and patronizing. I'm as interested in buying a Ford Focus as a younger guy. (2002: 109)

Television thus engages older viewers in a struggle to define what being old means where, unlike Wood's talk show viewers, their 'reflexive subjectivity' at work here dismantled media discourse.

Of course, we need to allow for the fact that media and self identity can work in mutually enriching ways. Rasolofondraosolo and Meinhof (2003) review this via the use of music from Madagascar in the lives of Malagasy women living in Europe. The lyrical content of this music is an important resource in cultural mediation, as it allowed the women to explain the rationality of cultural practices that appear bizarre to European eyes. For example, songs about the tradition of disinterring, reclothing and reburying the dead let one woman relate Malagasay spirituality to familiar western themes of commemoration and consumption. As strange as this practice may look, wrapping dead bodies in expensive clothing is no different to spending vast amounts of money on lavish funerals, and Madagascan music provides a means to explain this.

Evidently, latter day u&g is mistaken in trying to make media pleasure and significance the exclusive province of brain chemistry and switching off. Focussing on audience sense-making shows how media are often the conduit for thinking our way into the social, not wishing it away. And in these actions, the individual is subject to all sorts of cultural forces beyond his or her gift. However, the problem is that looking at 'meaningful' media runs the risk of accepting the terms of Henning and Vorderer's debate. It assumes that there is a sphere of meaningless media; places where people have little to say about what they are looking at or hearing because there is little to say. In the next section, we will consider how meaningless moments are vital in understanding the pertinence of audience research.

## THE MEANING OF THE MEANINGLESS

**3.5** Imagine you find yourself in London on the evening of December 26th, 1908. Cinema is all the rage. Feeling extravagant, you decide to round off Christmas by experiencing the new century's defining marvel. Except, having spent your meagre wages on presents, food and drink, you cannot afford to play the libertine. So you wander down to Mare Street, where Arthur J. Gale has converted a shop into one of the city's many 'penny gaffes' that show the latest films from France. Admission is cheap, as Gale pays his staff a pittance. So you can afford a place in the upper auditorium. The lights go down, and you marvel at life on the screen. Suddenly, someone downstairs yells 'fire'! You smell smoke. You panic in the dark. There is only one way out, down a single set of stairs, and you have to fight 150 people for it. You run, you push, you climb, then somehow you're out in the open air. You have escaped. You stagger home, thanking your stars. For a few years, you regale people with the tale of how you dodged incineration, but as World War One dawns, grimmer tales fill your thoughts. Soon, you can't remember the flames at all.

The description of Gale's premises, and the real fire that happened there, is taken from John Burrows' research on cinema audiences in Edwardian London (2004). Burrows sets out with the difficult task of reconstructing the history of a popular cultural form that many dismissed as trivial. He is motivated to do so by records that show that 'penny gaffes', or rather the people who attended them, were the subject of acute social concern. The fire in Gale's establishment was a catalyst for the 1909 Cinematography Act, which subjected the nascent exhibition industry to licensing. Ostensibly, this was justified on public safety grounds. But Metropolitan Police records intimate more sinister motives.

In the early 19th century, the Whitechapel police force, which had once hunted Jack the Ripper, pursued a new prey; urban degenerates who stoked their debauchery in picture palaces. In the view of police commissioner Sir Edward Henry, such establishments:

> [Pandered] to the appetite of the lowest classes in order to fill their halls with spectators ... [showing films which] ... are calculated to teach crime and, being attended, especially in the Whitechapel district, by a large number of foreign children of the lowest class, the teaching is likely to be fruitful in results. (cited in Burrows, 2004: 183)

In pushing for the 1909 Cinematography Act, then, the police were not simply concerned *for* the movie audience, they were worried *about* them. In particular, moviegoing was associated with fear of foreign radicals. 'Penny gaffes' often doubled as meeting places for Eastern European émigrés, seen as a source of an anarchist threat that gripped the capital in the late Edwardian era. That the Act gave police the right to enter any such establishment on suspicion of unsafe conditions was not, in Burrows' view, coincidental.

Regrettably, Burrows' research on what it was actually like to be in such dens of iniquity is hampered by the complete absence of first-hand accounts from their patrons. Presumably this is because few thought popular pastimes to be of cerebral merit. This suggests that things that seem meaningless at the time can end up being anything but. Studying 'meaningless media' might, therefore, be the very stuff of history.

The exciting thing about this insight is that it alerts us to the idea that audience research lives in a time of great promise. Livingstone, Allen and Reiner pursue this in their research on *Audiences for Crime Media 1946–91* (2001), which takes advantage of the fact that we still have viewers who can attest to the televisual evolution of the UK police drama. The authors justify this work against the charge of trivia by arguing that the perception of television watching as meaningless is produced by structural factors. One of these relates to the way we understand television viewing as a private activity. This, they point out, is a historical peculiarity, as individualized audiences are relatively novel. Second, oral historians have established that people are better at recalling social practices than meanings. Clifford's investigation of Mexican telenovela viewers (2005) finds, in complementary fashion, that viewers are often reticent to speak about their media preferences as they cannot believe they possess any social value. So, one of the reasons why media appear meaningless is due to a conspiracy of silence surrounding them. Having overcome these obstacles, Livingstone, Allen and Reiner discover that the ordinary police drama is a key resource that seems to express generational identities. Despite differences between age groups, all hold in common that the most fondly remembered shows are those that were encountered in respondents' youth and young adulthood. Even if the stories fade, the reception of police dramas is related, if not central, to favourable and unfavourable comparisons between past and present.

Returning to textual matters, Alice Hall (2003) holds that television viewers work quite hard to establish what is meaningless. She reaches this conclusion via a consideration of how audiences understand and use the idea of realism. From the reception vantage, realism consists of six factors; plausibility, typicality, factuality, emotional involvement, narrative consistency and perceptual persuasiveness. So, *Erin Brockovitch*, based on the true story of a single mother's transition into a powerful environmental advocate, is 'real' in the sense that it was inspired by actual events, but 'unreal' in that it was atypical, and Julia Roberts simply does not look like the real character. Amusingly, given that the research was carried out among US undergraduates, *Star Wars* was considered more realistic than *Dawson's Creek*. However many light years away it is, *Star Wars* is set in a visually convincing and emotionally involving universe far more believable than *Dawson Creek's* existential teen angst: 'they talk like so sophisticated and they overanalyze everything' (2003: 630).

Furthering the theme of 'produced meaninglessness', Christine Williams (2001) explored the consequences for how we understand associations between music and identification. Interviewing UK teenagers on their musical inclinations, Williams demonstrated how positioning chart music as valueless has great value for their determination to assert a sense of individualism. On the surface, the identificatory aspects of music could barely be taken seriously. As one girl said about the *Spice Girls*:

> Like they're the only reason a girl will stand up to their boyfriend or their husband ... it's got nothing to do with it. People stand up cos they want to and cos they feel they can. Not just 'cause the *Spice Girls* stick their fingers out and go 'girl power'! (2001: 235)

This lack of meaning correlated with the perception that the pop music scene offered little more than a parade of the same products, each one as useless as the last:

> [On boy bands] ... they're not real, they're just like five people they think you fancy they get a list and you have to, like, y'know, it's the same for every boyband, you have the sweet blond one who's the main lead singer, you have the ugly tall one ... it's not hard to do, you just find a song and copy it. (2001: 230–231)

Yet there are two ways in which this ennui took on a cultural energy. One could argue that the second quote is a function of designed obsolescence in the charts. However, turnover had reached a speed where Williams' teens no longer saw the purpose of buying music. Downloading and home taping became the norm as nothing more than a rational reaction to the industrial aspects of media. As Metallica's pursuit of Napster testified, this response to the meaningless had profound economic consequences.

Also, the refusal to identify closely with any particular performer indicated, according to Williams, a desire to be seen as an individual. Her teenagers saw the sorts of subcultural affiliations noted by Dick Hebdige (1979) as characteristic of youth in post-war Britain as an anathema to personal identity. Regarding the latter, if individual songs and performers are meaningless, their cumulative presence as a way of filling and announcing the teen space (the bedroom, the car) as a private area of personal expression is anything but.

Such private identities became the basis for new connections with other people made on the basis of taste, not demographics or space.

> I have never met anybody else who has ever heard of the show! You have answered all of my dreams! I wasn't even sure the show actually existed! How can I get the tape? (Bjarkman, 2004: 224)

The above quote is taken from Bjarkman's exploration of the world of the video collector; people who tape all they can from television, based on a love of video itself as a media form, and the belief that recordings will come to have a broader significance. These cognoscenti are involved in a conscious project turning objects generally considered temporary, valueless and even ugly (the recorded video cassette is not normally deemed appropriate for domestic display) into precious aesthetic and historical artifacts.

The collectors understand that their actions appear outlandish due to the ephemeral nature of television programming and viewers' associations with it. Yet it is precisely the 'here today, gone tomorrow' nature of the medium that has made their work historically important. Indeed, their actions are manifestly related to central archival dilemmas; what gets recorded and what is ignored? Whose history is told and whose disappears en route?

Hence the above quote. It is written to one of the collectors by someone who has discovered that the former's archive includes tapes of the 1970s ITV children's science-fiction show *Tomorrow People*. For the author, *Tomorrow People* was a mnemonic for valued childhood memories. However, it lived on only as a memory, and as images and stories faded, so too did the picture of what it was like to be the child who was thrilled by them. So, as television content disappears into the ether, so do certain cultural experiences and ways of life. As the video collectors realized, positioning television fare as disposable has a profound impact on how society creates a historical record of who mattered and who did not: 'While museums turn history into spectacle, video archives turn spectacle into history'. (Bjarkman, 2004: 235). So, trivia formed the basis for far from trivial actions where people carve a place in society.

The meaninglessness of media in fact complements the fluidity of identity and identification processes, as Dafne Lemish discusses in her work on the centrality of the Eurovision Song Contest (ESC) in Israeli gay culture. Lemish directly addresses what Hermes (1995) calls the 'fallacy of meaning'. Hermes contends that we can only understand the role that media texts, in her case women's magazines, play by acknowledging their disposability. Lemish explored what this means in two dimensions in which the ESC can be seen as an empty experience. The first is its ordinariness. For the gay men she interviewed, the ESC always had been and always is a material part of their life; videos of the competition lay scattered around their apartments; its songs were frequently on in the background; they made unthinking annual pilgrimages to the same bars to watch the live event. But, this ordinariness is vital. The ESC formed the soundtrack to Israeli gay lives – particular songs being used to trigger memories of epiphanel moments. The physical presence of ESC material was a means of announcing sexual identity. Third, the 'camp' qualities of the ESC allowed the articulation of certain gay sensibilities. So, if camp:

> generally refers to counter-cultural tastes that mock and challenge mainstream cultural assumptions and aesthetics and is often associated with forms of parody, irony, exaggeration, stylisation, nostalgia, humour, theatricality and artificiality (Lemish, 2004: 52)

so we understand why this is how some of its gay viewers feel:

> For many gays, loving the Eurovision Song Contests is built in from childhood ... but later, when they mature, they see it in ironic light ... they know it's crap .... But it's lots of fun. (Lemish, 2004: 50)

A second way in which the ESC is significantly meaningless surrounds the victory of the transgendered Israeli Dana International (DI) in the 1998 competition. DI became important as someone who was meaningless in that she refused to mean. Her performance embraced many subjectivities without being defined by any one of them. A woman, she claimed a gay sensibility. A Jewish Israeli, she appeared in Amnesty International posters dressed as a Palestinian, and attracted a large Arab following. If her performance was about any one thing, it was about crossing borders, and the futility of trying to fix identity within any single dimension. Trash like the ESC is well placed to address the fluctuation of cultural experience, where one 'becomes' rather than 'is'.

## DIASPORA AND QUESTIONS OF IDENTITY

**3.6** So, we have the prospect that when we dismiss media as meaningless, what we are really expressing is confusion over where to place their significance. This returns us to the problem of individuality. As we saw, that both the individual and media pleasure is felt on a physical level, and that Roland Barthe's influential concept of *'jouissance'* defines pleasure as the moment where the body escapes culture, makes it difficult to assert the centrality of media to the project of the self. Yet DI's performance and its reception intimates something more. National celebrations of her victory represented multiple acts of thinking in, out and differently about what it meant to be an Israeli. If DI's body itself announced potential for 'border crossing' that few imagine, the key is the way that this created an imaginary that could potentially rewrite physical and social boundaries.

Enter researches on diasporic audiences, currently pivotal to the way that cultural studies understands identity as the relation between being and becoming, individual and cultural formation. DI represented the intersection and the dispersal of gendered, sexual, ethnic and national identities. Her physical manifestation raised questions about what all of these things mean. In the process, she made a point that is fundamental to diasporic studies; that cultural imageries of identity, made in and though media, have material consequences.

As an introductory example, consider Meenakshi Durham's 'Constructing the "New Ethnicities"; media, sexuality and diaspora identity in the lives of south asian immigrant girls' (2004). As the title suggests, Durham's ethnography explored how teenage girls of Hindu origin used media to negotiate multiple points of being, contradiction and even oppression that they encountered via the multiple identities they embodied. Again, the meaningless was counterintuitively crucial to these negotiations:

> Last year I really got into *Friends*, which I guess is unrealistic and I know is stupid and stereotypical, but I'm not really influenced by it ... I just love watching it, I love how fun they are and the fun they have. (Cited in Durham, 2004: 152)
> I love Hindi film songs ... I don't know what they're saying ... they're just cool ... just better than American songs. (2004: 153)

Both of these media experiences were meaningless on an explicitly textual level; *Friends* was just 'stupid', where Hindu musicals probably mean something, but the girls did not know what. But on a cultural level, both resources helped the girls mediate the different worlds they inhabited; *Friends* accessed a high school lingua franca, where musicals contained a sense of Indianness shared with parents. Importantly, of course, what this Indianness is was precisely the question; being Indian for the girls was different from what it meant for their progenitors. This usefully summarizes power relations within diaspora studies. The girls found themselves having to be Indian in Florida due to forces beyond their control. They had to figure out what this means, partly, by using media products made by multinational systems of production and delivery. But it was up to them to make these power dynamics real by embodying them in specific ways.

So how does American teenage, Hindu, female Indianness work? Media are medial to this question. As Wiley (2004) stated:

> If communication technologies both express the social relations of human community and shape these relations, the globalization of media and telecommunications infrastructure raises significant questions about what kinds of community can exist, what sorts of national spaces can persist, and how the shapes and purposes of communication technologies are being determined. (2004: 83)

Here, Wiley located the ontology of being in communication. This is important as it explains Tsagarousianou's criticism that 'diaspora' is often inaccurately used as a synonym for ethnicity, migration or displacement (2004). If diaspora has an essence in anything, it is the development of symbolic strategies for dealing with the cultural effects wrought both by the global flow of people and ideas. While diaspora might be grounded in questions of race and nationality, these forms of identity are the sites of diasporic conflicts, not the substratum for these struggles. On race, Stuart Hall has written; 'black is essentially a politically and culturally constructed category, which cannot be grounded in a set of fixed transcultural or transcendental racial categories, and which therefore has no guarantees in nature' (1996: 443). For Tsagarousianou, whatever their origins, diasporic *experiences* are defined by a sense of possibility rather than loss. That is, while Durham's teens had no power over where they lived, what it meant to be there was, in many important respects, up to them. But how can young women, economically dependent on parents who exercise real control over what they do, where they do it, and who they do it with, be seen as powerful? To understand this, we need to examine relations between diasporic studies and questions of cultural imperialism.

The cultural imperialism thesis originally posited the fear that western media could impose western values upon the non-western world. This is a fear that remains pertinent in south-east Asia (Chada & Kavoori, 2000). However, the theory has been complicated by several factors. Accepting that it is a real danger, some have illustrated that this form of power does not simply flow from west to east, north to south. Park (2005) notes that Korea has been flooded with Japanese media products since 1999. Survey research suggests that use of these goods correlates with positive evaluations of a nation with whom political relations have only recently been normalized. Sinclair and Harrison (2004) contend that western cable and satellite services have served as culturally liberating forces in India and China. In the former, the pre-satellite monopoly enjoyed by state broadcaster Doordarshan spawned fears that it:

> had the effect of asserting Hindutva, the 'Hindu–Hindi' religio-linguistic hegemony of the Northern Indian States over the rest of India and marginalizing the minority religions; Muslim, Christian, Sikh, Jain and others. (2005: 45)

It was not, therefore, the west that formed the primary cultural threat to much of the Indian audience. Faced with such diversity and numbers, Star TV was forced to 'Indianize', providing content that catered to different language groups.

Diasporic audience research emerges from the fact that the media's role in cultural mediation is influenced by the movement of people as well as goods. The vast audience for Indian and Chinese media, in its various dialects, exists on an international as well as national level. Consequently, questions of political economy and cultural relations came to focus on international media and their ability to provide: 'contemporaneity and synchronicity to the dispersed populations that make up a diaspora in their everyday lives' (Tsagarousianou, 2004: 62).

In prioritizing the idea that a cultural sense of self is both related to but also more than a product of racial, ethnic and national origin, diasporic studies have explicated media interpretation as more than the application of a mental template that somehow 'belongs' to gender, colour or place of birth. Harindranath (2005) is particularly acerbic about Katz and Liebes's study of reception of *Dallas* among Israeli immigrants (1990). He indicts Katz and Liebes for collapsing race, ethnicity and culture. The *Dallas* research contended that Arabs and Moroccan Jews preferred linear narratives reflecting the traditional nature of their cultural origin. This, for Harindranath, naturalizes difference, hence painting Arab society as indelibly pre-modern. Echoing Hall, Harindranath argues that since ethnicity is as cultural as it is natural, immigrants do not carry meanings like luggage. This is all the more so since diasporas are produced by a series of push–pull factors. Indian migration, for example, must make distinctions between old and new movements produced by 'the diaspora of plantation capital and the diaspora of late capital' (Mishra, cited in Harindranath, 2005). In considering differences within Indian diasporas, Harindranath connects with our consideration of individuality and the meaningless. How is he, as an Indian Hindu 'pulled' to Australia by career opportunities, to make sense of the fact that he does not like Bollywood films? Does that make him less Indian, or different Indian?

The answer, perspicuously, is that this question signals the project of writing a different sort of Indianness. This is explored in Marie Gillespie's (2003) research on British Hindu families and their reception of the Doordashan production of *The Mahabharata*. Although this programme has been seen as part of the Hindu nationalist project, Gillespie portrays it as a tool in the project of rewriting Britishness. Where Shi's work on media use among Chinese students in the US (2005) depicted unease that watching American media might levy the charge of westernization, Gillespie's research finds no such tension. Among young British Hindus there is no contradiction in enjoying both *Mahabharata* and *EastEnders*. Nor does pleasure in 'traditional' English media curtail a critique of media racism. The ability to switch between different sorts of media signals an empowering form of cultural capital – literally a fluency in different symbolic languages. Used to speaking in different discourses, Gillespie's respondents use the *Mahabharata* in a way that departs from the hegemonic agenda identified by Sinclair and Harrison (2004). Connecting the programme to concerns over women's rights, poverty and other forms of social inequality, the Hinduism expressed is of a multicultural variety:

> Even though representations of femininity in the epic are intricately interwoven with discourses of patriarchal and religious nationalism 'these same structures are subverted in Southall and Delhi by women who selectively appropriate and contest key narratives for their own purposes' (2003:145)

Nick Mai's (2004) work on watching Italian television in Albania sharpens relations between diaspora and the project of the individual. Liberalization in the 1990s gave Albanians unfettered access to Italian television. The taste for Italianness was, according to Mai, a direct response to 'a communist project which failed in providing access to the ultimate freedom lying beyond collective identities'. Young Albanians embraced the energy and abundance of Italian television as an expression of domestic desires. While this led some to often disappointing migratory adventures, the presence of Italian television was a vital cultural resource in the formation of a migratory imagination implicated in projects of the self – even for those who never left Albanian shores.

Still, the idea of audience autonomy and creativity should be used with circumspection. As much as diasporic experiences might paint the national as of dubious relevance to being, Camauer (2003) notes that new immigrant communities in Sweden have suffered from the absence of a coherent state policy to develop inclusive media representations. Even when non-western agendas do force their way into western media systems, important elements can be lost in translation. Bishop (2000) notes that although Tibetan exiles have successfully attracted Hollywood's attention to the *Free Tibet* campaign, this has come at a price. Films such as Martin Scorsese's *Kundon* have been criticized for their inauthenticity. Consequently the Tibetan cause has become embroiled with public scepticism about Hollywood and celebrity politics.

Access to media from a 'putative' home can also be a source of anxiety. Shi's Chinese students use their native media as the foundation for stories of 'going home'. Regardless of its likelihood, it is important for these migrants to hang on to the idea that one day they will return to China. To do this, they have to build an imaginary of the home. Applying this same idea to Korean subscribers to Korean satellite services in the US, Lee discovers that media from 'home' can have unsettling effects (2004). Drawing on news tendency to focus on conflict, Lee describes how Korean news broadcasts create the impression that such is the rate of domestic decline at 'home' that the 'home' no longer exists.

Nor can the desire for acculturation, a certain yearning to 'fit in' to dominant cultural forms, be entirely dismissed. Yang et al. (2004) note a preference for American media among Chinese undergraduates at a US university, born of desires to improve language skills and learn how to recognize cultural cues. Rios' work among young Latino audiences in America (2003) discovers disdain for telenovellas. Knowing that these programmes are dismissed as trash, some young Latinos/Latinas fear that they too will be dismissed if they become part of the audience. Finally, Juluri's work on the 'Indianization' of music television in India expresses the fear that the apparent localized appeal of global television opens a sort of cultural backdoor for capitalistic values.

> For future generations, such as the children born into an India of seventy channels of satellite television, personal gunmen and air conditioned classrooms ... the national and tradition may have lost their hope of redemption for making them see the insanity of their lives in relation to the teeming humanity on the doorsteps of their homes and cars before they flee to America. (2002: 383)

## WHITENESS

**3.7** Diasporic audience studies therefore develop the faculty to think the connection between individual and culture in a way that addresses both agency and external power. We have, then, a network of identification, where the hub is often located in media products and experiences that apparently have no meaning.

As a final demonstration of the political importance of these considerations, I will explore the consequences of Harindranath's critique that audience research has often collapsed race and ethnicity. Explicitly, the author claims that scholars making this mistake imply that ethnicity somehow only belongs to people of colour. He is, in other words, pointing to Dyer's critique that media work to 'exnominate' whiteness as a particular existential mode (1997).

The concept of exnomination refers to the way that repetitive patterns of representation have the ideological effect of naturalizing certain perspectives on the world (Fiske, 1982). Apropos race, Dyer analyses how whiteness speaks as the invisible centre of media discourse. This being the case, representations of and by people of colour appear manifestly different, and are placed under an obligation to explain that difference. For example, we have seen that Malagasay women have to work to make songs about their culture's death rituals rational, even though logically they make no more or less sense than, say, dressing a dead body in an expensive suit, putting it in an extravagant coffin, then burning the whole 'shebang'.

Regarding relations between media and the individual, the cultural effect of exnomination is to open possibilities for agency; white people, excused the task of explaining their whiteness, are free to explore other aspects of their identity. Recent work on audiences and race, however, suggests that not all media experiences divert our attention from how white exists as a cultural category, not just a natural norm. Gabriel (1996) looks at white responses to Joel Schumacher's film *Falling Down*. Starring Michael Douglas, the movie follows the adventures of 'D-Fens', a disgruntled white, middle-aged Los Angelan as he crosses the city, and its people, en route to visiting his estranged wife and daughter. His journey features violent encounters with a Korean shop owner, Latino gang members, burger bar employees, a white supremacist and elderly white golfers. In the first conflict, Douglas's character trashes a store in response to its extortionate pricing of a can of Coke. The shopkeeper's policy shows, in the white man's opinion, a lack of gratitude to an American public which has given huge financial support to Korea.

Studying white reactions to this scene, Gabriel notes a form of 'nomadic identification' which uncomfortably draws attention to whiteness and the ordinary nature of white racism. White viewers felt that D-Fens's reactions to the exploitative store practices were understandable, and even enjoyed cathartic pleasure as he set about the shelves with a baseball bat. However, the expression of his anger via racist comments (lampooning the Korean's mispronunciation of 'five') uncomfortably locates the viewer within the racist body: 'I hated myself in the end for liking him in the first place... why the hell did I like him? He's no hero. I didn't like him at all'. (Gabriel, 1996: 139)

As Gabriel notes, drawing attention to whiteness as *a* rather than *the* way of being intimates a loss of power; as something which is no longer centre stage, and as something that has to be managed. This has real consequences for everyday life. Bucholtz (1999) explores this in a linguistic analysis of a white American high school student's account of a violent encounter with a black pupil (from which an African American classmate delivers him). The event is retold using what the author calls a 'Cross Racial African American Vernacular', learned by the boy's passion for hip-hop. Unlike 'colour blind' versions of whiteness, the boy's account draws attention to race, gender, sexuality and the differences between them. As such, the student is caught in alternating moments of power and vulnerability, based on his recognition that his whiteness represents one among many existential possibilities. Moreover, like Durham's teenage Hindi girls, he is forced to make sense of what race means in his context. He is not 'acting black' but 'acting white' in a locale where a vernacular growing from black cultural formations has taken centre stage.

Being called to account for one's whiteness can be an uncomfortable experience. Studying how a white woman manages the criticism she receives for using racist language, Warren (2001) noted rhetorical strategies used to reclaim the high ground for whiteness. Audience researchers have identified the insistence on the meaninglessness of popular culture as one such strategy.

In their influential study of the enormously successful *Cosby Show*, a 1980s/1990s sitcom featuring a black doctor and his family, Jhally and Lewis connected interpretations of the show with an 'enlightened racism' (1993). Industrial fears that explicit reference to contemporary racial tensions would alienate manly white prime time audiences encouraged *The Cosby Show* to depict racism as something that used to happen. This allowed white audiences to locate Cosby comfortably in the entertainment sphere, hence avoiding any thoughts of the very real economic and social problems faced by real black families at that time. Rockler (2002) explored similar themes in her study of white and black readings of the US newspaper comic strip, *The Boondocks*. The strip features the experiences of Huey, a politicized black teenager sent to live in a predominantly white area. The story in question features Huey's angry reaction to a white schoolmate's attempt to cheer him up. This is done via a greetings card featuring white people; this reminds Huey of his symbolic invisibility.

Rockler's research showed that black readers were more likely to understand and appreciate this response. The story angered some white readers, as it punctured their understanding of what comic strips are supposed to do. Comic strips should be entertaining, should make you laugh, not make you think. Rockler did not argue that these different readings somehow belonged to whiteness or blackness. Her focus was on how both exist as interpretive strategies. White rejection was based on colour-blind language. Huey's reaction to the card was unseemly as its donor was simply trying to reach him as another human being. The colour of the people on the card should have been irrelevant, as colour *is* irrelevant. However, Rockler argued that this reading was more available to white readers, as their cultural experiences were less likely to demonstrate the many places where colour continues to matter. In this sense, trying to render *The Boondocks* within the realm of 'meaningless', i.e. 'non-serious' entertainment, was at the same time part of a strategy whose effect was to avoid discussions of systematic racism via a depiction of society as an agglomeration of individuals, rather than a network of collectives. It also excused them from the need to confront racism as an everyday phenomenon that, while speaking to social structures, only becomes real when reproduced by individuals.

## CONCLUSION

**3.8** So, if I could speak to my *Simpsons* family again, I would say two things. I would confess that my efforts to force a neo-Marxist analysis on them were misguided, if for no other reason than they were based on what I wanted to hear, rather than what they might have wanted to say. But I would also argue that their efforts to position the show as meaningless has a real social significance, tied up with all sorts of issues about how they understood themselves and the world that they lived in. As we have and shall see, trivia matters.

Understanding the importance of trivia is used as a device to create a space for cultural studies within media research. The contrast with u&g is not intended to paint experimental psychology as an illegitimate discipline, but simply to show that audiences are more than individuals with psychological needs determined by brain chemistry and unique history. Although we might think of media habits as mundane and idiosyncratic, the fact that we all have them shows structural forces afoot. Further, in not attending to where this 'patterned idiosyncracy' comes from and what it means, we risk losing important parts of our cultural history.

# 4 Fans, Power and Communication

## FAN RESEARCH AND COMMUNICATION STUDIES

**4.1** Ending the previous chapter in diasporic symbolic relations signals the political dimensions of audience research. Media are tools that audiences use to manage the cultural consequences of political and economic dispersion by maintaining collective identities that geography and governance repress. Fan studies thence merit their own chapter as key places where individual projects of the self have been connected with democratic imagined communities. That is, they have asked what forms of democratic speech are possible within specific systems of media production, distribution and consumption. Fan research also therefore implies an element of judgement. Yet the project cannot be reduced to separating 'good' and 'bad' audiences. So what sorts of distinctions are we to make, on what criteria? This answer I offer relates Matt Hills (2002) and Cornell Sandvoss' (2005b) analyses of how fans use media objects to create individual identities with Ian Angus's (2005) and Karl Otto Apel's (1977) theorization of democratic speech.

There are several stages to my thesis. First, I consider how Benedict Anderson's concept of 'imagined community' (1995) grounds both the apparently radical claims of fan scholars and the proposed détente. Next, I present contemporary examples of 'classic' fan pieces, considering how slick readings of them make the mistake of equating fan studies with the claim that audiences do as they please with media products. Continuing, I assert that the apparently 'radical' claims made about centrality of scholar subjectivity in fan inquiries in fact restate older discussions on the nature of social science. This grounds the association between Hills' and Sandvoss' deployment of psychoanalysis and Angus's and Apel's communicative definitions of democracy. Here, I propose that judgements on fan activities rest on empirically outlining the possibility of speaking and being heard.

Football supporters are offered in illustration. The sport is used on the criterion that it addresses a number of key political questions. Football fans are clearly and consciously related to the culture/politics nexus in the areas of nationalism, ethnicity, gender and consumption; moreover, they are often active participants in the theorization of their own actions. They also reference an interesting new turn in fan research; the figure of the 'anti-fan'. Jonathan Gray (2003; 2005) has researched the cultural logic of distaste. In doing so, he finds that the reasons why people hate or avoid certain texts and genres are complex, logical and worthy of attention. Gray's thesis addresses the limits of determination in commodified symbolic worlds; love it or hate it, an event such as the *Lord of the Rings* trilogy is something we all have to 'buy', as it is everywhere from the screen to drinks cups at fast food outlets (Barker, 2005a; Chin & Gray, 2001). Football 'fanspeak' demonstrates how a specific audience copes with the consequences of commodification, seen as a regrettable yet inevitable force. My own research, however, argues that it also depicts the folly of equating opposition with democracy and inclusivity.

## WHY IS FAN RESEARCH MISUNDERSTOOD?

**4.2** Why and how has fan research been simplified and caricatured? The source of this error rests in thinking that to advocate popular pleasure as worthy of scholarly attention means that we approve it in all forms. To ground this argument, I will consider some recent projects that might be seen to do the latter.

It is true that scholarly rationale is frequently presented in confessional form, indicating fan studies as more guilty pleasure than proper day job. So, Will Brooker writes a book on *Star Wars* fans: 'partly out of sheer love and loyalty for the saga and its culture' (2002: xiii). Deborah Jermyn's work (2004) on *Sex and the City* begins in personal joy. Matt Hills (2002) is compelled to explain his devotion to the 'uncool' bands *Level 42* and *Toto*. Alan McKee (2002) offers that such scholars are, at base, professional fans; given the luxury of the time, space and money to do what others do for fun. It is easy to see how casual readings discern a modern take on the tale of the emperor's new clothes; however elaborate the explanation of what's going on, and however much we want to believe this work has worth, there is just nothing there.

A sober revision reveals disinterested qualities among fan scholars standing closer to what would be widely recognized as proper scholarship. Cheryl Harris uses experiences in the US organization 'Viewers for Quality Television', an 'interpretive community [designed to] share and discuss fan issues with other like minded fans' (1998: 46), as a basis for the wider academic project of conceiving popular culture as the place where: 'individuals and social groups negotiate their own insertion into the message and language system of a culture' (1998: 42). The seemingly natural inferiority of popular vis-à-vis high culture disguises how 'the class-based notion of 'taste' arises and becomes politicized when applied to cultural products by social groups with competing interests' (1998: 42). Harris improves understanding of audiences by reversing views of influencability at play in areas such as effects research and cultivation analysis. That is, the more audiences are absorbed in media, the better they understand how texts and industry work, the clearer they are on how they would *like* them to work, and the more vocal they are when these expectations are not met.

Harris' is as succinct a summary of a central trajectory in the fan project as one is likely to find, and clarifies polysemic politics. Making meanings at variance with those that media and dominant social forces 'prefer' indicates that, sooner or later, resistive audiences would 'prefer' that media directly represent rather than hint at alternative social realities. For example, Jenkins' research (Hill & Jenkins, 2001) on *Star Trek* locates part of the original series' appeal in its sexual ambiguity. But as the genre developed over the decades, so gay fans became frustrated at the absence of openly gay characters. Organized fan groups such as the 'Gaylaxians' began to lobby Gene Rodenberry for redress. Thus, fan groups and fan research are part of a project that seeks not just to understand and interpret media texts, but to alter the course of their production. Scholars are, therefore, involved in normative questions of what inclusive public cultures should look like (Hills & Jenkins, 2001).

## IMAGINED COMMUNITIES AND THE CONSTITUTION OF THE RESEARCH OBJECT

**4.3** Inclusive public cultures are premised on the existence or at least the impression of non-hierarchal social relations in communication. This explains why it often seems that scholars join with fans. Indeed, using Benedict Anderson's idea of 'imagined community' as a key tool (1995), fan scholars play a role in forming the very objects they set out to study.

'Imagined', in this context, does not mean inauthentic, but rather recognizes that community exists as an idea grounded in a necessary mental abstraction; the impression of affective connections with people and places we rarely if ever meet or visit. The communities that audience researchers study, then, cannot be judged according to 'true' or 'false', but only by how they make ways of being in the world through creative acts. Within our lexicon, imagination appears as its own everyday antonym. The *impression* of the national has political resonance as a means of building 'horizontal comradeship' disguising 'actual inequality and exploitation' (1991: 7). Fan studies add by demonstrating how the force of an audience's imagination can take on a material form usurping media dominance.

As an example, *X-Files* research among 'X-philes' shows the reality of the virtual. Bury (2003) and Wakefield (2001) both investigate how women's internet fan sites provide opportunities to speak pleasures grounded in feminist critiques of both the series and media in general. Bury's 'David Duchovny Estrogen Brigade' (DDEB) was formed by women who objected to the text-inspired patriarchy of other *X-File* communities. DDEBs acknowledge that the *X-Files* is supposed to be about Fox Mulder's pursuit of a conspiracy to conceal evidence of human/alien encounters. But it is Dana Scully who drew their gaze. Although textually positioned as an annoying sidekick, who monotonously reminds the visionary Mulder of the scientific impossibility of his thesis, Scully was a DDEB vision of how television representation of women characters could be improved.

Wakefield makes the same case for the 'Order of the Blessed St Scully', another internet site modelling itself on the structure of an all-female religious order. Wakefield explores the transformation from imagined community to material presence. OBSS presented 'worshippers' with a virtual abbey, mapping out spaces of devotion and interaction. Within these walls, the beatification of a television character made perfect sense. In classic 'resistance' terms, participants rescued Scully from a series written by men, for men. This imaginative act was the bedrock for interaction between women, modelling the sorts of respectful, democratic communication they craved in society. Members often disagreed on themes such as 'Scullyangst' – narratives where Scully was hurt or disempowered. Some women read these storylines as reminder of their own subordination; others as exemplars of Scully's heroism and strength. Both interpretations, however, were subordinated to the wider ambition of building a culture where women are active, not reactive. This concrete project featured genuine interactions between real women. Both DDEB and OBSS witnessed audiences' desire for their own interpretive interstice, distinct from the place that is understood as the mainstream.

At the same time, if fan politics are implicated in building inclusive public cultures, there must be a mechanism for projecting the critique back to that centre. Increasingly, this involves the physical occupation of media territory. Nick Couldry (2000) notes how Princess Diana's death catalyzed the collapse between media and everyday spaces; here, ordinary people transformed ordinary places into special commemorative sites, subsequently drawing media attention. Audiences make established sites of media production 'ordinary' inasmuch as they are superimposed with personal histories via 'pilgrimages'. Manchester's Granada Studio Tours, for example, let viewers visit the set of *Coronation Street*, the UK's longest running soap opera. Using letters written by tourists, Couldry found a complex interplay of power relations. Visitors were awe-struck by the sense of crossing a boundary into a special symbolic world, but this was experienced in personal ways.

A part of everyday symbolic and domestic existence, *Coronation Street* had been 'there' during the defining moments of people's lives. A visit to the set commemorated these moments.

So fans appropriate not only media texts, but media places, giving physical shape to imagined communities. Akass and McCabe's *Reading Sex and the City* (2004) illustrates that media scholars can join in. *Sex and the City* (SATC) has spawned a tourist industry that redraws New York's topography. Its pilgrims eschew the Statue of Liberty for sights such as the Magnolia Bakery in Greenwich Village, where 'Carrie discusses her crush on Aidan with Miranda' with the added incentive of 'pink frosted cup cakes' (Akass & McCabe, 2004: 220). There is nothing subversive about giving large amounts of money to the travel and leisure industry in return for a symbolically rich dessert. The point, however, is that these sorts of experiences are stitched together into imaginative events exceeding their economic value. Speaking of a photograph they had taken on the SATC tour, the authors write: 'the photo bears witness to the fact that we were there in New York. Not the real New York … but the New York of fairy tales defined by nostalgia for old time romance and the staging of possibility in and from media texts'. (Akass & McCabe, 2004: 236)

What does Akass and McCabe's rationalization say about scholar status? Returning to Jermyn's piece in the same collection (2004), we find an explanation grounded within the 'horizontal relations' idealized in imagined communities. Jermyn's focus group research on Carrie et al. emerges from a series of personal experiences that were clearly shaped by SATC's iconography. Her viewers universally approved of SATC's thematization of women's pleasure in sharing other women's company. In fact, the interviews themselves became occasions of this joy. It appeared that the study had dissolved boundaries between scholar and non-scholar. The researcher became as much the object of analysis as the researched, reflecting: 'on their own place as consumers of popular culture … rather than [seeking] to construct themselves as observers somehow outside or beyond cultural consumptions' (2004: 203). Jermyn did not simply 'find' fan communities, but actively made them.

Do these blurred boundaries mark fan researchers as solipsists or narcissists? What purpose do 'horizontal relations' serve in valid insights on fan activity? Political engagements are implied here. By way of introduction, we should note many objections to the 'flattening' of media cultures, where industry, audience and academic move across a level plain. Couldry's consideration of media spaces leans toward media power. Although places of production are publicly accessible, at the same time the infrequency of boundary crossing maintains media as sacred ground. Turning to fan collectives, we should recall that Anderson's original conception of 'imagined community' was not a democratic vision. A community only becomes coherent by defining exclusionary outer limits. As Mark Jancovich (2002) puts it, fan 'communities' are often marked by vicious infighting between groups claiming sole right to the badge of authenticity. Christine Scodari (2003) elaborates in her exploration of women 'X-philes' who profoundly oppose the interpretations found among the DDEB and OBSS. For many female fans, Scully's resurrection as feminist icon is an anachronism, assuming a symbolic subordination that is no longer exists as it once did. These women see no need for an external symbolic object reflecting their own capabilities, and so feel free to find pleasure in apparently 'patriarchal' plots – and Dana Scully is getting in the way. One can hardly indulge in romantic fantasies about Fox Mulder, when his 'available' status is threatened by a constant female companion. Scodari thus points to apertures between women fan groups that disrupt a vision of horizontal feminist politics.

This rider explains why fan studies are not a simple celebration of popular culture. Desires to 'be with' the audience can simply reference the importance of spending enough time in their company to render their symbolic world meaningful. Nevertheless this often moves into, and indeed starts from, a desire to share not just meanings but pleasures, emotional investment and critique. We have, then, a shift from description/analysis into participation that implies a form of judgement. What sort of evaluations do fan scholars make? What purpose do their adjudications serve?

## FAN POLITICS

**4.4** Let us be clear; the question is not whether fan studies are political, it is what *sorts* of politics do they imply? Given that Anderson's work is such a frequent conceptual touchstone, it is worth indicating that his initial reference is to 'an imagined *political* community' (1995: 6). However, understanding politics as referring to official structures of economics and governance brings problems. Alan McKee discovered this in his time with *Dr Who* aficionados (2004). Dr Who's travels through the galaxies initiate a series of encounters with totalitarian regimes, which he usually manages to usurp. But when McKee tried to measure the show's politics via the question: 'If Dr Who landed in the UK today, who would he vote for?' he was met by either bewilderment or an answer which reflected the fan's political preferences rather than their engagement with the show. Thus, representative politics appeared an inappropriate frame for their devotion.

This leaves open the realm of other sorts of politics centred on local issues, morality or identity (McKee, 2004). Nash and Lahti (1999) elaborate in their research among a 'despised' audience for a 'despised' product. If we take a distaste for, or at least wariness of commodification as a foundational quality in critical audience research, the James Cameron blockbuster *Titanic* is an obvious target for critique. Massive costs were easily recouped in box office receipts, video sales, DVD sales and consumption of peripherals, such as the soundtrack and teen/gossip magazines devoted to Leonardo DiCaprio. Teenage girls were the core demographic. Curiously, they were also the most despised part of the audience, from the point of view of the director of *Titanic* and the male lead. Cameron wanted the film to be marketed as an action adventure, not a romance; DiCaprio wanted to be appreciated for his acting talent, not his looks. Moreover, teenage fans writing to girls' magazines or posting on internet message boards knew this. Nash and Lahti's analysis of these comments identified two strategies used to cope with public vilification. Some girls stood out from the crowd by articulating their pleasure within the aesthetic discourses offered by Cameron and DiCaprio. Others went for broke; if they were to be admonished for being silly teenage girls, they might as well enjoy it. This was a tremendously emancipatory moment for girls who could then lose themselves in the fantasy that one day they would indeed become Mrs. DiCaprio.

What does this sort of fantasy express, politically? On the one hand, there is no critique of capital here. Girls did not complain about blowing meagre financial resources on impossible dreams. But the dreams were possible because of tensions within 'media power'. Director and actor vocally objected to the film's reception because they exercised so little control over its promotion. Conflict, then, happened not between text and audience, but between the agents that made and circulated the film. Nash and Lahti proffer that teenage *Titanic* fans made the best of a bad deal, finding pleasure in staying in an identity that is widely viewed as immature and transitory. The girls recognized how media messages are organized and circulated. And they reflected on cultural relations; 'These girls are placed in the uncomfortable position of having to negotiate expressions of their fandom under the disapproving lens of the journalistic arbiters of [adult male] tastes'. (Nash & Lahti, 1999: 83)

The politics of fan studies, then, lies in lines of power running between different groups which may or may not relate to traditionally viewed political ideologies and structures. Such a relational definition of the political grounds the sorts of evaluations at play in the area of communication; something we can grasp by paying close attention to early 21st century theorization on the role of the fan researcher.

## HOW RADICAL ARE FAN SCHOLARS?

**4.5** Abercrombie and Longhurst (1998) tried to develop the politics of audience activity through differentiating consumption from actions that resemble production. All audiences are 'active', in the sense that they engage with rather than absorb what media offer. How much this intrudes into the materiality of life, however, differs. If we return to this issue of sexual identity, so-called 'slash' literature, stories written by and for fans positing romance between same sex characters from shows such as *Star Trek*, *The Professionals* and *Starsky and Hutch* (see for example Bacon-Smith, 1992; Jenkins, 1992; Green, Jenkins & Jenkins, 1998) signifies the point at which fans make public meaning. In the world of soap opera, Harrington and Bielby (1995) note that American producers recognize their viewers as skilled informants who should be consulted on narrative development. Some fans are so active, it seems, that they project themselves back into the media world. Will Young's previously mentioned homage to *Top Gun* shows just how high profile fan readings can be.

On this basis, Abercrombie and Longhurst place audiences on a continuum running from consumer through fan, cultist and enthusiast to the ultimate category of 'petty producer'. In the final destination, fans make the ultimate resistive act by evolving their own universe of textual creation and circulation. No conscious or sustained conflict with mainstream media cultures is necessarily implied. On the one hand it could be that: 'oppositional readings that might be developed by audiences are relatively codified and almost politicized accounts directed at a unified force of power that can be identified by audience members'. But it might also be true that: 'opposition is rather more an evasion, a kind of determined unseriousness, a form of play that refuses to take power seriously and is thus undermining' (Abercrombie & Longhurst, 1998: 28).

Celebratory fancies are further curtailed by a suturing of material fan cultures to narcissist tendencies in consumer logic. The idea of *reception* as a form of *production* is expressed in a performative understanding of audiences. The idea that 'performance' belonged in media, not audience, was tied to an environment with rigid distances between the two. This environment no longer exists: as we increasingly draw on media imagery to articulate the self, so everyday life becomes a performance where we are both audience and actor of and for symbolic representations. That the world and its people have now become objects of display, meaningful only insofar as they are looked at, represents the final victory for commodity capitalism (Abercrombie & Longhurst, 1998).

Despite this move, Matt Hills (2002) argues that Abercrombie and Longhurst's typology grounds an unhelpful dualism, where 'good' and 'bad' fans are placed either inside or outside consumer relations in accordance with academic desires rather than audience ontology. His argument is grounded in an interpretation of the work of the Frankfurt School's Theodor Adorno, informing an important take on the scholar subject, and the theme of 'horizontal' fan/scholar relations. The Frankfurt School have been summarized as a collective of 'Marxist theorists who saw mass culture as a tool of mass repression' (Tudor, 1999: 24). Hills prefers to define Adorno as an advocate of dialectic method, rather than a denouncer of all things popular. Although Adorno did identify a qualitative shift in the era of mass media, where electronically produced artifacts were commodities before they were anything else, for Hills the attention paid to this feature overshadows Adorno's more fundamental ontological argument; that the significance of a cultural phenomenon will always exceed our descriptive and analytic powers. Moreover, the essence of that phenomenon exists neither in the thing itself, nor the researcher's account of the object, but in the interplay between the two. The problem, therefore, with Abercrombie and Longhurst's continuum is that it affects stasis in a fluid field; fandom is identified as a fixed object, assigned a positive or negative political value according to its anti-racist, antisexist, anti-homophobic, anticapitalist content.

Logically, this contradicts Abercrombie and Longhurst's own conclusion that fan cultures can only be understood within their everyday material contexts. If they were studied in this manner, Hills continues, scholars would see that if fandom can be defined as anything, it is as a network of intersecting tastes. One is never just a *Star Wars* fan. Everyday fans draw on a variety of media materials in projects that centre on the construction of the self, rather than the preservation and reification of an external media experience. Consider again the 'X-philes' discussed by Wakefield (2001), Bury (2003) and Scodari (2003). While the same series inspires each fan group, the sense made of Dana Scully differs to the point where they are literally speaking of different texts; one where the lone male's pursuit of a conspiracy is central, the other were it is irrelevant. Attention to this sort of detail tells us that we cannot coherently use the term 'X-phile' in the singular.

Clumsy efforts to jam diverse fan cultures into preordained hegemonic/subversive categories have resulted in degrees of plain misrepresentation. Aforementioned 'slash' literature is a case in point. Green, Jenkins and Jenkins (1998) complain that scholars have foolishly sought a unifying theory of slash – what it is and what it does – when those who write and use it know there can be no such thing. Brooker (2002) accuses the concentration on slash as encouraging the view that the subgenre has a high profile in science fiction communities; most of the *Star Wars* fans he encountered had never heard of it.

The persistent quest for explicitly political subversion speaks, in Hills's view, to a latent project to secure academic legitimacy. The 'problem' of audiences remains power related. However, the tone of qualitative audience research implies that the gap between how popular culture *could* work as a democratic space and how it *does* operate can be defined analytically before empirical engagement. As a result: 'theory ... is granted status as pure conceptually, being held apart form the polluting notions of narrative' (2004: 135). What this amounts to is a call for more horizontal fan/scholar relations. While figures such as John Tulloch and Janice Radway (1983) began their research, on Dr Who and women romance novel readers respectively, from positions of empathy, the empirical analyses they offered are deficient in the sense that they remained subordinate to academic theoretical projects that themselves remain untheorized (Hills & Jenkins, 2001). The result, consciously or not, is the impression that theory only happens within the academy (Hills, 2004). A great deal of empirical energy is wasted in the fallout. One cannot hear what data might be saying if one only listens for their ability to resonate the known. A key specimen in this argument is fan scholarship's failure to study how fans themselves use and develop media theory (Hills, 2004), an issue that will become important in the pursuant discussion of football.

Debating the place of media theory has an enormous importance for understanding why some fan scholars advocate the importance of dissecting the writer's subjectivity. The Hills/Jenkins conversation superficially appears to invert traditional 'scientific' relations; scholars are criticized for *not* presenting themselves in their accounts. Yet at the same time, Hills is eager to point out that the autoethnographic turn is not a call to 'navel-gazing'. So what exactly is being claimed here?

His argument has precedence in Thomas Kuhn's comments about the processes of normal science (1974), and Glaser and Strauss's championing of 'grounded theory' within ethnographic practice (1967). Like the former, Hills argues that fan scholars have achieved a certain level of consensus, meaning that key theoretical concepts have been accepted as true statements rather than testable propositions. Like the latter, he proffers the way out of this dilemma as being a closer attention to what real fans actually say and do, conceiving individual experience as a material concentration of diverse influences (Hills, 2005). Here, then, 'being with' fans means listening to what they are trying to say on *their* terms. Horizontal relations between fan and scholar do not imply unanimity. They are simply necessary to understand why the things that fans do are rational within their own frames of reference. Consider similarities between Barker's encounter with a fascist *Judge Dredd* fan (1997), and John Brewer's ethnography among men who had joined Oswald Mosley's British Union of Fascists in the 1930s. Brewer's contention was that it is only possible to confront fascism if one understands how its ideology appeals to ordinary people (2000). In his work, therefore, description and understanding form the basis of judgement. But what sort of judgement? And how does this translate to discussing audience's tastes?

## DIALECTICS, MORALS, POLITICS

**4.6** The answer to this question resides, I believe, in understanding the moral dimensions of an analytic project that asks how communication is possible. Canadian scholar Ian Angus elucidates. For Angus, communication begins as a discipline with the distinction between philosophy and rhetoric, wherein the persuasive intent of a message is divided from its truth claim. Commodification expands this gap, such that communication becomes indifferent to matters of true and false. That is, the attractiveness of a message, and the conditions that make and circulate that message, are more important than what it says. The political consequence is that democracy is emptied of content. This ceases to be true, however, if communication is understood as the place where truth claims become effective. In this case, the question shifts from representation, with its incarnations of true and false, toward an understanding of how: 'the plurality of media ... actualizes the multiplicity through which a specific cultural form emerges' (Angus, 2005). In this environment, the only constant is the presence of communication itself. Democracy, Angus concludes, can be found in the tension between the claims that truth is more than expression, and the only truth that counts is expressible. In doing so, he locks the judgemental component of critique within the diversity of expressive opportunities available to subjects in the political field. Judgement, then, does not imply distinguishing right from wrong, but identifying the range of possibilities that are considered as possibly true.

Let us return to Will Brooker's research among *Star Wars* fans to consider how Angus's ideas enlighten audience interpretation. That *Star Wars* persisted as a 'cultural form', despite a quarter-century hiatus between films, speaks to the presence of the 'plurality of media' sustaining its cultural presence. The force remained in comic books, action figures, novels, video games and, indeed, fan communities. George Lucas's status as ultimate arbiter of the trilogy's meaning was queried. By the time *The Phantom Menace* was released, then, the only 'stable' feature in the universe was the certainty that people would care and communicate about a thing called *Star Wars*; even if the negative criticism rained on the new prequels *by the fans* questioned what the 'thing' was.

They cared, in some cases, as *Star Wars* offered a canvas to present a variety of visions: Christian spirituality; straight edge (anti-drug) morality; American democracy. Members of the US armed forces saw parallels between the Jedi struggle with an evil empire and the part they played in eroding Saddam Hussein's Iraqi regime. So, *Star Wars* provided a language to express how they viewed their role as subjects in the 'proper' politics of foreign relations (Brooker, 2002). Presumably, then, it would also serve as the place where the possibility might be raised that from an antiwar perspective, it was they who served the 'Empire'.

So the politics of fan research involves asking how rich an interaction the fan has with an external cultural world. This is the question Hills and Cornell Sandvoss pursue via the psychoanalytic domain of object relations. Sandvoss' opening gambit would seem to mitigate 'political' understandings of fan scholarship:

> The centre of gravity of social signification has shifted from objectively identifiable textual structures associated with particular class positions to subjectivelyconstituted readings and appropriations of fan texts which also reflect a multi-polar distribution of power in the complex connectivity between class gender and ethnicity. Thus the object of distinction ... is no longer the text ... but theinteraction between text and reader. By the same token, the key to understandingthe emotional rewards of fandom ... shifts from the macro questions of power, hegemony and subversion to questions of self and identity in fandom (2005b: 42)

However, object relations move from the individual back to 'macro questions of power'. According to Hills, 'object relations work emphasizes the way we can use a variety of externally existing, cultural, aesthetic objects to process, experience and sustain aspects of the self' (2005: 807). Sandvoss intimates the underlying theme that the self is formed in a dialogue between inner states and external phenomena. In particular, he focuses on Janet Winnicott's notion of the 'transitional object'. Here, individuals find security in a changing world through external objects whose familiarity creates feelings of comfort and power.

The political dynamic within this process is explored via the related concept of narcissism. Fans find pleasure in seeing their own reflection in the media. So, media offer a means of *projecting* the self into the public realm. Abercrombie and Longhurst stipulate narcissism as folly, given the objective gap between what the commodity world is and what fans want it to be. That is, *Star Trek's* existence as a source of sustainable profit has more importance than its contribution to public discussions of sexuality. In distinction, Sandvoss is persuaded that since narcissism is spurred by the desire to integrate self and nature, it offers a 'kernel of social and economic change' (2005b: 118). Consider William Shatner's oft-cited appearance on the long-running American comedy sketch show, *Saturday Night Live*. Here, Shatner performed a skit where he horrified *Star Trek* conventioneers by revealing that he was not really the captain of the 'Enterprise', before advising them to 'get a life'. In doing so, he stoked the widespread perception that *Star Trek* fans are mentally deficient, externalizing their hopes for utopia into a television world that never was. In contrast, slash literature shows how the attempt to integrate self and fan object, or in the case of slash, real sexual identity with a fictional series, 'heals' by creating communities where same sex relations are natural.

Continuing with 'healing', it is no accident that Karl-Otto Apel's description of communicative democracy (1977) draws on psychoanalysis for analogies. Psychoanalysis begins with an estrangement between a patient's thoughts and actions. A patient presents as ill because he or she cannot see how his or her internal life associates with damaging external behaviour. Enter communication, where behaviour is the 'mediating text' between patient and analyst. The ultimate goal is to use the resultant patient/analyst dialogue to allow self insight. But the 'patient' is both the source of the problem and the solution, not only as the provider of 'data', but ultimately as the person who makes analysis real by integrating it within self.

None of this is to suggest that audience researchers are tasked with curing the sick by unmasking the link between popular cultural taste and psychocultural need. What Apel does do, however, is express the sort of 'horizontal' relations required in scholarship which respects audiences as active agents in the materialization of media effects *and* the development of media theory. This does not mean that we have to agree with or validate what audiences say. Returning to Brooker's military personnel, we could point out that their account excludes alternative experiences. Or they do not communicate with certain constituencies in the conversation of US Middle Eastern policy.

Enter evaluation. Sandvoss frames fan activities as 'possibilities', not fully-fledged solutions, since they depend on commodified media objects. The potential of media discourse is constrained by the fact that texts are things to be bought and sold above what they may or may not express. What is new about his argument, however, is that Sandvoss understands the ultimate power of media texts to reside in the fact that very often they express nothing. That is, Sandvoss reintroduces a notion of 'containment' by replacing polysemy with 'neutrosemy'.

The idea of the neutrosemic first emerges in his research among football fans (2003). Interviewing supporters of London's uber-chic Chelsea, Sandvoss found that they projected a variety of narratives onto the club; socialists, giddy consumers, traditional fans, racists and multiculturalists all saw their colours flying over Stamford Bridge. The question of what Chelsea really is became irrelevant; it existed as a cultural object in the life worlds of supporters who made it mean very different things. Chelsea, in and of itself, expressed nothing.

How can saying nothing express deep political power? We can understand this by returning to Angus's theory of communication. Sandvoss (2005a) contends that audience autonomy is an illusion created by the inappropriate use of 'reading' as a metaphor to explain the interaction between audiences and media objects. Citing Wolfgang Iser, Sandvoss defines the purpose of reading as the creation of a disruptive experience, where the reader is presented with an object that unsettles how he or she understands self and society. It is a reflexive experience. The Chelsea example, however, was reflective. That some supporters continued to espouse racist views about a club with so many black players displayed a certain impotence, where the object failed to penetrate the supporter's idealized world.

It is here that Sandvoss confronts the mistake of equating semiotic democracy with autonomy. Polysemy erroneously locates the question of media power in the text, and the audience's ability to rip that text from its preferred ideological mooring. Neutrosemy pinpoints media power in the individual. Recall that cultivation analysis concluded that the main effect of media is lethargy; scared people do nothing. Sandvoss makes a similar argument. Neutrosemic texts make no truth claims, thereby allowing audiences to project variant desires onto the same spaces. The effect is that audiences never have to meaningfully engage with an external world that can revise the inner self. How else can we explain the fact that racist white Chelsea fans, for whom the club stands as a representation of white working class tradition, could welcome black French international Marcel Desailly as one of their own (Sandvoss, 2003)? The problem is one of communication, as the fans refused to engage with symbolic changes. They could do so because the only constant in 'Chelsea' is commercial availability. Match day tickets, merchandise and television appearances (increasingly in subscription and pay-per-view form) have a use value saying nothing more than 'buy me'.

Recall that fan cultures become 'political' as they insert ordinary voices into discussions of how public culture should work. In the case of Chelsea, it is obvious that racism has no place in a democratic multicultural society. The racist reading of Chelsea is, therefore, wrong both morally and normatively. But how does this moral conviction translate into empirical projects respecting the cultural worlds of the audiences we study? Doesn't Sandvoss' work simply return us to questions of good and bad?

A critique of Bettina Roccor's account of the meaning of heavy metal for its performers and its fans (2000) provides a useful analogy. Roccor seeks to debunk the view of: 'the average headbanger ... [as] a latent right-wing, radical, sexist, violent, alcoholic, debilitated and, even more, satanically asocial' (2000: 84) by unpacking the controversy surrounding the German band Die Böhsen Onkelz and their performed but never recorded piece, 'Turks Go Home'.

Roccor is keen to show that this performance was not racist, in the way that we would normally understand the term. Roccor asserts that 'the fan is always expert' (2000: 92). Seen from the headbanger's perspective, the many variants of the heavy metal scene are united by an enthusiasm for a particular musical tradition focused on a celebration of outsider status and freedom.

Heavy metal is first and foremost a sign system where everything, from music to dress to lyrics, is subordinate to the expression of a rebellion designed to shock. It follows that any political statements heavy metal bands do make are primarily ways of expressing 'outsiderdom'. When bands make apparently political statements, they rarely reflect on content. According to Roccor, these songs express an overall feeling of authenticity, existing over and above lyrical meaning – which is why objectionable lyrics can be perfectly acceptable for people who do not espouse such politics. A generation earlier, Dick Hebdige (1979) made the same argument about punks who sported swastikas. That this was not a fascist expression was demonstrated by the leading role the subculture played in the 'Rock Against Racism' campaign of the late 1970s.

The problem with Roccor's exegesis is that it relies on self-contained understandings of fan cultures. Her faith in the validity of 'insider accounts' only makes sense if heavy metal fans are *only* heavy metal fans, and their music *only* circulates among other headbangers. Neither statement is true. Ironically, Roccor's insistence on the importance of context leads her to ignore the context of heavy metal as a social relation: the desire to shock, for example, can only be fulfilled under the gaze of a non-fan audience. As a result, we cannot accept that 'Turks Go Home' was not a racist song. Insiders' views are important as a gauge to the sort of racism at play here; that Die Böhsen Onkelz went on to stage an anti-racism concert indicates that 'Turks Go Home' did not originate in the same sort of xenophobia that drives the extreme right wing. But perhaps it was all the more disturbing for that. What we can say is that in reducing racial hatred to an aesthetic device, Roccor's account gives little thought to relations between citizenship and fandom. The critique of her work is certainly moral; but it is also evidenced by the empirical tracing of the absence of communication between fan and object world, where the latter refers not just to the song, but its circulation in a context of rising racial tension in Germany. Insider accounts are 'bad' in that they present a demonstrably insufficient account of a material cultural moment. To put it another way, they reflect how fans would like to be seen.

Of course part of the problem also lies in the academic recounting of this event. That Die Böhsen Onkelz staged the anti-racist 'gig' does acknowledge the resonance 'Turks Go Home' had a beyond heavy metal culture. This gets lost in an account that relies heavily on notions of resistance, where heavy metal is located entirely outside dominant power positions. Contextualizing this critique within the previous discussion of object relations and their parallels with ideas of democratic speech, the political evaluation available in fan research rests on the empirical investigation of the diversity of voices heard in 'fanspeak' and their relation to the structure of media cultures.

What ideas are expressible in fan cultures? Under what conditions can these expressions change media structures, and the way that academics conceive of media power? What are the limitations placed on expression, and where do they come from?

## FOOTBALL, CONSUMERISM, ANTI-RACISM AND DEMOCRATIC SPEECH

**4.7** To conclude, I will discuss my own research on issues of racism and fandom as they coalesced around the white English footballer Lee Bowyer (Ruddock, 2005). In January 2003, Bowyer made his debut for West Ham United, an English Premier League club located in London's East End. His appearance was controversial due to his recent trial over the beating of an Asian man which, the prosecution alleged, was racially inspired. Although he had been acquitted, some felt that the player had not adequately defended the racist accusation. Bowyer's debut was thus the occasion of both an anti-racist protest, and a spirited defence of club and player mounted by West Ham fans contributing to the website *Knees Up Mother Brown* (KUMB) (named after a traditional London song which supporters have adopted as their signature tune). The fans' posts provided the data for the study.

Bowyer's case represents associations between sport, politics and media that in turn reflect many of the topics driving fan studies, particularly around 'imagined community' and consumption. Football imbricates nationalist projects. In the post-World War Two Soviet Union, a tale circulated of how in Kiev in 1942, a ragtag football team of starved Ukrainian slave labourers defeated a well nourished Luftwaffe eleven by five goals to three, despite being warned to throw the match on pain of death. A game that had been intended to corroborate the supremacy of the 'master race' rather testified to an indefatigable Soviet spirit (Riordan, 2003). Of course many Ukrainians did not think of themselves as Soviet. To boot, Riordan's research asserts that the victors had not been threatened (although many were punished as collaborators after the war), that the team they played were not glamorous, athletic pilots, but anti-aircraft gunners, and that both sides parted on terms as amicable as one could expect between populations at war. But the Ukrainians did win 5–3. The myth springing from the game had more to do with Soviet propagandizing than anything that happened on the pitch.

Economically, Ericson (2003) provides a compelling account of relations between sport and capital in research on football's ideological role in 20th century Swedish industrial relations. We can look 'upon sports as a means of neutralizing the socio-political demands of the working classes, as a

mechanism for the achievement of consensus between the classes and ultimately as a tool for the achievement of hegemony' (2003: 22). But Ericson
prefers the humbler task of asking how these dynamics worked in the formation
of *Bruksanden* (foundry spirit) within the *folkhemsmodellin* (Swedish
welfare state system, characterized by paternalism) as experienced in the town
of Sandvikens from the turn of the century to the 1950s. Ericson describes
how Karl Frederick Goransson, director of the Sandvikens ironworks, finan-
cially supported Sandviken AIK (a football club founded by ironworkers that
went on to achieve professional status) as agent of the 'company' concept,
which reflected wider state antipathy to Marxism. Ericson argues that the
Sandvikens case illustrates hegemony, how a form of popular culture was
used to secure Goransson's civic leadership through the consent of his workforce. Here, community and company were as one, with the understanding
that workers owed the quality of their lives to the economic success of the
ironworks, but also that the company had to commit economic success to
longevity of the community. This meant investing in healthcare, education and
leisure to produce a healthy, happy and committed workforce. The community
model that Goransson imagined was one in which it was important to have
'informal' spaces of interaction, or communication, between management and
workforce. Sport was one such arena. So, Sandvikens AIK was explicitly
intended to merge leisure and economy.

Continuing the economic theme, football in the UK has witnessed compa-
rable efforts to merge the economic and the cultural by equating the status of
citizen and consumer. In 2002, the journal *Soccer and Society* published a
special edition inspired by the launch of Supporters Direct, a Labour government initiative designed to help and advise supporters who wished to become
involved in the governance of their clubs. Chris Smith, then Minister for
Culture, Media and Sport, contributed with an essay remarkable for its
attempted synthesis of socialist ideology with free market economics – melting
fan, citizen and consumer into a single entity. Reviewing football in the
1990s, Smith proudly proclaimed that 'crowds are healthier and more
diverse than at any other time'. (2002: 13) But, at the same time 'huge inflation
in the cost of supporting football' meant 'many people on lower incomes are
now unable to attend matches' (2002: 13) At the same time, the problems
this caused were described in economic, not cultural terms: 'Football
supporters ... are the game's greatest asset, the people who pay the ticket
prices, TV subscriptions, and buy the merchandise'. (2002: 14)

Smith then retreated to culture by defining clubs as 'community assets'.
Supporters Direct was 'based on the same core values as the Labour
movement – community self-help, mutual support, social responsibility'
(2002:14). Hence, Smith attempted to merge commerce and culture
through an initiative theoretically enabling supporters to become economic

stakeholders in clubs – as long, according to the website, as they were 'democratic' in structure.

Smith opened the issue of how, in the logic of Abercrombie and Longhurst's scale, authentic fans transcend commercial relations (2002). In contrast, he saw no contradiction between true fan and consumer. He was supported by Trevor Watkins (2002). A supporter of Bournemouth AFC, an English club in the lower reaches of the professional game, Watkins led a consortium which bought the debt ridden team out of receivership, restoring it to the status of 'local community asset that it should have always been' (2002: 58).

Watkins's language reflected questions of distinction and economic consciousness in 'fanspeak'. He eagerly displayed badges of the 'authentic', articulated in two load-bearing ideas in fan distinction. First, the familiar narrative about how his love affair with the club began with the epiphanal first visit:

> It was a ... February afternoon in 1974 when my dad first dragged me along to watch AFC Bournemouth ... We stood on a clapped out old terrace and drank hot Bovril as the old man with the flat cap teetered on a rickety wooden ladder leaning to hang the half time scores on a board behind us ... the football may have been mediocre second division fare but it was good enough to hook me ... 27 seasons on, the excitement is still there. (2002: 58)

The second claim regarded Watkins's move from 'fan' to 'enthusiast'. There are such as he who are willing to become involved in running clubs; others might be willing to lend less time-committed support as parts of supporters' organizations; for some, support begins and ends with paying to attend games. For still others, they will never attend, but the club's presence nevertheless has a vague sort of community meaning. At the top of the tree, Watkins shed his claim to the ordinary, having established his credentials. His lofty position in the fan hierarchy, however, relied on understanding that football clubs can only be community resources insofar as they perform economically.

At face value, that Watkins and Smith appear as minority voices, as the 'consumer' category, is incommensurate with the nature of club/supporter dependencies. While one can switch brands if a product is not working for one, this is not possible with football teams; as Oppenhuisen and van Zoonen indicate in their work on Dutch fans (2006), club preference is tied to issues of locality, tradition and identity. Clubs cannot be differentiated by marketing strategies. They cannot be welded onto a sponsor's company values. Nor can one simply switch allegiances when a team fails to deliver on the pitch.

But elsewhere, consumer discourses become important and unexpected oppositional resources. The weight of evidence certainly suggests that most fans accept commerce as a necessary evil. Noted football scholar Richard Giulianotti's time among Scottish fans (2005) finds 'communities' that are no longer 'imagined' outside of economic relations. While his sympathies lie with 'authentic' fans – those with long-standing traditions of match day attendance, whose performances provide the raw material for the media spectacle that the game has become (Giulianotti, 2002) – Giulianotti also notes how consumerist logic has created an oppositional lexicon. Although supporters cannot change what they consume, they can change how they consume; swapping wet, poorly resourced stadia for warm pubs where they enjoy panoramic views of games while drinking alcohol, all for a fraction of the price (Giulianotti, 2005). This speaks to a wider dynamic, where in accepting consumer status, fans feel they have a right to demand satisfaction. Often, this has as much to do with human dignity as value for money. Having paid expensive ticket and merchandizing prices, today's fans feel they have paid for the right to be treated with respect, not herded like animals. So, consumer identities are not simply imposed categories, but also resources for finding an effective voice within the game's structure.

Giulianotti's work flags two themes in the Bowyer study. The first is that football fans consciously engage with how 'fan' is theorized, supporting Hill's thesis on the importance of understanding them as research participants rather than subjects. The second is the presence of media. Television emerged as a tool that can be used to opt out of the staggeringly inflated prices Scottish football clubs have imposed. This contrasts with the suspicion toward the media displayed by those blaming television for attracting bands of 'armchair' supporters who dilute the authenticity of the game's fan base. Media represent something of an unwelcome presence. Note how Watkins' earlier claim to being a real supporter rested on an unmediated experience. In this sense, football supporters demonstrate aspects of Jonathan Gray's anti-fandom; distrust and distaste for mediated football is a tool that fans use to argue that they belong.

Consider the following post to KUMB in response to Bowyer's debut:

> At approx 2.15pm Sky [television] showed scenes outside Upton Park of a demo against M. Bowyer. By what I saw on the TV there looked like there was a few there, giving some verbal and taking some back.
>
> After leaving the Stanley after a pre-match bevvy (apologies on a separate post due soon, sorry gents) I proceeded along to the ground. Outside the main stand was a group of no more than 12, well basically dickheads, with lovely homemade banners and plenty of gob. The old bill were trying to usher the rest of us way, for the dickheads were taking loads of verbal and getting a bit humpy.
>
> Now this whole shenanigan has really pissed me off. Upon recognising one of the officers in charge of the situation, I asked whether I could ask the assembled throng what their motives and aims were. The police officer ... replied and I quote 'Rio (I play cricket alongside him) don't antagonise them, they've taken a load of abuse all day

from everyone from fans to locals. They're just seeking attention; I doubt any of them have set foot inside the ground since puberty. They're here to get on telly, nothing more'.

Well I'd like to say to those who made the effort to protest, f\*\*k back into you little semi-detached with a copy of *The Guardian* (Rio B.)

How can the preceding discussion of the politics and pragmatics of fan research build social significance into this statement? Connecting object relations with conceptualizations of democratic speech acts, we have connected fandom with politics by defining the imaginative community as a utopian space where different sorts of people can speak across a horizontal plane of social relations. Fan/scholar bonds have been exemplified as one such plane. The political project of fan research thus involves outlining speech possibilities. In football, Giulianotti (2005) and Oppenhuisen and van Zoonen (2006) demonstrate that consumerist logic is not just experienced as an oppressive force, but also gives fans a voice that the game's structure must hear according to its own economic principles. Joke Hermes (2005) extends this into the realm of identity politics. Giulianotti complains that the growing influence of television has reduced football to a commoditized spectacle, where fan performances are primarily useful as a means of securing the football's exchange value as a saleable asset (something that armchair supporters want to watch). Equally Hermes' research among Dutch supporters shows that one aspect of this 'spectacular', the tabloidization of football gossip around players, has opened participatory spaces normally closed to women.

The Bowyer episode spoke to equivalent race themes. The relative absence of Asian fans and players demonstrates that English football does not serve a multicultural audience. Regardless of whether Bowyer was or was not racist, we can ask if his presence at West Ham *and its mediation* prompted a dialogue on this state of affairs where all were empowered to speak, and where the core of traditional fans were willing to listen to others.

In 'Rio's' account, anti-fan tendencies are evident insofar as media presence is an important tool in distinguishing the writer from 'fake' protestors. The quote is indicative of general strategies, where the protest position was assigned to those who understood neither football nor West Ham, one of the first English clubs to feature black players. 'Rio' draws distinctions between media representations and the reality of match day attendance, suggesting that the protest may have looked more spectacular on television than it actually was. The new fans are invited to f\*\*\* off home clutching a newspaper that the fan regards as the standard bearer for the oppressive force of political correctness.

We can be persuaded of the fan's credentials; this is an authoritative insider account. On what basis can it be critiqued? If we do so, does this make the writer 'bad', a racist? I would argue the answer is no, as the problem is more communicative than moral. The study argued that Bowyer supporters were not racist; they simply had nothing to *say* about race. This was because, to use Sandvoss's ideas, they were primarily involved in a projective exercise, where mapping their own authenticity onto the West Ham canvas mattered more than cultural politics. The community imagined was that of the committed supporter, not the multiculturalist. As one supporter put it: 'OK. Most of you don't like him about the fuckin racist incident. I agree. For a club with our history it is bad etc … but we still need a decent centreback'.

In arguing that football is not the proper place to discuss these issues, many of the posters to KUMB refused to listen to those who saw Bowyer's presence as an affront to the Asian community, many of whom counted themselves as traditional supporters. So, in this instance, a discourse that had roots in an 'oppositional' anti-consumerist theme also complemented reactionary sentiments on which the far right British National Party tried to capitalize. The problem, then, was Rio's failure to consider how West Ham fandom connected with the wider sphere of cultural politics, based on the inability to interact with the object of the Asian and anti-racist supporter.

## CONCLUSION

**4.8** It is misleading to read fan research as an introspective, self-congratulatory field where academics wallow in their own pleasure and, worse still, provide excuses for avoiding difficult questions about the political economy of the media. Questions of power remain central, although what and where this power is and how it works is open to revision. Nor does any of this conclude that one can only meaningfully study media cultures in which one has an affective investment. We must consider, however, how scholars and their methods are implicated in the expressive possibilities of media based cultures. Empirical evidence of these opportunities forms the basis for the judgements that are appropriate within qualitative inquiry.

# 5 Objectionable Content: Sex, Violence and Audiences

## INTRODUCTION

**5.1** The fear that prurient media content does bad things to good people predates audience research by some centuries. Persistent consternation over sex, violence and audiences partly reflects changing frequencies and modes of access to such content. For W. James Potter (2004), it also shows the intellectual poverty of debates on what representations of savagery and lust 'do' to us. A jaundiced eye might argue that scholarship on sex, violence and audiences merely supports things we already 'know'; that bad media make both deviant and normal people more aggressive and hateful (especially toward women) under short-term experimental conditions, with probable real life consequences. Alternatively, all that has been proven is the impossibility of analysing human culture in scientific laboratories.

This chapter offers that dominant worries over media sex and violence *underestimate* their impact by *limiting* the questions we ask. Four problems are posed. What is objectionable media content? Where do we find it? What does it do, and to whom (as subdivided into the ideas that violence and porn do bad things to bad people, do bad things to good people, do a variety of things over long periods of time that are difficult to measure, and might have positive social roles)? Who wants to know about it, and why? Concluding that old debates about effects should be informed with new problems and studies, I will then offer two examples of these new directions, represented by Alan McKee's (2006) work on pornography consumption, and my own nascent research on audience reactions to media coverage of alcohol abuse in the UK. The common thread is that in using both quantitative and qualitative techniques, they illustrate that conflicts between scholars are driven more by the way we conceive rather than gather evidence of cultural influence. There are no bad methods, only bad reasons for using them in inappropriate ways. Also, one can accept the critique of the experimental effects tradition without dismissing public concerns over sex and violence out of hand.

One of the difficulties in this topic is that it can be hard to distinguish evidence from common sense. As Potter continues, if violence deliberations are conducted between parties who are sure that they already know what is happening among audiences, differences are inflamed by the fact that none of their misgivings is *entirely* misplaced. As Karen Boyle notes (2005), difficulties in establishing associations between on-screen and real life aggression means little to those feeling they have real experience of media-inspired brutality. Yet this is an opportunity, not an impasse. In travelling from general questions in the topic of the objectionable, to my own study of a small sliver of British 'booze culture', I also show how casual observation can act as the starting point for more formalized inquiry. As we will see, even effects scholars do this, for all their use of numbers and labs.

## THE DILEMMA OF THE PROBLEM

**5.2** Framing sex and violence as objects of inquiry, three questions initially emerge. To begin, one must justify topical merger. For many, pornography is violence, involving both symbolic and real aggression and domination (Carter & Weaver, 2003). From here, it is difficult *not* to advance on media sex and violence as anything other than deleterious forces bent on wreaking social havoc. But what is the nature of the harm they visit? And what is lost in assuming that there is a problem?

For Potter (2004), the effects question is blinkered by the dogmatic pursuit of the 'Holy Grail' of violence research; the manufacture of aggressive behaviour. This obsession limits what we can say about the cultural influence of savage media environments. In agreement with cultural studies scholars such as Henry Jenkins (1999), Potter charges that behaviourist studies tend to concentrate on extreme examples of violent texts. In doing so, such work distracts attention from less spectacular forms of aggression that routinely riddle media narratives. What really disgusts Potter about media violence is its commodity status. Cheap crowd-pleasers, brutal media are the progeny of the industrial desire to develop easily replicable formulae for narratives that deliver audiences. Economic dimensions render spurious efforts to define violence as a freedom of expression issue. The free speech concept is inapplicable to the sale of goods. Even if it were, the real question would be what does it mean to live in a symbolic world with so little consumer choice?

Potter argues that media violence is a far bigger problem than anyone, including academics, has imagined. But what is lost in such a determined footing? As Martin Barker (2005b) asserts, those who enjoy media violence are constantly told to justify their tastes. It makes just as much sense, in his view, to start by asking why people object. This is more than a whimsical suggestion, as moral objections to salacious material are often mere gambits in the pursuit of grander social goals. Alan McKee's research (2006) convincingly argues that even those concerned about the negative impact of apparently antisocial content need to know why such material is a source of pleasure for not just deviant, but also normal audiences.

Yet the preponderance of these opening remarks clearly draws on a 'there is a problem' rather than 'is there a problem?' frame. This must be justified, and it is here that I begin to outline the transition from casual observation to formal analysis. I frame the reception of messages about sex and violence as troubling because they have ever been so in my lecturing career. Images of men and women fighting and fornicating have caused a number of uncomfortable and embarrassing moments which, on reflection, have raised evocative questions about how we make sense of the objectionable. These, in turn, have influenced my investigation of alcohol issues.

Pornography has proved to be more of an irritant than violence. Without doubt, the most cringeworthy experience of my lecturing career came during a tour of the New Zealand Board of Film Classification in 1995. I had taken two bus loads of undergraduates to a talk on censorship. Gathered in a cinema, we were told that we could only truly understand what the job entailed if we viewed some of the distasteful content the office had been asked to consider. Having watched a stand-up comedian deliver an expletive filled act, and a scene from a karate film where barely a second passed without someone being kicked in the head, it was time for our third serving. Suddenly, the screen filled with porcine porn star Ron Jeremy doing that which has made him famous.

It was no fun watching porn with my students. They obviously agreed; within forty seconds, two-thirds of them had walked out. Speaking later, we all agreed that we were glad when it was over. But we were less unanimous on what made the incident so disconcerting. Some objected to pornography on moral grounds. For others, economic issues intruded as the film represented the commodification of women's bodies. Some of the students had aesthetic qualms; they did not mind watching people have sex, they minded watching the hirsute, corpulent Jeremy having sex. Alternatively, the problem was contextual; this was simply the wrong place, the wrong time and the wrong company for porn.

What these unsystematically gathered observations demonstrate is that the offensive is not just there for all to see, which makes teaching and researching sex and violence difficult. While I have never shown explicit pornography to students as part of teaching, I have fewer reservations about screen violence; a short-sighted distinction, as someone pointed out to me following a lecture in which I had shown a scene from the UK gangster saga *The Krays*. Afterwards, a male attendee complained that he had found the images extremely disturbing. As violence was a recurrent threat in his life, the man requested that in future I should give equal consideration to how upsetting violent images can be. The point was valid and well put, questioning my own 'common sense'.

Indeed Annette Hill's study of complaints made to UK media regulatory bodies (2000) signals that the scale of public concern about media content is overestimated. According to Hill, complaining was a once only experience for most people contacting the Broadcasting Standards Commission and the Independent Television Commission in the 1990s. Radio and television seemingly pleased most of the people most of the time, questioning our certainty that sex and violence is an obvious public issue.

Instead of asking what harmful content does to people, we need to know why people are offended, hurt or entertained by media content of questionable taste. For instance, Sarah Hardy understands pornography as an 'ordinary' genre, to be addressed in the same way as any other cultural phenomenon. It is perfectly sensible to ask how porn works as a resource in a conversation with the self on sexual and gender identities (Hardy, 2004).

On the resource theme, it might also be the case that in some circumstances there is too little violence in the media. Research on public reactions to the murder of Ken Bigley, a British civilian engineer kidnapped and slaughtered by Iraqi militia, revealed that some people resented the media's under-representation of violence in the Iraq War. Some complained that the focus on Bigley's indubitably tragic demise drew attention away from scores of equally agonizing deaths suffered by soldiers and civilians (Ruddock, 2006b).

With these caveats in place, we can now address the four questions one must ask in the sex and violence problem, understanding that there might not be a problem and, if there is, that its nature is unclear.

## WHAT *IS* OBJECTIONABLE?

**5.3** Take what would appear to be a perfectly reasonable definition of media violence: 'The overt expression of physical force, with or without a weapon, against self or other, compelling action against one's will on pain of being hurt or killed, or actually hurting or killing' (Gerbner et al., 1978: 179).

In her account of how quantitative survey and experimental research hegemonized violence debates in 1960s America, Sandra Ball-Rokeach (2001) notes how many examples of media aggression so defined were excluded from analysis. In a period where police routinely and brutally suppressed civil rights and antiwar protestors, it was significant that images of state sponsored assault were not deemed relevant. Boyle points to a similar irony in Bill Clinton's admonishing of television for increasing images of violence, when his own foreign policy had added to the trend in the news.

Peter Wilkin (2004) also highlights definitional problems in pornography, especially in efforts to distinguish porn from the erotic. Wilkin presents Dianne Russell's statement that:

> I define heterosexual pornography as material created for heterosexual males that combines sex and/or the exposure of genitals with the abuse or degradation of females in a manner that appears to endorse, condone or encourage such behaviour... erotica refers to sexually suggestive or arousing material that is free of sexism, racism and homophobia, and respectful to all human beings and animals portrayed'. (see Wilkin, 2004: 349)

Accepting feminist concerns, Wilkin nonetheless accuses Russell of ignoring what pornography means to the people who use it.

Violence and pornography are not homogenous categories. They are crossed by subgenres influencing the sorts of social impact we should look for (Carter & Weaver, 2003). Potter and Tomasello outline six factors that affect what violence expresses; justification, realism, explicitness, humour, consequences for victims and attractiveness of perpetrators (2003: 317). Before making judgments about what media violence does, then: 'we need to understand more about how people encounter all elements in a violent story, to what elements they attend, [and] how they use these elements to construct an interpretation about ... what violence means' (2003: 325). Until such time as these questions are answered, we cannot begin to understand the social impact that these images have.

Interpretation is important, as studies have shown that audiences do not necessarily view messages of sex and violence as being about sex and violence. While *Buffy the Vampire Slayer* apparently pushes black magic and martial arts at impressionable teenagers, much of the target audience see friendship as the serial's main theme (Jenkins, 1999). Brigid Cherry (2001) finds women who like horror because they view 'monsters' such as Frankenstein, Jason from the *Friday the 13th* series or *Halloween's* Michael Myers as embodiments of loneliness. One of Alan McKee's respondents watches porn for the shoes.

Even scholars who accept that images of sex and violence do damage have complained that behavioural concerns mask the cumulative ideological effects. George Gerbner maintains that media violence affects everybody as a representation of social power.

> a dramatic demonstration of the power of certain individuals ... and the tendency of others to fall victim to it ... [the effects may be] lessons of victimisation and ways to avoid as well as commit violence; caution and prudence as well as pugnacity; a calculus of one's risks as well as opportunities to be gained from violence ... a tendency to assume high levels of violence; to acquiesce to the use of violence by others ... a sense of fear and need for protection. (Gerbner et al., 1978: 184)

Simlarly, one of the primary influences of media violence, according to Karen Boyle, is to naturalize gender inequalities; violence tells us that women are 'naturally' socially vulnerable and inert. It plays a part in naturalizing a world where women are not only hurt, but hired less, paid less and voiceless.

## *WHERE* **IS THE OBJECTIONABLE?**

**5.4** That much of my Ron Jeremy experience 'wrong' was about 'where', not 'what', is supported by literature on the place of the offensive. Here, place takes on both physical and mental dynamics. Questions of taste are implicated in the mental maps that people build around their cultural geography.

Offensive material constantly breaks new territory. Echoing Ball-Rokeach and Boyle, Walma van der Molen (2004) warns that the changing quantity and quality of news violence places the genre in the frame as agent of social harm. The Iraq war has produced footage coloured with the glamour and sensationalization of fictional violence. Viewers find themselves racing to battle alongside troops thanks to the technology at hand for embedded journalists. Many of these viewers are children, due to the routinized presence of news as part of the pre-watershed evening meal milieu. Here, they see all sorts of natural, accidental and political violence which can be just as upsetting or exhilarating as fabricated brutality.

Questions of place are also important in grasping the scale and nature of the pornographic. As an industry which in 2002 made over $57 billion (Simpson, 2004), pornography cannot be regarded as a marginal media phenomenon. This is all the more the case given its connections with 'respectable' parts of the leisure business, such as the hotel industry (Jacobs, 2004).

Porn is therefore mainstream, signifying for Reading (2005) new socio-spatial sexual relations. Cyberspace combines with the adult entertainment industry's capital muscle to subvert orthodoxies of taste and desire. Porn is no longer bound to sex shops in bad parts of town. It now sits directly next to mainstream content (hence Mitchell, Finkelhor and Wolak's (2003) research on the impact of inadvertent exposure). Virtuality also frees the consumer from fears over storage and capture. No longer bound to the limitations of the secret stash, porn users can explore a greater range of images and possibilities. Combined with the dominance of concern over child pornography, Reading suggests that the new anytime, any place porn culture creates the belief that anything else goes. The internet has even made the workplace part of the pornographic environment. Given the possibilities opened by portable technologies, it might be easier to ask where porn isn't than to ask where it is.

Beth Eck (2001) demonstrates how place influences the interpretation of the offensive. Eck asked forty-nine women and men to interpret four nude images; Titian's *Venus of Urbino*, a *Penthouse* picture, a photograph of an African woman nursing her child (taken from *National Geographic*) and a Calvin Klein ad featuring a nude Kate Moss. The advertisement was the most disturbing image, as people were unsure of its purpose. The Titian, the *Penthouse* and the *National Geographic* pictures were 'comfortable', in that people read their form and function with ease. The idea of pornography as comforting is challenging. But consider the following quote. In response to the *Penthouse* image, 'Kathy' stated 'that's a *Penthouse*, not a *Playboy* ... it's nasty'. As 'nasty' as the picture might be, Kathy's ability to distinguish a *Penthouse* from a *Playboy* indicated a level of mastery based on the power to locate pornography in its proper place. While the men Eck interviewed were more likely to find pleasure in the image, often related to nostalgia for the role that this sort of pornography played in adolescence, women were equally comfortable with *Penthouse* as something that could be held at arm's length. Hidden away in drawers and under beds, the magazine rarely confronted women directly. The same cannot be said for commercial nudes. While Eck's women objected to the commodification of women in *Penthouse*, the exploitation of the Calvin Klein ad seemed worse. First, nudity at least has a utilitarian function in pornography which is completely superfluous in advertising. Second, where pornography is a 'bounded category', the commercial nude is more offensive as it represents a very public and widespread form of sexual exploitation. Such evaluations rest on context, not content.

## WHAT DOES MEDIA SEX AND VIOLENCE DO?
## WHO DOES IT INFLUENCE?

**5.5** Although meta-analyses such as that provided by Browne and Hamilton-Giachritsis (2005) maintain that there is now a robust link between exposure to media violence and short-term increases in aggression, as observed and measured under experimental conditions, we should recognize that this is a humble claim. No-one believes in the 'magic bullet', the media message that can turn ordinary people into monsters.

To illustrate, consider Malamuth, Addison and Koss's *Pornography and Sexual Aggression: are there reliable effects and can we understand them?* (2000). Although the authors agree that experiments consistently find 'the existence of reliable associations between frequent pornography use and sexually aggressive behaviours, particularly for violent pornography and/or for men at high risk for sexual aggression' (2000: 26), they also recognize that it is not clear what this means given the validity problems that dog experimental research. Observed effects tend to be very small, only appearing under 'careful and precise assessment that is specifically geared to the manipulations used'; another way of saying that results are more 'made' than 'found'. Malamuth et al. also recognize differences between experimental and real world violence render experimental data a dubious foundation for policy, especially given the lack of attention effects researchers pay to culture:

> We believe ... moderators [of effects] include ... a culture that emphasizes or de-emphasizes equality between genders ... home background ... personality characteristics and dispositions ... current temporary emotional state ... content of stimuli ... and the environment in which the individual is exposed

Notwithstanding these reservations, contemporary researchers fall into four positions on what violence and porn does. The most high profile one is that *media sex and violence does bad things to bad or weak people*. Quayle and Taylor (2003) develop Reading's technological apprehension by noting the new possibilities the internet opens for child sex offenders. Stack, Wasserman and Kern (2004) put deviance theory to the test in a survey of 531 internet users. Here, indicators of antisocial and criminal impulses were positioned as independent variables which might predict internet use. Paying for sex, lack of religiosity and not being part of a happy marriage accounted for forty per cent of the variance in porn use, as measured by this survey.

From a u&g vantage, some have explored how personality affects media tastes. Greene and Krcmar's survey (2005) correlates pleasure in violence to a tendency to be verbally aggressive and sensation seeking. Sensation seeking is the constant need for new physiological experiences, and is interpreted in this literature as a fundamentally biological impulse (Slater, 2003). Experimentally, Grimes et al. (2004) used heart rate monitors to show that children with established psychological disorders and disruptive behaviour patterns were the most likely to react to screen savagery. In a survey of pornography use among US male undergraduates, Bogaert (2001) associated intelligence and aggression with different sorts of substantive preferences. A general pattern emerged where less intelligent, more aggressive men were more likely to choose porn featuring violence and insatiable, ergo continually sexually available, women.

How should we interpret the argument that sex and violence merely exacerbates that which is already there? First, there is no 'mere' about it.

Reinforcement, as cultivation analysts have long argued, is a powerful effect in itself. Second, we must ask who the 'sick individual' frame favours. Boyle points to the huge help that the effects tradition has provided to serial killers such as Ted Bundy, who eagerly grasped the idea that pornography made him hate and kill women as a means of avoiding his demise. Finally, while looking for the media's power to prey on the sick and the weak, this body of research claims to have found far wider patterns of influence. Slater's survey of 3000 US high school students in the wake of the Columbine murders observed that students who felt alienated from school or the family tended to seek out violent media. On this basis, Slater, Henry, Swaim and Anderson (2003) propose a 'downward spiral' model, where media cultivate antisocial feelings among more than a handful of radical outsiders.

That so much of the effects tradition is represented by experimental research pressed upon university undergraduates speaks to the fear that *media can make otherwise good people bad*. Bartholemew and Anderson (2002) provide a classic example of a behaviourist experimental study asking this question; that is, a study where media stimuli are tested for their power to evoke immediate and observable changes in aggression among apparently normal people. Twenty-two male and twenty-one female students were asked to play either *Mortal Kombat* or *PGA Golf Tournament*, then they: 'competed with a confederate in a reaction time task that allowed for provocation and retaliation' (2002: 283). Participants were led to believe that they were competing with one another in a game involving speedily clicking a mouse. When a participant was deemed to have lost, he or she was punished by a blast of white noise. In the second round, he or she had the opportunity to determine the length and severity of the blast delivered when the rival lost. Men who had played the violent game were significantly more likely to inflict the most severe punishments. Although this conclusion supports Malamuth et al.'s signal that gender influences effects, in Anderson and Murphy's experiments (2003) playing violent video games led to significantly increased aggression among young women, especially when the avatar was also female.

Returning to pornography, Rogala and Tyden (2003) tried to escape the artificiality of experiments by surveying women patients in a Stockholm family planning clinic to look for links between pornography use and unsafe sexual practices. Of the 1000 respondents, eighty per cent claimed to have used pornography, with one-third feeling that this had influenced both what they did and how they did it. One consequence, the researchers concluded, was that pornography aided the spread of sexually transmitted diseases by encouraging unprotected anal sex.

Schneider et al. (2004) studied associations between media sex, violence, and damaging social attitudes. As with Anderson and Murphy, identification emerged as a key independent in the effects of first person shooters. Arousal and pleasure were enhanced by games where players identified with avatars and the narrative built around them. The authors were troubled by this, as to them it spoke to the power of video games to promote the belief that violence is, under many circumstances, a valid tactic in conflict resolution.

The idea that media encourage violence indirectly by glamorizing and justifying aggression has been the subject of many projects. This work is significant as it develops the idea that media are key independent variables in the production of inclinations toward violence, having more than an already powerful reinforcing role. Vidal, Clemente and Espinosa's quantification of teenage television viewing habits and attitudes articulates this view with great clarity:

> it may well be that there is not a predisposition toward watching violent films in people with violent impulses but rather an early learning that generates a selective attentional or observational process when exposed to rewarded violent behaviours. This is coherent with the idea that young people perceive violence more positively as they watch more and more violence (2003: 389)

Worse still, Grana et al.'s experiments on reactions to televised bullfighting in Spain (2004) intimates that framing can overcome disinhibitions toward aggression. A survey of two hundred and forty-eight children aged between 8 and 12 measured their attitudes toward the practice. Most expressed distaste for the public taunting and slaughtering of animals. Nevertheless, experimental treatments where bullfighting images were accompanied by commentaries celebrating its cultural relevance produced significantly increased willingness among boys to express aggressive feelings, as measured in a questionnaire. Golde et al. (2000) found similarly disturbing short-term attitudinal effects produced by certain sorts of pornography. Eighty-three male students were split into four groups, each shown different sorts of pornography; those viewing content featuring degradation were more likely to blame the victim when questioned post-test about rape scenarios; this was especially the case when humiliation was combined with explicit sexual content.

Finally, pornography has been studied as a form of addiction. Griffiths (2000) notes the internet's power to encourage 'excessive' sexual behaviour and obsessions. Furthermore, she fears that, like a drug problem, internet porn can lead into 'harder stuff', tempting people toward criminal activity such as cyberstalking.

As all agree, short-term effects are only relevant insofar as they associate with long-term consequences. This has led some to ask the question of how *long-term exposure has effects that are hard to see because they are multiple, not directly behavioural, and happen to everyone.* The third person effect is an obvious example of such an influence, with Lynxwiler (2000) illustrating the power that music videos have in amplifying fears over rap and heavy metal's socially corrosive features. Long-term ideological effects are the foundation of cultivation analysis, with the argument that regular, frequent exposure to media violence creates fear, distrust of others, the degradation of anyone who isn't a middle-class, middle-aged male and a desire for punishment over rehabilitation in attitudes to crime (Gerbner et al., 1978). Qualitative work explores how violence and sex present resources and obstacles for those who use media in their explorations of identity.

Gender is often central. It is here that porn and violence become conjoined in concerns over the social damage caused by a cultural environment filled with messages about women's social and sexual subordination. Evans-DeCicco and Cowan's survey (2001) locates a trend where both women and men tend to evaluate female adult stars far more pejoratively than their male counterparts. Porn insiders often credit the industry as being the only place where women are valued and paid more than men. That male performers are often referred to as 'stunt dicks' would offer that in some ways porn inverts the sexist objectification found in mainstream media. Without venturing into the problems in this argument, Evans-DeCicco and Cowan found the reverse. Immediately after watching a porn film, both women and men were more likely to believe of the female performers that they were under the influence of drugs, of low intelligence, came from broken homes or were sex abuse survivors than they were of the men.

While short-term aggression studies have stressed desensitization as a media effect (where people become less shocked by violence and less empathetic toward its victims) other research argues just the opposite; that violence and sex can unpleasantly increase sensitivity. Absence of pleasure is an important idea as much of our media exposure is inadvertent. Schlesinger et al. (1992) point to the chilling effect that media violence has in reminding women of their physical vulnerability. But more recently, qualitative researchers have explored the discomfort caused when pleasure in sex and violence gives way to guilt.

Karen Ciclitira's interviews with thirty-four women porn users (2004) is a case in point. Feminist anti-pornography positions, stressing causal relations between representations of and real subordination, are problematic as pornography is no longer an all male preserve in terms of either production or consumption. The women resented a perceived 'anti-sex' bias in these positions, compounded by issues of race and class; a black former sex worker criticized the white, middle-class bias of this discourse. But the women recognized that they did not live in a porn utopia. Much as they liked it, the pornography they watch centred on male pleasure. Women of colour were largely invisible, and misogyny a regular occurrence. Pleasure/pain differences were largely coloured by reception context also. The women were comfortable with certain images when viewed with partners; however, for heterosexual respondents these same images became 'offensive' when used by partners as masturbation fodder.

But guilt is a male thing too, according to Thomas Austin's (1999) work on the soft porn classic *Basic Instinct*, featuring Michael Douglas as a detective (Nick) in pursuit of a serial killer who may or may not be Sharon Stone (Catherine). Austin asked male fans of this film to write to him explaining why they liked it. In response, 14-year-old 'Shane' wrote:

> I won't give my address because you know what parents are like! I've got a video in my room so I stayed up until 5.0 a.m. and watched it with my earphones on desperate heah! ... you see pictures of Sharon Stone and you just have to watch it. I'm sure you felt the same at 14! (1999: 156)

Here, the lengths that 'Shane' goes to see Sharon Stone cross and uncross her legs forces him to confront the power differential between Douglas/Nick (who gets to sleep with Stone/Catherine) and himself (who gets to sleep alone). This was a profoundly impotent moment as Shane confessed to his status as a sexual initiate.

Lisle (2004) looks at how unanalysed forms of media violence can have unexpected effects in his work on relations between news, tourism and guilt. 9/11 stands as a perfect example of Walma van der Molen's thesis on news and the glamorization/commodification of violence. In 2002, more people visited Ground Zero viewing platforms than had ever journeyed to the World Trade Center. If, however, tourists were drawn by news media's aping of disaster movies, the experience soon disabused them of the impression that this was an exciting event. Using press reporting of public reactions to the Ground Zero experience, Lisle notes a common guilt reaction. Tourists were met by overt attempts to commodify the disaster; organized walking tours and street vendors hawking 9/11 souvenirs, sitting right next to bereaved families trying to mourn privately in this commercial space. The effect, on tourists, was a feeling of guilt.

Of course, that *Basic Instinct* offered 'Shane' a pleasurable experience that also prompted reflection on what it means to 'be 14' opens the fourth possibility that media sex and violence can be good for you. Henry Jenkins presented this idea to an American Congressional hearing on media violence. The hearing was prompted by the Columbine shootings, and the apparent role that media images played in formulating and fuelling Harris and Klebold's psychotic rage. Against this suggestion, Jenkins argued that the condemnation rained on Goth culture demonstrated the imperative need to understand how young people use what might appear to be disturbing media content to achieve positive goals. The MIT professor's testimony was premised on the belief that the key variable was fundamental alienation Harris and Klebold felt toward mainstream US high school culture. It is true that, like many, the killers turned to gothic culture, but only as a part of a wider and eclectic media diet. But having interviewed teen Goths, Jenkins concluded that the killers had aberrantly decoded a distinctly non-violent subculture. Key informants claimed that content related to violence and death was appealing as a means of announcing a sombre disposition distancing teens from the norms of school 'jock' cultures. It was, then, a symbolic tool used to withdraw from rather than confront elements of the teen environment that Goths find uncomfortable, or just boring. Jenkins warned that actions taken to deny these resources to teens (who were being sent home from school for wearing items such as black leather coats) might push teens toward, not away from, extreme action. Also, Goths told Jenkins that they *liked* being miserable, which to them meant listening to music and watching movies with friends, while contemplating what the next life might be like.

Adult audiences also find pleasure in media violence by treating it as an aesthetic device designed to deliver a certain sort of media experience. Barker (2005b) studied undergraduate reception of Sam Peckinpah's *Straw Dogs*, a 1970s film denied classification in the UK for years as it contains a rape scene where, in the eyes of many, the female victim enjoys the experience. Some students read the sequence as a textual device. Acceptability, in the eyes of this audience, depended on the rape's role in narrative and character development. Viewing context was important as well. In the screening, one female viewer was forced to leave by the perception that male co-spectators were aroused or amused. Others, however, felt the scene was necessary, helping them grasp the film's anti-violence message.

Annette Hill's study of Quentin Tarrantino films locates aestheticized violence more squarely within pleasure's province (1997). Addressing the tendency of 'new brutalism' fans to watch favourite scenes over and over again, Hill explains that this is prompted by a thirst for aesthetic knowledge and the thrill of anticipation, not bloodlust. The pleasure of Tarrantino is found in the moments before ears are sliced, experiencing 'what's gonna happen' anxiety, then watching again to note how Tarrantino uses dialogue, music, settings and lighting to create an anticipation unmatched by other directors. Here, violence becomes 'tasteful'. The ability to appreciate art depends on the capacity to read a cultural phenomenon in terms of form rather than content (Freeland, 2002). Hill's viewers wanted an experience only satisfied by well-crafted representations. Violence was a means of announcing cultural capital; viewing pleasure lay in distinguishing themselves from filmgoers who accept any old violence.

So media sex and violence happens in many places, doing a variety of things to all kinds of people, who in turn do all kinds of things with this content. A wealth of data illustrates the damaging consequences this material can have in particular contexts, especially experimental ones. But this is just the beginning of the puzzle. Interpretation and context are recognized as key variables in determining the impact such content has. As we move closer to real reception places, so these variables multiply (Hovland, 1959), meaning there remains much controversy over the long-term consequences of liking violence and porn. Amidst this confusion, it has become clear that these tastes often have rational bases and positive consequences.

## WHO WANTS TO KNOW?

**5.6** Not a particularly novel or surprising conclusion. Looking at the research alone, it appears that researchers from different traditions agree on many things. Consider Glascock's study on the impact of degrading porn on gender relations (2005). Cosmetically, this ticks all boxes as a classic piece of effects research: an experiment, using US undergraduates, exposing them to violent misogynist porn, then measuring their attitudes to sex and gender relations. Superficially, its conclusion is just as classic: men were more likely to be aroused by scenes of female degradation.

But Glascock ends the research with a series of questions, not conclusions:

> male participants ... may become more aroused because they identify more with the male character who is not perceived as degraded ... perhaps some combination of arousal to male affirmation as well as female degradation is at work here. (2005:51)

A pattern had been found, but how it came about and what it means is open to question, as the researcher notes. This calls for more research, considering more variables studied in different treatments. So why the hostility between scholars?

The answer lies in 'before' and 'after' questions of why research is commissioned, and how its findings are used selectively. Speaking before the US Congress, Henry Jenkins complained that the overwhelming financial support given to experimental research created the impression that media violence is *the* rather than *a* variable driving real crime and aggression. This suits the political agenda of those looking for a quick and easy fix for certain sorts of social issues; far better to blame the media for Columbine than to recommend a root and branch revamping of the education system. Annette Hill (2000) and Martin Barker (2001) pursue the political motivations of violence research in the UK setting: the former uses third person logic to assert that the main effect of violence is as a catalyst for a moral crusade. For the latter, the refusal to acknowledge what qualitative cultural studies has to say on the matter reflects an institutional cynicism about media studies as a discipline.

Yet again, effects researchers do not disagree with these accounts. Sandra Ball-Rokeach was co-director of the Media and Violence Task Force, a sub-division of the National Commission on the Causes and Prevention of Violence established by US President Lyndon Johnson in 1968. While her thesis is that short-term effects have been replicated to the point where they can be accepted as facts, thereby serving a legitimate base for policy and citizen action, she is more than aware that this conclusion was reached via a highly politicized research process. In a narrative that would do justice to an Oliver Stone movie, Ball-Rokeach describes being the subject of FBI surveillance, and being placed under the jurisdiction of lawyers who determined her role as being to 'prove' the violence case, where she would have preferred to explore if the case should have been made at all.

The idea that researchers lose control over the way their ideas are used in the public domain is not exclusive to quantitative experimental research. Luff (2001) argues that one of the reasons why Ciclitira's female porn fans had a hard time reconciling their pleasure with sympathy to feminism is because the latter's anti-porn position has been hijacked by the religious right. But Jhally's (1994) criticism of sexist music videos in the early 1990s suffered a similar fate. His argument was not against sexual representation per se, but objected to objectification in its present form that targeted women, not men. In essence advocating *more* sex on television, Jhally was horrified to find his work being championed by those who would ban all sexual imagery.

Audience researchers must therefore recognize that they work in political contexts that not only shape the questions they ask, but also create the danger that findings can be selectively reported with unintended or unimagined public reverberations. Just as the effects of violence and pornography are contextual, so too might be the apparent conflicts in academic studies of the same. Having surveyed key issues in the theory and method in this field, we can now examine how they shape contemporary work.

## NEW STUDIES IN PORNOGRAPHY:
## ALAN McKEE AND THE MORAL PORN FAN

**5.7** It is impossible in good conscience to disagree when Dianne Russell states:

> if most pornography consisted of pictures of gangs of women raping men, sticking broomsticks up their rectums as the men smile as the men ejaculate and say 'encore',

> or pictures of men holding their male victims down and forcing anal and oral sex on them as women watch and applaud, or women snipping their testicles off with pliers, or women sticking wire up their penile openings, then men would have put a stop to pornography long ago .... Women must unite to fight this form of discrimination. (1998: 168)

In this statement, Russell draws on the work of Catherine Mackinnon and Andrea Dworkin in redefining pornography as a civil rights issue which in some ways decentres the effects question. The images she describes are a form of hate speech. They should be censored on the grounds that a society committed to equality finds them offensive on moral grounds. Overtly racist expressions are widely understood to be unacceptable in the media landscape. Why, Russell asks, is the same not true of pornography that degrades women?

Russell's work has been criticized for its strategic and unproblematic acceptance of the experimental research (Wilkin, 2004). Her moral point, however, stands independent of method questions, and makes questions of consumers' interpretations superfluous to the problem at hand. To justify continued research into pornography and its consumption, then, it is necessary to show how practical questions reach into the moral realm.

The most systematic attempt at this so far has been provided by Alan McKee, who has used both qualitative and quantitative methods to describe the cultural meaning pornography carries for its ordinary users in Australia. By ordinary, I mean that McKee's research reaches for a sample that does not comprise of university students or sex offenders, whose over-representation has skewed the findings of experimental studies. And it dispenses with experiments as:

> the vast majority of pornography in natural settings is done for pleasure. It is possible to imagine that sitting in public watching ninety minutes of pornography which you personally do not like, with no other distractions (pornography offers few pleasures in terms of narrative, performance or visual pleasures outside of the sexual), unable to masturbate ... could be a distressing experience. (2006: 7)

Using a survey of 1023 porn consumers, with forty-nine follow up qualitative interviews, where those who wished were given free rein to explain their tastes, McKee builds a series of arguments. First, he gathered empirical evidence to support doubts over the validity of experimental research. The survey studied correlations between a series of independent variables including not just pornography use but also location, age, education, political affiliation and education, and the dependent variable of attitudes toward women. While 'heavier' porn users were no more likely to take patriarchal or misogynistic attitudes, older, poorly educated rural conservatives were significantly more likely to believe that women should not get equal pay, should not be in positions of social power, or meant 'yes' when they said 'no'.

Crucially, none of this disagrees with Russell. In interviews with forty-nine consumers, McKee found people who would agree that these sorts of violent images should be banned. Accounts depart, however, over Russell's argument that barbarous misogyny is the adult entertainment industry's lingua franca.

McKee's work takes an unusual step in privileging description over analysis. No friend of anti-porn initiatives, McKee's rationale was to place the voices of 'normal consumers' within the public censorship debate. He therefore placed greater weight on reporting comments than analysing them. What his means is that his work represents something of an open text; and in this regard, it suggests more than it states.

In descriptive mode, the first insight emerging from the data was that porn consumers have a variety of often conflicting tastes that in turn dissolve the 'pornographic' as a unified category (McKee, 2006). Some were turned on by the perfect bodies of professional performers; others preferred the 'reality' of ostensibly amateur productions. Some did in fact like the stories. Although many interviewees represented conventional gender differences, where women criticized pornography's obsession with the male orgasm and vigorous sex, other female consumers objected to this as a sexist policing of their own desires.

The sample agreed, however, that their use of pornography was entirely compatible with family values and respect for women. They were at pains to ensure their children did not have access to their collections. They were vehemently opposed to violent, paedophilic and bestial porn, and were perfectly happy to support censorship in these areas. The problem, as they saw it, was that public porn debates tend to blend criminal, depraved genres with porn productions made by consenting adults who take experience pleasure in what they do. Despite regular and frequent porn use, McKee's interviewees claimed to have never encountered the sorts of images Russell describes.

Picking up on the final point, McKee identified key judging criteria showing that consumers' porn tastes had little to do with generic conventions used by the industry. The key variable distinguishing good from bad porn, in terms of its ability to deliver pleasure, was if performers themselves appeared to be having a good time. Productions where talent appeared to be going through the motions, or where viewers felt they could detect evidence of drug use or coercion, were dismissed as bad, i.e. impossible to enjoy. McKee's sample thus accepted the Russell critique. They also demonstrated a knowing take on porn's complicated realist aesthetic; scripted or 'gonzo', porn always features real people having real sex which is really good, bad, indifferent or painful.

Despite the onus on presenting audiences as actors rather than evidence in the porn conversation, McKee did conclude that their words indicate a range of positive uses standing independently of the adult industry's economic ambitions. Pornography, for these people, was a versatile cultural building block for healthy relationships and a sense of self. One woman described using a taste for porn as an indicator of compatibility with prospective partners. Couples used pornography as a way of describing the pragmatic maturity of their relationships, where masturbation was seen as legitimate self-expression that is essentially other to sexual partnership.

But in my view, in giving words precedence over analysis, McKee's work stands as a clear representation of a dynamic where data is rarely exhausted by analysts' discussions. In this regard, I would suggest that his interviews give evidence of the insecurity of the pleasure pornography provides. The idea that porn is only fun when it features willing participants in an industry that treats them with moral, physical and economic respect means that this pleasure depends not only on the text, but on the story that consumers tell themselves about how the adult entertainment industry works. What do they do, then, when presented with Linda Lovelace's claim that her apparently exuberant performance in the seminal 1970s chic porn flick *Deep Throat* was delivered at gunpoint (Boyle, 2005)? Do they have to ask if their pleasure means more than someone else's pain? To what extent is this less about pornography, and more about global economic relations, since the question could equally be asked of people buying cheap trainers and T-shirts made by slave labour? While McKee is critical of the assumption that porn is a bad phenomenon that does harm, and while his consumers resented being corralled alongside sex offenders, damage is an issue the interviewees raised of their own volition. Liking porn does not stop its fans from worrying about it. McKee's work therefore represents both the importance of considering interpretation, but also the contradictions of audience power. Interpretation is only relatively autonomous within cultures of media production that audiences neither understand nor control.

## NEW STUDIES IN VIOLENCE: BRITAIN'S BINGE DRINKERS

**5.8** On the evening of 20 September 2005, 25-year-old Christopher McBride sat quietly sipping a beer in Liverpool's 'Jacaranda' bar. He was approached by John Frazer, who demanded a cigarette. When McBride refused, Frazer punched him twice in the head. At first, the victim thought little of the assault, finishing his drink before heading home to nurse his bruises. Later that night, Christopher McBride fell into a coma and died (Glover, 2005).

Three months on, I was asked to design and analyse a survey assessing the effectiveness of local alcohol awareness initiatives in Merseyside. CitySafe, a local government organization which aimed to counteract the safety issues related to excessive drinking, had sponsored a pre-Christmas alcohol awareness campaign on Liverpool's 'Juice FM' radio station. The campaign consisted of a series of vox pop comments on the social embarrassment drunkenness can cause (e.g. 'I was so hammered last night ... I can't even remember getting into the taxi'). Additionally, DJs encouraged listeners to complete a quiz on the effects of drinking, offering Robbie Williams concert tickets as a prize. Quiz answers could be found on an internet microsite. While there, listeners were encouraged to complete a survey on their drinking habits and concerns. My research was based on the 179 responses received. Unexpectedly, the study became about media violence.

Bearing in mind that not even effects researchers believe in magic bullets, the first task in completing the report for CitySafe was to explain that it was not possible to measure the effects that the *Countdown to Christmas* campaign had. The spots were simply a few among thousands of messages that audiences received about alcohol and its consumption. What we could do, however, was to begin to map a 'cultural geography' of drinking, outlining the where, when, what and how of alcohol consumption, then asking what drink-related themes were most relevant/appealing/memorable/shocking for those listeners who responded to the measure.

The 'modal' drinker answering the survey was a woman, aged between eighteen and thirty-five. Unsurprisingly, given levels of UK concern about binge drinking, ninety-five per cent of our sample denied drunkenness as their goal. Despite this, seventy per cent of the sample spent between £20 and £100 on alcohol alone in the city's bars once or twice a week. Even at the lower figure, this meant that most of our drinkers regularly exceeded safe per diem unit consumption. What, we wondered, were the alcohol related risks that worried our drinkers? The overwhelming response was violence. We also asked if they had seen anything in the media which had raised their concerns about drinking. The same answer was returned.

Alcohol, for the listeners, was violence related as both a social and media issue. Consequently, the research accessed a number of general themes in representations of aggression. First, we have the idea that violence has a ubiquitous symbolic presence, meaning its analysis has to stretch beyond the familiar concerns over action adventure and horror films, music videos or gaming. Given this omniscience, audiences make intertextual connections between messages that appear unconnected. As Michael Frazer was tried and sentenced in December 2005, it is highly likely that when we asked if people had seen anything in the media which struck a chord about drinking dangers, they were thinking of Christopher McBride's murder. Contrary to the question of what media do to people, with the passivity implied, our listeners made active sense of alcohol related issues. While Porter's data (2004) shows drinkers who feel that the news exaggerates the scale of Britain's booze problem, we cannot dismiss Juice FM listeners' fear as the irrational product of symbolic artifice. In the UK, the risk of drink inspired assault is significantly greater than in the rest of Europe (McVeigh et al., 2005)

Building on the idea that violent images can have cumulative, contradictory, long-term effects that are difficult to see, it was important to explore the consequences that the solid drink/violence connection the listeners made might have for other alcohol related issues. To begin to do this, the survey constructed an 'aversion index'. We asked people to rate a series of alcohol related problems on a scale of 1–8, where 1 indicates a high level of concern, and 8 a low level. Our question read:

What puts you off drinking? Please number in order of priority, with item 1 being the most important.

- Hangovers
- Cost
- Weight gain
- The way drinking makes you look
- Making a fool of yourself
- Being around drunk people
- Violence
- Long-term health risks.

The question produced the following results:

| Item | Mean Score |
| --- | --- |
| 1. Violence | 3.6 |
| 2. Hangover | 3.8 |
| 3. Health risks | 3.9 |
| 4. Cost | 4.2 |
| 5. Weight gain | 4.8 |
| 6. Behaving foolishly | 5.0 |
| 7. Effects on looks | 5.4 |
| 8. Drunk people | 5.4 |

Violence appeared as the leading theme. A Friedman test revealed the differences between these mean scores to be statistically significant ($p < 001$). This had a particular relevance for the Juice FM campaign. Our drinkers worried far more about violence than social humiliation, or the embarrassing behaviour of other people. They were also slightly more concerned about short-term consequences rather than long-term physical and mental effects.

To this point, the numbers supported George Gerbner's 'mean world' hypothesis. The fear of violent assault while drinking was both rational and irrational. That is, while a UK drinker should worry about it more than a colleague in Denmark, what he or she should worry about far more are the long-term health risks of frequent intoxication. But when we asked listeners an open-ended question on the sorts of messages they thought would effectively give pause for thought, they moved toward a more Hill/Barker like position relating violence to cultural literacy and environmental control. People wanted to see graphic images of injuries and illnesses. In their minds, good violence/health messages would merge into a category we might call the 'gruesome', the explicit image whose veracity can be neither ignored not denied. Respondents actually wanted *more* media violence, which in this context would do more good than harm.

The other pattern that does not fit Gerbner's thinking is that if media prompted fears over the dangers of the night economy, this did not keep the drinkers away from bars. Strangely, it is in this very pattern that we can find the damage that media violence might do. Invited to expand on their perceptions and fears in open-ended questions, it became clear that the drinkers viewed assault as a tangible, but distant, risk. When they spoke of aggression, it was generally as an experience done by other people to other people. The focus on violence, then, provided a rhetorical means of absenting oneself from social concerns over alcohol abuse, especially as time spent discussing this was time not devoted to considering long-term health risks that are the product of design, not chance. For our drinkers, the damage of media violence lay in the support it gave to those who did not want to think about long term health issues.

## CONCLUSION

**5.9** My drinking research raises a fifth possibility in the question of what media violence does to people. If we accept that it makes sense to publicize the effects of drink fuelled aggression, nevertheless drinkers in Liverpool – good people who do not set out to get drunk and avoid public disorder – used this content to reach 'bad' or rather unhelpful conclusions.

What does this say about the general field of sex and violence research? For anyone involved in media education, the area is an unavoidable academic and practical problem. The realities of teaching the topics alert us to the difficulties in defining and delimiting the objectionable and its social impact. Although common sense, everyday observations have hampered public debates on 'antisocial' media, scholars have used various methods to expand the range of questions that we can ask about sex and violence. A sober reading of quantitative experimental research reveals that effects have not been proven, although disturbing patterns have been observed under controlled conditions. Hugely reliant on criminal and student samples, effects researchers would agree the need for more real world research considering ordinary audiences and their use of a wider variety of media. As my alcohol study shows, media violence happens in unexpected places, with unimagined results.

# 6 Reality, Media and Celebrity

## INTRODUCTION

**6.1** Can we speak of reality television as a genre, given its exponential expansion? In practice, audiences make distinctions between 'gamedocs' such as *Big Brother* and 'slice of life' alternatives like *Pet Rescue*. Actually, it is more accurate to speak of reality media; many shows exist across a variety of forms, to the point where the pragmatic question is, who is not watching, reading or gossiping about their events and characters?

Early in the academic reaction to reality media, Nick Couldry (2002) concluded that the phenomenon's main impact was the production of celebrity. In 2006, his thesis was supported by the formerly unknown Chantalle Houghton, who achieved fame by convincing contestants on the UK's *Celebrity Big Brother* that she was already famous. So dense is Britain's A to Z star universe that house-mates found Chantalle's charade, including a hoax girl band with a non-existent minor hit, plausible. None seemed surprised or shocked by the presence of a celebrity no-one had ever heard of. By the first week's end, the fake star had become the real thing.

Reality and celebrity therefore appear as an immense, twinned symbolic presence. But this is not the reason for devoting a chapter to how audiences react. Instead, I will argue that studying the cultural significance of reality and celebrity sharpens our ability to explore media power if we replace the question 'how real is reality?' with that of 'how *live* is reality?', or better, 'how is the reality *event experienced as live?*'. The trouble is, considering reality television as a conduit to people and places as they exist before acts of mediation is a bit like eating chocolate cake because you fancy an egg. Chocolate cake would not be chocolate cake without eggs. But if its taste might be, faintly, of eggs, it is not like eggs. Similarly, an exploration of reality media has to acknowledge that reality and reality media are analytically and experientially distinct.

Nevertheless, reality media provide fresh insights on associations between information, knowledge and pleasure. We have seen how learning and entertainment are rarely divisible in receptive moments. Fiction, we know, feels authentic when 'reality' is understood as a complex concept in both scholarly theory and audience understanding; people mean very different things when they denote a media text as real or not, and indeed can see the same object as simultaneously credible and implausible *vis-à-vis* its claims to truth.

Reality media join this trajectory in offering a mirror process where the real can be said to have a fiction effect; programming using the raw material of people and places ostensibly playing themselves is designed to be engaging and entertaining before it is informative. Strangely, in contrast to classic realist texts that work hard to disguise the evidence of artifice, a show like *Pop Idol* apparently behaves like a professionally malevolent magician; it is only too happy to show the audience how the celebrity trick is done (Holmes, 2004b). However, it might be that this strategy can increase the influence of reality shows when they are understood as media *events*.

To set the scene in a different way, studying reality audiences is not about searching for the moments where people are duped or not into thinking the things that they see, hear and read (for reality media cross the senses) represent a world that would exist without staging and re-presentation. This premise avoids the issue of how media experiences exist in their own right. Tempting as it is to bewail the artificiality of media reality, and the uncharismatic, untalented celebrities it regurgitates, these commonsense qualms say little about a more important question; what do these genres and characters tell us about the centrality of mediation in building a sense of the social?

It is this question that prompts the thesis that the significance of reality media and celebrity are better grasped via the idea of 'liveness', particularly as it evolves in the work of Nick Couldry. 'Liveness' allows a model of cultural power that respects audiences as people who are, on the whole, sufficiently attuned to re-presentational strategies as to be able to easily pierce some of the more obvious ideological claims media make. Nevertheless, Couldry's analysis offers that beneath the confusion of multiple reactions to multiple texts, media remain the link between self and social; such is the nature of their power.

The empirical use of these ideas will be illustrated via the study of political celebrity. Just as reality programming converts the everyday into a spectacular pleasure site, so too the concern has been expressed that for politicians, appeal now counts for more than political acumen. Using an archive of letters written to UK Tory Member of Parliament (MP) Boris Johnson in the wake of a highly public scandal in 2004, I will show how Johnson served a fictional role, inasmuch as he allowed audiences to express a range of opinions that often had little relation to anything he had said or done. Diverse as these responses were, however, they relied on underlying structures of the scandal as a live event. While people who wrote to the MP often criticized media handling of politics and politicians, their responses remained dependent on the presence of media.

## REALITY MEDIA: THE DAMAGE DONE

**6.2** In the closing stages of World War Two, a teenager named Rudy Boesch enlisted in the US Navy. The sea suited him, and by 1961 he had become a diver in the elite SEAL Special Forces. Scoffing at middle-age, Boesch served two tours of duty in Vietnam, engaging in forty-five combat missions and winning the Bronze Star for valour. Retiring in 1990, Boesch completed an astonishing forty-five years of active service (www.nightscribe.com/Military/rudy_boesch_bio.htm). Evidently an extraordinarily resilient fellow, Boesch's powers won him fame only when, at the age of seventy-two, he was unable to hold on to a log for as long as a much younger opponent on the American 'gamedoc' *Survivor* (Fraser & Brown, 2002).

The Navy man's story encapsulates our darkest fears over reality media's capacity to erode traditional markers of authentic human value. We must understand, however, that this is a subset of larger anxieties over the faith we can place in *any* media. A trust crisis has infected many genres. In the UK, the circulation of faked photographs of British troops abusing Iraqi prisoners provoked a public debate on the credibility of visual images. In the other direction, the US news media's decision to censor genuine pictures of torture perpetrated by US guards for reasons of taste (the prisoners in question being naked) shattered 'window on the world' pretence (Taylor, 2005).

Authenticity can be just as important to entertainers. In hip-hop, a performer's appeal often has relatively little to do with musical or lyrical gifts. White rappers combat the perennial problem of assumed fakeness by publicizing back stories emphasizing humble origin (Hess, 2005). Or, in the case of Eminem, authenticity is fabricated by a resolute refusal to occupy any fixed gendered, raced or classed space; a homophobe who hugs Elton John, a loving father who hates his mother, a white man whose entire cultural world is black, Marshall Mathers cannot be fake since he does not claim to be anything (Calhoun, 2005).

So the question of the real, or rather what we can trust, pervades media culture. What is more worrying, the fear of the fake has also bled into real life. Staying with hip-hop, Melissa Campbell (2004) defined 'booty dancing' as a cultural practice premised on a superficial engagement with race; white dancers ironically sample a culture that can be easily picked up and put down again. On the same lines, Tracy Shaffer (2004) differentiated between 'real' and 'fake' tourist forms in an analysis of backpacking as a symbolic practice. The clothes you wear, the places you go, the way you move through them and, vitally, the stories you tell about your travels determine whether you are having an 'experience' or just a holiday.

What all of these studies express is the anxiety that life is being detrimentally colonized by the symbolic. Even real people doing real things in real places can be fake in intention, action and effect. A prevailing suspicion of fraudulence reduces genuine mediated suffering to a vehicle for pleasure. Reality media are the vanguard of this move, with its common currency of humiliation (Mendible, 2004). Talk shows appeal, according to Mahan-Hays and Aden (2003), as they allow viewers to feel above the wretches who lay bare intimate and tragic details. Human beings are caught in the tension between wanting to be both social and individual. The structure of the television talk show errs toward individuality in making it easier for viewers to feel superiority rather than sympathy. Reiss and Wiltz (2003) offered support in the form of psychological research. Correlating sixteen personality types with preferences for reality shows, the authors found that pleasure was positively correlated with a taste for vengeance, and negatively associated with morality.

However, this is a social rather than a psychological problem, as reality media systematically pick on the same sorts of victims; echoing cultivation analysis, some scholars argue that the cumulative lesson of reality genres is that it's a straight man's world. Fairclough (2004) expressed disappointment that although *Wife Swap* takes the gendered nature of domestic work as a core subject, the theme is subordinated to narrative set-ups that guarantee conflict between wives who could plausibly join forces against errant partners. Graham-Bertolini (2004) and Yep and Camacho (2004) explained this as the product of the persistent assumption of misogyny-tinged heterosexuality; shows such as *The Bachelor* and *Joe Millionaire* are contests that naturalize women's sexual and social subordination. This is particularly troubling given their success as international franchises, telling the same story across a variety of cultures. It is certainly tempting to look at reality shows as global bullies, fond of picking on women, the working class, or preferably both. Yet others are less pessimistic. *Queer Eye for the Straight Guy* has been identified as a programme that turns an unflattering spotlight on the male heterosexuals who are the innocent bystanders in *Wife Swap* (Morrish & O'Mara, 2004).

The franchise issue returns us to the disquiet expressed over the commodified elements of media culture. Mark Andrejevic (2002) sees little point in engaging with 'positive' or 'negative' content of reality media. More important is what they say about economics and governance. To understand his point, consider the question that is constantly asked of 'gamedoc' contestants; why on earth did you do it? For Andrejevic, the decision is less bizarre when set against the information economy's demand that we constantly disclose personal details. The really remarkable thing about *Big Brother*, Andrejevic continues, is its success in transforming a reference to omniscient totalitarianism into a system where confession and disclosure are offered as a means of release. This mirrors shifts in the wider economy. Just as reality media depend on ordinary people's willingness to bare all, so too the information economy can only survive if consumers take on the burden of providing information about spending habits and tastes. Information society has developed two rhetorical tricks to mask potential objections to surveillance; the idea that only people with something to hide will object, and that confession is good. Marketing companies argue that their research promises to reduce the number of commercial messages we are subjected to; if they understand us better, they will be able to target us with information about those goods and services we really want. Money might make the world go around, but only by riding on information. Reality media encourages a structure of feeling that lubricates the process.

## HOW DOES REALITY BECOME REAL?

**6.3** Andrejevic made a pretty grand claim; that reality media are in some ways the glue cementing politics, the economy and the individual. What remains to be explored is the role that audiences play in this cohesion. An early answer was provided in by the idea of 'parasociality'. Reviewing the development of the parasocial from 1956 to the present, while David Giles summarized the main question here as being 'how similar are parasocial relations to ordinary relations' (2002: 283), it is more accurate to say that the proper query is 'what sort of social relation is implied by the parasocial?'. As originally conceived, parasocial studies set out to study how audiences came to relate to media figures. These relations were often conceived as 'resulting from deficiencies in social life and dependency on television' (2002: 280). Yet the deficiency model failed to sustain since, as research developed, it became clear that although relations between audiences and media figures appeared to mirror other sorts of relationships, they were unique in many respects. Hence the shift from the first to the second question.

The idea of the deficient relation can still be seen at play in recent parasocial studies, and explains their limitations. Brown, Basil and Bocarnea (2003) and Casey et al. (2003) study the impact that celebrity can have on health awareness. When basketball player Magic Johnson announced he was HIV positive in 1993, surveys showed increased public awareness and knowledge of the disease. Health centres reported greater numbers of patients asking to be tested for the virus (Casey et al., 2003). When Mark McGwire broke Babe Ruth's legendary record for home runs in baseball, the public was discovered to be conversant with the previously little known supplement androstenedione that had helped him swat many a ball beyond the last fielder. Both public figures felt 'known' by the public as they activated important narratives that people enjoyed, understood and cared about; the American dream of success for all, the foreboding knowledge that tragedy can strike anytime, anywhere to anyone. What these studies also noted, however, was that the spikes in public consciousness that happen when triumph and disaster meet celebrity are unsustained; public interest in HIV infection waned soon after the Johnson announcement. Ultimately, then, it seems that however much we feel that we know them, celebrities are not real enough to make a difference; they are a distant cousin, not a lover or a sibling. Giles' review of the parasocial concluded, however, that these weak 'celebrity effects' are the product of studies that look at individual celebrities rather than the phenomenon of celebrity in general; to 'sample' Louis Althusser's distinction between ideology and ideologies (1972), *celebrities* may have short term effects, but *celebrity* might be a different matter. Audience scholars need an understanding of how multiple encounters with a variety of media figures, both fictional and real, make for an engagement with the social. To appreciate how this can be done, we need to turn to recent work on reality media that leads toward the idea of 'liveness'.

Liveness is offered as a better way of understanding how reality media come to matter to a sceptical public. While notions of 'real' and 'authentic' remain important, for our purposes they are too analytically vague to express what reality genres tell us about the integration of media and everyday life. This is *not* to say that they are inconsequential. Quite the reverse; the more we question what the authentic is or can be in media culture, the more significant it becomes.

In the most systematic analysis of reality media audiences to date, Annette Hill (2005) indicates the need for a new term to understand the genre's relevance through two conclusions. First, audiences seek moments of authenticity in gamedocs, despite the general feeling that such shows are wildly contrived. Second, although audiences value the reality of shows taking place in every-day settings, their verisimilitude can be upsetting. *Pet Rescue* and *Animal Hospital* can show sick animals, as long as they do not die (at least, not very often). So, combining large sample survey research with qualitative inter-viewing, Hill found a tremendously bargained relationship between audi-ences and reality media. On the one hand, viewers recognize the feigned nature of gamedocs, to the point where the genre is nearing exhaustion as a pleasure source. At the same time, Hill also found that a show like *Big Brother* retains a powerful role in shaping audiences' sense of true and false and right and wrong as social categories. Recognizing that reality televi-sion's entertainment ethic determines it cannot be straightforwardly mimetic does not mean that it abandons all claims to *any* sort of veracity. The pleas-ure of *Big Brother* does not lie in its voyeuristic display of flesh and bodily functions, but in the moments where the performances of contestants who act up for the cameras unravel under constant surveillance (Hill, 2005).

Exploring the apparent contradictions in how audiences negotiate the reality of reality television is important, as the ontology of reality media is tied to governance issues; as British media institutions are organized along lines that make meaningful distinctions between fact and fiction, the way that these categories come into being through public discussion and organizational arrangement is of great importance. Indeed, Hill concurred with Biltereyst (2004) that audience suspicion of gamedocs cannot be taken as an independent reaction, as it tends to reflect the form and function of elite concerns; media itself complains about reality media.

What reconciles the arguments that viewers know reality media is not real, yet turn to even its most staged versions for an authentic experience? The answer is not that audiences are stupid; it is that we have to understand that reality media offer a distinct form of authenticity to be understood according to its own aesthetic.

Thomas Austin (2007) reached the same conclusion via a study of public reactions to *Capturing the Friedmans* (CTF). The documentary, made by Home Box Office and Notorious Pictures, covered the case of Arnold and Jesse Freidman, a father and son jailed in 1987 for sexually abusing children. Made sixteen years later, the documentary was remarkable for its extensive use of home footage shot by the actual family. According to Austin, this exaggerated the tensions inherent in the form. Documentarists by definition make compromises between aesthetics and evidence, and the public versus the private. In these cross hairs, CTF repositioned private, naturally produced artefacts of ordinary family life as public evidence of the nature of abusive families. Or did it? Did these ordinary images prove that Arnold and Jesse could not possibly be guilty of the crimes for which they were imprisoned, or did they illustrate the fact that most of the time sexual abuse is perpetrated by people who appear to be normal? Looking at reactions to the film on internet message boards, Austin concluded that the result for audiences was an ambiguous, intriguing and upsetting viewing experience. But this could not be taken as a product of the brute reality of the evidence to hand. The shocking qualities of the home movies were a product of an editing process that imbued them with a deliberate sense of ambiguity that had more to do with the conventions of European cinema than documentary. Additionally, this aesthetisization of real footage was the product of commercial motives that make profitable documentary possible. But Austin's conclusion is that these intersecting tensions actually increase the responsibilities faced by documentary makers. Just because something is aesthetic, entertaining and voyeuristic does not mean it is only these things. Nor is it naïve to expect documentaries to tell us something about the parts of our world that are beyond our experience. CTF did push audiences into discussing real issues; the nature of child abuse, the operations of the justice system. That it was a commercial success shows that it is possible to find and therefore demand moments of truth within current systems of production and distribution.

We need, then, an idea that expresses both the recognition of the space between media and real and the expectations that audiences can reasonably make about the media's duty to respect the ontology of experiences without their own production practices.

## LIVENESS

**6.4** Liveness offers one solution. At first blush, it may seem an anachronistic term to use. Jerome Bourdon's exploration of liveness (2000) began with the acknowledgement that far less television is live, inasmuch as the moment of performance and broadcast are one and the same, than used to be the case. Liveness, however, refers more to a sensibility fostered by the knowledge that television is a potentially disruptable medium. In 2006, Channels 4 and 5 were fond of filling airtime with compendium shows that documented 'television's most shocking moments', commemorating occasions where slick production techniques imploded before our eyes. Bourdon postulated that television's appeal rests on the promise that these moments can happen at any time; although the fact that the medium's prolific output can be contained into '100 shocking moments' tells us that in practice this is rarely true.

The point to be made here is that one does not have to behold events as they occur in real time to have the sense that one is watching cultural evolution as it happens. For example, in October 2005, David Cameron, leader elect of the UK Conservative Party, found himself sitting in front of verbal pugilist Jerome Paxman, host of BBC 2's prestigious *Newsnight*. The programme was broadcast long after the actual interview had been recorded. This did not prevent, however, a feeling of shock at Paxman's opening question: 'Mr Cameron, do you know what a pink pussy is?'. The answer was, on this occasion, 'a cocktail'; Paxman was alluding to a discrepancy between Cameron's ability to act on binge drinking and his board membership of a brewery. The time lag between the question being asked and its broadcast did nothing to disguise Cameron's bewilderment and the collapse of any rehearsed speeches he might have had in mind. The unravelling felt live, even if it was not actually so. It is events such as these that create the impression that audiences are live witnesses and therefore participants in cultural processes. If little television remains live in the purest sense, this does not stop the feeling that anything can happen, which is the essence of liveness as a cultural form.

The idea has been developed most notably by Nick Couldry as part of his explorations of power and media rituals (2004). In my view, Couldry's central thesis is that the unpredictability of live media is systematically produced. This is not to say that audiences' reactions to media are a reflex of institutional design, but it is to say that responses are organized, in the sense that they are the product of traceable institutional processes.

Uncoincidentally, Couldry's thinking in this area began with *Big Brother*. He originally signalled an interest in addressing media power in terms of the commodity relations identified by Andrejevic. So, speaking of the first UK series that catapulted a dozen unknowns into what then seemed an unlikely fame, he wrote:

> It is striking that so much effort should now be expended on television's represen-
> tation of the ordinary ... rather than the spectacular; we have reached, it seems, the
> opposite of the society of the spectacle. But the contradiction is only apparent ...
> the self-effacing presentation of everyday 'reality' arguably constitutes the purest
> form of legitimation of the media frame. (2002: 291)

Here, Couldry expressed the view that reality television is worthy of attention as a demonstration of media power par excellence. Television's commodity form had disguised itself in a show that appeared to *reverse* the process of spectacularization.

Recall that fan researchers trace pleasure in the opportunities that texts create for their devotees to project themselves into media spheres. Reality television seems to work in reverse, as media infiltrate the ordinary in an effort to mirror its rhythms and spaces. However, this solidifies the role the media play in defining the social, or the world of organization that exists beyond our individuality. The net effect is that if specific sorts of represen-tations are questioned, the general right of the media to represent what counts as social is unassailable (Couldry, 2004).

Liveness is the mechanism that allows this to work. The Cameron/Paxman clash illustrated Couldry's idea that the phenomenon is an institu-tional creature. The public unravelling of the up-and-coming Tory was the result, in part, not of Paxman's tenacity but the very form of the political interview, which assumes that politicians have something to hide (Richardson, 2001). It is structures such as these which explain how media create the impression that audiences are following events from within (Couldry, 2002). What we have, then, is a predictable unpredictability inherent in the nature of the media event (Scannell, 2002). Although the 'pink pussy' question came as a shock, anyone familiar with Paxman's style would have known that a question like that was on its way. The moment of surprise was curiously anticipated.

Predictable unpredictability explains why Holmes (2004a) argued that rhetoric around reality gamedocs vastly overestimates the role that interactivity plays in explaining audience pleasure. While various voting mechanisms and forms of access to reality events create possibilities for audiences to intervene in how narratives evolve, television broadcasts remain the pivot of pleasure. Both Hill (2002, 2005) and Jones (2003) found that eviction night was the most popular feature of *Big Brother*, with other forms of access mattering little. Eviction night illustrates the idea that live media represents a resource that allows the particular organization of social life. Scannell (2002) pointed to the synchronicity of *Big Brother* and the working week; each day is branded, culminating in eviction night that signals the start of the weekend. While we do not know exactly what will happen when we tune in, we can prepare for the event.

Having said this, Couldry argued that this represents an anti-essentialist model of power; if media institutions offer structured experiences, the multiplicity of both the institutions and experiences means that it is left to the audience to stitch them together and determine the nature of their social impact. So, while we know that the audience for eviction night will have expectations about what they are to encounter, the precise nature of these expectations will be the product of the peculiar patterns that viewers make of the various speculations offered by television, newspapers, new media and everyday gossip. If the social happens in media, it also happens across media, where audiences have a say in determining the path. The shift is from asking what people are doing with texts to: 'what ... are people doing in relation to media across a range of situations and contexts' (Couldry, 2004: 119). Social life can thus be orchestrated by media without reflecting a central order.

This is of great political importance, as it addresses Nina Eliasoph's critique that institutionally focussed research tends to assume the public as a given existing entirely outside those institutions (2004). Eliasoph complains that the analysis of relations between media and political organizations frame the public as a simple product of those bodies; influence is a unidirectional flow from government and media to audience. Although we can gather evidence to show that this is often the case, space needs to be made for considering situations where the public play a role in forming both what 'public' means and in determining how social institutions function and cohere. It follows that liveness is a model functioning as a reflexive approach to the institution concept, where audiences influence how reality, or more accurately authenticity, and celebrity circulate as social phenomena.

Reality media are 'real' in their organizing capacity. At this juncture, it is pertinent to note that the mechanisms of celebrity have a similarly ordinary aspect. Although it is now de rigueur to lament mundane stars, what this ignores is that we sometimes value the former as a positive feature of the latter. Indeed, when we praise stars who appear 'down-to-earth', what we express is recognition of a certain sort of performance where a public figure manages to appear ordinary under extraordinary circumstances.

The processes of stardom are, in this respect, not so very different from the 'performances' that Erving Goffman saw in everyday life (Tolson, 2001). The ordinariness of stardom helps us to describe the inadequacies of parasociality since one of the consequences of the explosion of celebrity is that our encounters with it now often come in real, everyday contexts. Drawing on Goffman again, Ferris (2003) described the common experience for Beverly Hills residents of bumping into film stars. Encountering the likes of Bruce Willis while driving or shopping is a special case of the 'stranger/intimate' relations common to human interactions. Normally, we treat people we do not know with 'civil inattention'; we do not acknowledge their presence. Star encounters do not quite fit this model; they don't know us, but we know them, and they know we know them. A form of communication ensues, set around subtle devices that both star and audience use to acknowledge their co-presence. For example, both parties appear aware that there are some circumstances where asking for an autograph is appropriate, and others where it is not. This does nothing more than draw on the art of the everyday, where we constantly make these calls in relation to others; so, in this respect, celebrity *is* ordinary.

Reality media understand this. Speaking of *Pop Idol*, Sue Holmes (2004b) identified the paradox of the programme as being its ability to produce stars while at the same time showing exactly how the trick is done. On the surface, this apparently confirms the commodity-inspired disposability of popular culture; given that the music industry has now admitted success lies in marketing not talent, anyone literally can make it. Missing from this critique, however, is the distinct role that *Pop Idol* played in making this happen. Unlike actors, pop/rock stars have always depended on a sense of authenticity that draws upon the closing of the space between on and offstage (Ellis, cited in Holmes (2004b); this is also what Calhoun (2005) argues about hip-hop). Reality aspects of *Pop Idol*, revealing off-stage trials and tribulations, explained how the show could display a winning hand before playing it. Displaying the process made it credible (Holmes, 2004b). And, of course, it created the impression that we participated in it since it happened 'live', whether live on-stage or in the lives of contestants as they were filmed in the preceding week.

If *Big Brother* and *Pop Idol* both affirm the symbiosis of the reality/celebrity phenomena, it has yet to be shown what this has to do with politics. As a foundational point, my argument is that scholarship in this field helps us think through debates on citizenship that hinge the occasionally unhelpful ideas of apathy and ignorance. The compatibility of authenticity and performance concepts help us to explain the sorts of truth audiences can reasonably expect from the media, and therefore from the political systems using them. Moreover, the Boris Johnson incident illustrates how audiences *can* connect with politics under existing institutional arrangements that depend on 'liveness'. It also demonstrates that the outcomes of the mixing and matching of these moments in the acts of reception result in unpredictable consequences beyond the control of actors within the media frame.

## POLITICAL CELEBRITY: THE ASSUMPTION OF THE INAUTHENTIC

**6.5** The easiest connection between celebrity and politics is found in the emergence of celebrities who become politicians. Bob Geldof and Bono are now accepted as bona fide authorities on global poverty and famine, while Arnold Schwarzenegger presides as Governor of California. It is vital that these events are *not* dismissed as evidence of voter apathy or a world gone mad, but as the absolutely predictable outcome of specific sorts of organized political communication. Although it might appear that Geldof spontaneously appeared as the 'voice of Africa', what this disguises is that this could only happen within music's industrial and cultural processes, imbuing certain sorts of genres and performers with political credibility, meaning that they are positioned to react to crises as they happen (Street, 2002).

Although Babcock and Whitehouse (2005) begin by concluding that celebrity and politics should be incompatible with democratic systems dependent on rational, adversarial and participatory media, they concede Schwarzenegger's success in synthesizing screen persona and policy agenda has to be understood before it can be dismissed. This was not simply a case of casual and/or ignorant voters. 'Arnie's' celebrity supported a media campaign building political credibility (ergo trust) by skilfully avoiding traditional channels of political communication (ergo difficult questions about his qualifications for the job). Hence the anomaly that although the fiscal mismanagement of Gray Davis was frequently cited as the catalyst for Schwarzenegger's intervention, Arnold rarely spoke about what policies he would pursue to correct the problem: when he did, he would admit that he had no concrete plans for tackling the debt. He successfully concealed this contradiction by running the campaign through the familiar territory of entertainment talk shows. The race came to resemble reality television, capitalizing on the trust 'fallout' produced by the fact that voters felt they knew Schwarzenegger. In playing to the entertainment media, he terminated equal time regulations, thus gaining more coverage of a more positive style and becoming more familiar to voters.

The situation is different for career politicians. Where the above examples reference cases where stars have projected their already formed images of authenticity and credibility into politics, politicians face the reverse problem.

The bias of political communication imposes inauthenticity by default. Barry Richards (2006) sees this as resulting in a prevailing media cynicism that can only disengage citizens from political processes. However, paying close attention to the performance aspects of politics offers an understanding, in my view, of how authenticity can be housed in representation.

The fear is that politicians look upon someone like Arnold Schwarzenegger as a role model. So we commonly confront comments such as this:

> Tony Blair likes telling the story of how, in his youth, he ran away from home and got on board a plane bound for the Bahamas, but was caught by flight attendants and sent back to his parents. Malicious tongues say that at the time, in 1967, there were no flights to the Bahamas from the place where Tony lived. His well-wisher's comment is: Well, you know he is a brilliant actor. (Ozerov, 2002:178)

There is certainly a persuasive argument to be made that the mediation of politics fuels public disengagement. Jackson and Lilleker (2004) found a common sentiment among UK politicians that their job was influenced by the importance of pursuing actions likely to attract positive media coverage. James Stanyer (2002) places this within a global perspective. The quantity and quality of political coverage has been eroded by a number of factors. Infotainment is driven by a worldwide economic stagnation that has cut advertising revenues and hence profit margins in the media, meaning that audience share has become more important than public service. As evidence, he cites the fact that during the Iraq War of 2003, the only UK newspaper that saw increased sales was the *Daily Star*, which took the conscious decision to never even mention the fighting. Adding to this television's hostility to the increasing number of stage-managed political events, one is left with a vacuum that cannot help but have an impact on citizens and the voting choices they make:

> One key theme that emerges from reports on audiences' media consumption is a process of selective disengagement from electoral programming. A large proportion of voters sought to avoid election output initiated by the parties and the media; and even for those who did watch such material, they did so only fleetingly. The evidence – and it is far from comprehensive – suggests that in a media saturated environment a significant proportion of the public will filter the sources of political information they are exposed to and will avoid any prolonged exposure if possible. This means that politicians will find it increasingly difficult to reach a mass audience with their message and the media will find it harder to attract audiences to political information and programming. (2002: 386)

Joseph Capella (2002) argued that the effects of media cynicism toward the political correlate with a general disengagement with any matters of public policy, not just elections. His research in the US connects with institutional analysis in offering that the overall 'product' of political coverage is the general feeling that politicians are insincere, being motivated by ego and self-interest above all else.

All of these points are consistent with Richardson's thesis concerning the assumed inauthenticity at the root of the political interview as media form. However, Richardson also provides a solution to the dilemma in relating this 'inauthenticity' to schisms in the speech act and therefore the sorts of 'performance' that have more to do with the everyday rather than media projection of persona. Beginning in pessimistic mode, Richardson asserts that one cannot be surprised about the assumption of inauthenticity, given that when a politician speaks we are unsure of whose voice we hear. Goffman emerges as a key figure again: a speech act involves three actors; the person who speaks, the author of those words and the party on whose behalf they are crafted. The trick is to create the impression that this trinity are one and the same. But this is very difficult for the politician who, as everyone knows, employs a speechwriter and who has a professional duty to represent party line over personal opinion.

As if to make matters worse, we cannot even be sure that public reactions to this charade are any more trustworthy. It has long been argued that 'public opinion' is a myth created by opinion polls and media. Regarding the former, surveys lump together considered judgements with those of the ill informed, who are unwilling to admit that they know and care little about the political world (Converse, 1975). However, even monosyllabic, uninformed reactions to the political have become part of the spectacle, as Montgomery (2001) elucidated in considering a 2001 Conservative Party political broadcast that featured ordinary voters recounting their experiences of living under a Labour government. The campaign piece witnesses the difficulty of defining 'authentic' even in ordinary speech. On one hand, the sincerity of the speakers' words appeared beyond reproach, as those on camera did nothing more than give testament to things that had happened to them. However, that these testaments were packaged into a party political broadcast illustrates their aesthetic dimensions; the flawed speech patterns indicative of everyday discourse became signifying practices, a performed signal of the real. John Durham Peters' identification of the duality of wit-nessing (2001) clarifies the point. A witness is someone who sees something happen. A person who bears witness speaks about that event. In this segue, we see a shift in the nature of the truth claim asserted; from 'I was there' to 'this says something about our world'. Indubitable physical experience is used as an alibi for the assertion of less concrete claims.

Still, I would argue that it is precisely at the point where even non-mediated talk becomes suspect that we can explain the sort of authenticity provided and sought in political representations that materialize as tied to the structures of reality media and celebrity. Returning to Richardson, although the question 'who speaks?' is a problem for all politicians, some handle it better than others through the force of personality. In the UK, figures such as Clare Short, Ken Livingstone, George Galloway and the late Robin Cook achieved credibility in high-profile departures from the Labour whip. When this happens, the question is often asked how far these rebellions are a function of ego rather than conscience; it is apropos to mention, in this context, that such accusations were levelled at Galloway in 2006 following his decision to participate in *Celebrity Big Brother* rather than attend to his duties as a sitting MP. Nevertheless the profile of figures such as these indicate that performance relates to authenticity, in that what both public and public figures desire are images that are credible because they are *coherent*. Personality is important in politics since it seems to offer a guarantee on the limits of performance. In his idea of the 'idiolect', John Street (2002) posits that politicians are constrained in what they can do by the structure of their being. Writing of John Major and Michael Howard, Deborah Cameron (1996) determined that neither could ever be a great Tory leader as, regardless of what they did or said, they simply did not *sound* like great Tory leaders. Her words became prophetic, given the general conclusion in the wake of the 2005 General Election that while the British public agreed with most of the things Michael Howard said, they simply did not like the fact that *he* said them.

This is far from a new claim; the idea that politics works through the presence of special figures who appear to personify authenticity via coherence of thought, word and action is to be found in the analysis of *charisma*, as explored by 19th-century sociologist Max Weber. In its barest form, charisma is a form of political authority located within the extraordinary gift of the individual, rather than the impersonal forces of tradition and legality (Giddens, 1971). There are two elements of the charismatic that help the analysis of political celebrity. The first is that the idea is evidently tied to institutions and institutional crisis; charismatic leaders are seen as filling a vacuum left by the inadequacies of political conventions. However, while the charismatic locates authority in the individual, this happens because the public invest this faith in a specific personality:

> Whether a man [*sic*] 'really' possesses any or all of the characteristics attributed to him by his followers is not an issue; what matters is that the extraordinary qualities should be attributed to him by others. (cited in Giddens, 1971: 160)

Less specific is the role that media play in the communication and reception of charisma. Fieschi and Heywood (2004) dismissed the charismatic as something of a charade, given that charisma is itself an institutional product. The emergence of personal trust as electoral issue is connected with the way that figures such as George Bush have used media to promote the idea that government is *not* to be trusted, as part of the project of shedding the state's responsibility to act in the areas of economy, environment and welfare. Ryfe's study of letters written to Franklin Delano Roosevelt in reaction to his 'fireside chat' radio broadcasts during the depression (2001) also argued that the unique sense of intimacy felt between president and public could only happen via such an intimate, domestically located medium.

Nevertheless it is also clear that the importance of feedback and the wide variety of instances that are labelled as charismatic means that the concept cannot be exclusively understood with reference to sweeping political and historical judgements. The term charisma has been applied to figures as diverse as Joseph Smith, 19th-century founder of the Mormon Church (King, Sawyer & Behnke, 1998) and Vladimir Zhironosky, leader of Russia's right-wing Liberal Democratic Party in the 1990s, who courted public favour with the promise of cheap vodka (Eatwell, 2002). What this means is that the general idea that personality emerges as a political tool in times of institutional tension has to be carefully applied to specific case studies. In the current context, the question is: 'how does charisma allow us to understand how audiences find truth in a political world reliant on media systems whose credibility have been questioned by disenchantment with the reality/celebrity phenomenon?'. In answer, let us consider the scandal that enveloped Boris Johnson in October 2004.

## BORIS JOHNSON VERSUS LIVERPOOL

**6.6** In October 2004, Englishman Ken Bigley was kidnapped by Iraqi militia while working as a civilian contractor in Iraq. Despite an international campaign to secure his release, the Liverpool-born engineer was eventually executed in reprisal for the continued presence of British troops in Iraq. Some days later, a right-leaning political commentary magazine called *The Spectator* published an anonymous editorial denouncing the two minute silence held in Bigley's honour at a football match between Manchester United and Liverpool Football Club. Certainly, Bigley's death had been a tragedy; but one mitigated by the engineer's decision to accept a lucrative yet risky assignment. The public reaction to his execution was, the editorial opined, excessive. However, this was not surprising given the City of Liverpool's predilection for self-pity.

The article provoked a furious public backlash that became directed at Boris Johnson, Tory MP for Henley-on-Thames and editor of the magazine. In Liverpool, many were enraged by the fact that the editorial had repeated long-discredited charges made in the wake of the 1989 Hillsborough tragedy, where ninety-six Liverpool Football Club fans were crushed to death in an overcrowded football stadium. At the time, the tabloid newspaper *The Sun* had erroneously reported that the dead and dying had been abused by fellow supporters. Fifteen years later, *The Spectator* chose to repeat these allegations, while lazily reporting the casualty figure as 'more than fifty'. Local MP Peter Kilfoyle demanded an apology. In due course Tory leader Michael Howard ordered Johnson to travel to the north of England to deliver his regrets in person. This he did, visiting the city and meeting its people in a series of awkward encounters beset with justifiable fears for the errant MP's personal safety. None of this could prevent the excruciating moment where Johnson was confronted by Paul Bigley, Ken Bigley's brother, on a local radio call in show. As the bereaved sibling demanded that Johnson leave public life, the then Tory shadow minister for culture could do nothing but sit in silence. Although he was to later claim that he was glad he had confronted his critics in Merseyside (Johnson, 2004), at face value the Liverpool incident appeared a significant political reversal.

That its punch line was delivered during a radio broadcast signalled that this was an example of liveness and disruptability. I therefore determined that the incident was a suitable topic for audience research. I wanted to know how people had understood the incident; if they had felt its relevance, and if so, why? My first inclination was to contact the local press to arrange access to readers' letters. However, Liverpool's *Daily Post* and *Echo* newspapers had no usable archive. Fearing the project was stillborn, I contacted Boris Johnson to ask if he had received any public feedback on the matter, and if so if I could use these comments as the basis for my research. Johnson's office immediately agreed, providing me with 314 letters received from members of the public. I mention this as a useful lesson on the contingencies of research; the direction of the project was undoubtedly changed by the nature of the data I was able to secure.

Reading through the letters, what was most striking was the fact that they were overwhelmingly written to offer support to the MP. But what did this mean, and what were the wider conceptual claims made by this 'fact'? Stating the obvious, although this was a rich data set it was evidently not representative; letters to other media outlets and locally produced vox pops on television and radio confirmed that many had been incensed by both the editorial and Johnson's efforts to make good. The latter were seen by many as a pathetic attempt at spin designed more to repair damage done in the Tory heartland than offer a genuine apology to Liverpool or the families of Ken Bigley and the Hillsborough dead. The other danger was that the data could be selectively used to support almost any argument one might wish to make about political engagement or the absence thereof. That is, the temptation was to revert to a bipolar position where the letters could be seen as a good or improper reflection of citizenship. In the papers that followed (Ruddock, 2006b; 2006c), I certainly entertained the idea that the event illuminated key absences in public political deliberations; but this was stitched within the wider recognition that the key questions at hand were; 'what was it about the Johnson scandal that encouraged and enabled the letter writers to make their views public?' and 'what did it allow them to say, and via what mechanisms?'. Qualitative and quantitative dimensions were explored; although it was important to respect the reasons why each letter writer felt the need to communicate, it was equally important to map the frequency of certain sorts of responses, given the argument that media events, and our reactions to them, are in part institutionally made.

It was the decision to quantify the reasons why people were moved to contact Johnson that related the project to the wider issue of liveness, celebrity and authenticity. Forty-one per cent of the writers mentioned that they admired Johnson (even if they disagreed with the opinions expressed in the editorial) as he appeared to be a 'real' person who spoke his mind. This was the most frequent theme in the letters. Indeed, such was the force of Johnson's personality that it appeared to burst outside of the media frame into the everyday, such that Johnson was seen, in charismatic terms, as the personification of a political position:

> I was incensed to read yet more negative comments about the city I love. We're always copping it in the media, and we're sick of it. But it takes a big man to say sorry, and an even bigger man to say sorry face-to-face. (Male, Liverpool)
>
> How come you're a Tory? You always seem to make sense ... I've grown up thinking that all Tories I happen upon haven't got an original thought in their body. But you continue to be witty and strangely alluring ... if anyone can explain the whole Tory ideals thing to me, it's got to be you. (Female, North of England)

Given that it was possible to use the data to argue that letter writers displayed both 'shallow' and 'deep' involvement with political issues, the most sensible course of action was rather to try and trace what factors motivated people to take the now relatively rare step of writing to an MP using paper and ink. On this question, the first point to make is that there was much evidence connecting these actions with ideas of liveness and the resultant sense of cultural participation. Much like a Friday night *Big Brother* eviction, the period before the Liverpool visit was filled with gossip. Where would Johnson be staying? Who would he visit? How sincere were his intentions? Would he survive in one piece? The radio confrontation with Paul Bigley provided a Paxmanesque demolition, but here in real time. What would this do to Johnson's political career? That this was an open question prompted some of the letter writers to offer the MP their own interpretation of events, as a means of helping him understand what Liverpool meant for his career. Three writers offered Churchillian comfort:

> You will rise again. Winston Churchill suffered wilderness years. He was more effective and impressive afterwards – and how! (Female, South Coast of England)
>
> Think of Churchill. At your age, as I remember, he was sacked over the Dardanelles. It must have seemed as if everything was over. (Male, South Coast of England)
>
> It has been said ... that Churchill had a sense of destiny throughout his Parliamentary career. However, on several occasions he had to regroup and reposition, and fight off the black dog-depression – as well as his enemies. I hope you and your loved ones are able to overcome the current crisis. (Male, Oxfordshire)

But what was it about Johnson that inspired this sort of affection? There was clear evidence connecting perceptions of Johnson with the ideas of charisma and coherence. Many letter writers appreciated the fact that Johnson appeared willing to accept responsibility for the error he had made in allowing the editorial to be published despite its offensive rhetoric based on factual errors. As one Liverpool resident put it:

> You yourself would be the first to admit that certain aspects of the first article were ill-advised ... but to your immense credit you had the good grace to sincerely apologise. We all drop clangers ... there must be many people in Liverpool and elsewhere who feel about you as I do, but unlike myself may not write and tell you so. I wish there were more like you in political life. I feel that your approach to life and politics is refreshing. I love your self deprecating sense of humour. No Boris, don't ever change mate. (Male, Liverpool)

Several of the authors were critical of Michael Howard's decision to force the public apology. Taken in combination, the qualitative and quantitative data opened the possibility that Johnson was perceived as authentic in his willingness to speak beyond the Tory party line. While he had apologized and was apparently glad he had done so, at the same time he had refused to denounce the central theme of the offending piece; the need to accept personal responsibility for one's actions. In journeying north, Johnson was living the message. This meant, in charismatic terms, that he was perceived as someone prepared to break with his parent political institution, in order to create a coherent speaking position where his words and actions articulated personal rather than party conviction.

Nevertheless, it is also true that he was able to do this precisely because of the way he was positioned in the circuit of political communication. First, his willingness to risk the wrath of his leader was clearly aided by the fact that Michael Howard was, at that time, the unpopular leader of an unpopular party. Longevity wise, it risked little to rebel.

The other reason why Johnson's actions might have been less risky than they appeared is that the MP could always fall back on his original media day job. Beginning life as a political journalist, Johnson was also a familiar figure on the television punditry circuit, famous for his dishevelled appearance and eccentric 'public schoolboy' charm. This had crossed into the sphere of entertainment, with regular stints on the satirical quiz show *Have I Got News for You?* What all of this meant was that the Liverpool scandal was accessible as it centred on a media figure who brought with him a series of ready-made narratives, in particular that of the upper class amateur. The original editorial had commented on the way that British polar explorer Robert Falcon Scott had accepted his death on a 1912 expedition to reach the South Pole as being a result of his own errors. One of the letters presented the same image of Johnson stumbling into a quagmire despite his own best intentions:

> Oh Boris Johnson
> What can you do?
> Opened your gob again
> What will they do to you?
> Mind you no-one's perfect
> It's just a little impasse
> But think twice before you open it
> Or you'll sound like a silly Arse!
> I still love you Boris. (Female, South of England)

What this ode celebrates was the perception that Johnson had little truck with 'spin'. If he offended, this was because he said what was on his mind, not what he thought people wanted to hear.

So what did the letters reveal about the nature of political celebrity? While not representative, they did illustrate the processes through which people came to relate to a political event. Second, they also showed how the nature of media power lies in the structure of communication itself rather than the intention of any particular effort at persuasion. In terms of media presentation, Johnson's brush with Liverpool had no preferred meaning; the MP, the national press and the local press all provided different interpretations of what the story was about. Audiences were therefore provided with a series of possibilities in negotiating the scandal. As an example, one of the notable things about many of the letters was that they agreed with the original editorial's depiction of Liverpool, despite the fact that Johnson had been keen to disown these comments.

Overall, the letters supported the idea that what people want from media figures is a form of authenticity based on coherence; people trusted Johnson as they perceived a consistency between the MP's thoughts and actions, signalled by a willingness to say what he thought rather than parrot party ideology or public relations gloss. But, examining the structure of the event, we also see how this perception was associated with Johnson's structural position as a celebrity within a party in crisis, a situation making it easier to portray himself as a maverick. Moreover, the idea that audiences could contribute to the coherence of his performance, offering advice on what it all meant, relied on structures of media liveness.

## CONCLUSION

**6.7** As reality media becomes less real, and as celebrities grow ever duller, it appears there is nothing to do other than treat them as cultural cancers; cutting off the blood supply that allows them to pulverize society's vital organs. However, this chapter has argued two things. First, reality and celebrity are symptoms rather than causes of a wider credibility crisis between media and audiences. Second, there is much to be understood about how people make sense of the authentic before we can make judgements about negative impact. The case of political celebrity is offered as a case in point. Instead of complaining of the 'dumbing down' of politics, evidenced by the rise of the celebrity politician, we should ask by what mechanisms these figures allow audiences to speak of and to a political world that is often regarded as an alien presence.

# 7 Young People, Technology and Cultural Citizenship

## INTRODUCTION

**7.1** This book began by situating audience research as a subdiscipline of communications studies. I further claimed that the task at hand is not to solve the problem of audiences, but rather to unravel the things that we think we know about relations between people and media. Statements about the damage media inflict on the young illustrated gaps in commonsense views of what media do. It feels appropriate to revisit these questions in this concluding chapter, which explores the everyday life of media technologies through a project that I am currently struggling with. I have been commissioned to research the role that media play in informing young people about fire risk. A UK fire service runs 'Lantern', a youth outreach programme which, over the course of twelve weeks, gives young people basic fire training, culminating in a 'passing out' parade, where students display their new skills to an audience of parents, fire officers and local dignitaries. The programme has a series of goals. One is to reduce fire offending among young people. A second goal is to reduce attacks on fire crews by showing the human faces behind the uniforms. Third, many of the young people who take part have truancy issues; it is hoped that the course will help improve school attendance and performance by showing young people that they can achieve difficult goals. Lantern is a pseudonym selected to protect the anonymity of the project. Similarly, the names of staff and students used in the following accounts are fictional.

I had applied for a research grant from the fire service to study the programme. I had written a research proposal hypothesizing that media representations of fire and firefighters were instrumental in forming young people's attitudes toward the service and its role. I intended to assess this via media writing exercises similar to those used by Kitzinger (2004) and Philo and Berry (2004). I was also interested in how any processes of change could be related to the way that the young people narrated their experience of the programme. The proposal was accepted, and as I write I am a month into the project. However, the media writing exercise has usurped the hypothesis; when thinking about fire-risk, the young people I work with draw mostly on often alarming personal experiences. Indeed, mainstream media representations appear to be largely irrelevant. And it is on this finding that I wish to structure this chapter and conclude the book. I have found the young people's indifference to media enormously helpful in reconfiguring the problems I was having in thinking through issues of media power. Specifically, they have highlighted the significance of seeing life as media related rather than media centred. At the same time, the project has posed a series of challenges to my 'expertise' as an audience scholar that can only be met by recognizing and learning from the wisdom of the programme's students and staff. Further, the relevance of audience as a concept has been questioned. A multimethod approach has also been required, if for no other reason than to compensate for the inadequacies of techniques that look far better on paper than they do in the field.

I have decided to end the book with an unfinished project for two reasons. First, it demonstrates the importance of being willing to revise one's ideas about the nature of the media's social role. Second, it has shown that the question of what media 'do' to young people, or anybody for that matter, can only be explored via a journey that considers how media technologies come to have a cultural life. This in turn involves revisiting the power question, particularly in the convergence between media and general human communication. The convergence concept queries the validity of power models premised on antagonisms between production and consumption. Methodologically, it also interrogates research techniques that focus on how people respond to, rather than participate in, communication environments. The latter point has inspired new creative audience research methods that I have endeavoured to employ in my fire-risk research. Consequently, this concluding chapter will consider what sort of power model is appropriate within contemporary media environments where audiences are involved in a good deal of media production. It will ask what happens when concerns over the vulnerability of young people are couched in the language of cultural citizenship. Finally, it will revisit the 'I' question. The fire project involves participant observation; to study the course, I have to participate in it. As a result, data generation is based on my ability to achieve a rapport with both staff and students. Although this becomes a personality matter, I will argue that creative research methods provide a structured way to overcome this practical challenge.

## CONTEXT: ASBO BRITAIN

**7.2** Over and above these questions is a larger issue: why am I doing research on young people and fire-risk? What is the validity of the project?

The brief for the study is to describe how Lantern acts as a positive force in the lives of the young people who take part. Speaking with the course team, it quickly became clear that they faced a communication challenge interpretable via the framing issues discussed in Chapter 2. The team were highly conscious of the importance of their public profile. As an example, the team leader mentioned a particularly damaging newspaper story that had run in the local press. While some of the young people participating had been involved in fire offending, most had not. Equally, while many had problems with school discipline, the team preferred to think of the students as young people who deserved support in making the most of their potential. It had therefore been distressing to programme staff, students and their parents and carers when a local newspaper ran a story on Lantern, labelling participants as 'young arsonists'. Where the team saw young people as social resources, carrying the power to improve relations between the fire service and local communities, the story had instead framed them as liabilities.

This vignette is in keeping with the way that ASB issues are discussed in the UK. In a small survey commissioned by Liverpool city council, I found that concern over aggressive young people was the leading ASB concern among the 186 respondents, and that seventy-seven per cent of the sample directly blamed young people for the severity of the apparent crisis in the UK (Ruddock, 2006a). At face value this reaction, in combination with the way that local media framed Lantern, bears the hallmarks of a moral panic as explored by Hall et al. in the seminal *Policing the Crisis* (1978). When Mr. Justice Lawson remarked in 1969:

> With all this violence that young people are indulging in today, I am wondering whether leniency with the young is best for the public. In my view, this kind of violence to other people in our streets is not going to be cured by probation, fines or day attendance centres and the like. Word has got to go round that anyone who commits this kind of offence has got to lose his liberty (Hall et al., 1978: 34)

he could have been speaking today. The concern that Hall and colleagues expressed was that in coming to the unanimous conclusion that late 1960s and early 1970s Britain was in the grip of a mugging crisis, the police, judiciary and media set a socially destructive course:

> When the official reaction to a person, group of persons or series of events is *out of all proportion* to the actual threat offered, when 'experts', in the form of police chiefs, the judiciary, politicians and editors *perceive* the threat in all but identical terms, and appear to talk 'with one voice' of the rates, diagnoses, prognoses and solutions, when the media representation universally stresses 'sudden and dramatic increases' (in numbers involved or events) and 'novelty', above and beyond which a sober, realistic appraisal could sustain, then we believe if is appropriate to speak of the beginnings of a *moral panic* (Hall et al., 1978: 16)

The blanket labelling of Lantern students as 'young arsonists' seemingly painted a similar picture, where media created the impression that pyromania is a common youth affliction. Moreover, some scholars who have studied the ASB issue in the UK argue, as in *Policing the Crisis*, that one of the reasons why there appears to be so much youth disorder is because the police are looking for it. Just as Hall et al. believed that the main effect of the moral panic was that 'the behaviour of the stigmatized or deviant group comes progressively to fit the stereotype of it which the control agencies already hold' (1978: 42), so too McAra and McVie (2005) argue, on the basis of data collected from young people in Edinburgh, that police find suspicious youth since they look for suspicious youth who are suspicious by virtue of their youth. And again, the homogenization of ASB as a youth problem hampers policy by failing to attend to a series of important differentiations between types and locations of offences (Williamson, Ashby & Webber, 2005) and gender differences (Jarman, 2005).

However, the similarities between ASB and the archetypal moral panic are cosmetic. There is much evidence to suggest that the elite/media consensus that grounded the mugging crisis does not exist in this context. It is unsurprising to learn that academics have stressed that even if ASB *is* primarily a youth issue, this does not clarify whether young people are victims or villains (Goldson, 2000). The gradual veering of Labour policy toward individualistic and punitive measures (Payne, 2003; Flint, 2004; Fitzpatrick & Jones, 2005; Squires & Stephen, 2005) ignores the fact that even if young people do have to accept responsibility for their own actions, their ability to recognize this is a matter of socialization (Such & Walker, 2005). Yet these insights are not confined within the academy; Youth Offending Teams in the UK have expressed disquiet at the erosion of welfare as the cornerstone of their work (Burnett & Appleton, 2004). And notwithstanding McAra and McVie's critique, UK police officers are dismayed by the lack of time they have to prevent ASB, and indeed the lack of attention and credit devoted to such activities (Ahmed, 2004). In fact, the police object to the fact that ASB tends to be framed as a criminal rather than a social concern.

In approaching youths as people with rights who, if permitted, have the potential to act as social resources, and in appreciating the importance of communicating this sympathy both to the students and the public, the Lantern project conspicuously addresses framing. As such, it provides a means to engage not only with the wider subject of antisocial behaviour, but also the role that communication plays in shaping how we perceive and therefore act toward young people. To understand Lantern, then, we need to consider how audience scholars have conceived connections between media and childhood.

## WHAT DO MEDIA 'DO' TO YOUNG PEOPLE?

**7.3** One can certainly find studies reflecting the suspicion that media exploit children's innate vulnerability. Murray et al. (2006) designed a project where young subjects had their brains scanned as they watched violent films. They claimed that this technique showed how violent scenes activated networks on the right side of the brain that influenced emotions, arousal, attention, behaviour and memory. However, this Pavlovian thesis simplifies child/media relations, understanding of which in fact reflects broader tensions between structure and agency in audience conceptualization.

Reviewing recent scholarship, it becomes clear that one of the reasons why childhood is such an important issue is because it accesses more fundamental areas around the relationships between media technologies and social formations. Analysing media reporting, parliamentary discussions and commercial speech, Selwyn (2003) identified contradictory patterns of framing relations between young people and new media technologies. Often, youths are regarded as pioneers who use IT to smooth their transition into majority, more at home with new gadgets than technophobic adults. However, they are also presented as 'dangerous' users, for whom media are tools to evade parental supervision. Finally, young people are sometimes portrayed as victims of the new media age, particularly around issues such as cyberstalking.

In Sonia Livingstone's view, these ideas spring from the tendency to think of relations between media and society in reverse. Dismayed by the fact that UK internet policy is made largely in the absence of empirical data to show how children actually use the technology, Livingstone asserts that research on the topic should be child rather than technology centred (2003; 2005). In making this claim, she points to the inadequacies of what Brian Winston calls 'technological determinism' (1990). It is an error to see new media as devices whose real applications are directed by technical capacities alone. Ellen Seiter's research into the introduction of computers into Californian classrooms (2004) provides a trenchant illustration. Observing how children at an after school club used the new devices, Seiter argued that their introduction actually eroded the educational environment. First, children became embroiled in fights over access to computer time. When they did log on, it was difficult to stop them from celebrity surfing or shopping. Communication technologies are not, therefore, magic wands to be used to instantly transform established settings. The cultural lives they come to live are influenced by that which already is. For this reason, Livingstone makes the criticism that policy thinking on access issues ignores the fact that what a phenomenon such as the internet will be is influenced by the 'nature and quality, social conditions, cultural practices and personal meanings' (2004: 159) that surround it.

This is not to say that technologies exert no force; it is simply to ask us to step beyond the simple assumption that quicker access to more information will inevitably make the world a better place. For Livingstone, the vital question is how new technologies blur distinctions between accepted social categories; in particular, computers and the internet challenge the way we have been accustomed to distinguishing work from leisure, public from private, producer from consumer, citizen from consumer, education from entertainment and child from adult. As these categories shift, so young people are caught in a series of contradictions. Most notably, the common complaint that youth is apathetic and/or antisocial does not withstand society's failure to develop social spaces for them. Indeed, it is the absence of this space that explains why young people invest so much time in creating exclusive 'bedroom cultures'. Although childhood possibilities are fabricated from the intersections of law, commerce and culture, the reality of what this convergence means is determined by how children themselves make sense of their situation. In contrast to technological determination, 'as the empirical evidence repeatedly confirms, the driver of change in this public/private blurring is the activities of young people themselves' (2005: 46–7). When they venture into the real world of children and media, researchers find the error of approaching media ecology as a zero-sum game, where new devices inevitably confront and defeat their predecessors. The internet and mobile phones, for example, have found lucratively compatible niches in youth lifestyles. Each has a distinct communicative role; mobile phones being particularly useful on occasions when the user wants to avoid social etiquette (Madell & Muncer, 2005).

Livingstone's argument, then, is that understanding what media do to young people means understanding what they do *with* media. But this is not tantamount to arguing that the young are masters of their own media destinies. Her reading of bedroom cultures as a response to the absence of social space rather reframes the vulnerability of young people within wider issues around cultural citizenship. Instead of seeing weak children whose embedded naivety is being exploited, Livingstone presents young citizens with rights that are not being met.

For example, it is not to define the young as folk devils or imbeciles to suggest that social structures have failed to prevent the commercial colonization of those spaces that they are allowed to hold. In Boden's research into how young people read and imitate the fashion styles of celebrities and sports stars, the conclusion that:

> they have lived through a decade of economic boom and are now therefore fairly affluent, they are often from small families with dual earners ensuring households with sizable disposable incomes, they are able to draw upon strategies such as pester power to get their own way, and they have a high awareness of labels, media and technology. (Boden, 2006; 291)

casts the power of the young in economic terms. However, other researchers feel that their data casts doubt on the image of the youthful knowledgeable consumer. Chung and Grimes (2005) explore this in the practice of 'data mining'. Here, websites such as Neopets.com offer free online games in return for personal information which is aggregated, analysed and sold on to companies wishing to target youth consumers. So, these free games are nothing of the sort; one can only play them in exchange for surrendering privacy issues and doing unpaid work for the market research industry. Media literacy is bifurcated in the process; knowing how to access the games has nothing to do with appreciating the price the player pays. Shade, Porter and Sanchez (2005) support this in their interviews with thirty-five Canadian teen internet users. Complementing Chung and Grimes, Shade et al. found that their interviewees gave little thought to online privacy issues. For example, when one young person comments. 'I don't think anybody is interested in this 16-year-old kid on the internet ... I don't have any secret IRS files' (Shade et al., 2005: 518) he or she could not be more wrong. To begin, in thinking of surveillance as a governmental phenomenon, the comment ignores the invasive commercial exploitation endemic in data mining. To make matters worse, Shade et al. found that the absence of interest in privacy issues led to a lack of consideration for the online rights of others; illegal downloading and reading other people's emails were seen as a natural part of cyberspace. Therefore media literacy has moral and ethical as well as technological dimensions.

Young people themselves are prone to express disquiet over their own media habits. Discourses of addiction are familiar to them: 'I was spending like 15 hours a day on the computer ... I had dreams about playing games ... it corrupted my mind' (Shade et al., 2005: 516). Young role playing game players report feelings of inferiority in comparison to video game avatars such as Lara Croft (McDonald & Kim, 2001).

It seems we are turning back to issues discussed under the banner of fandom. Recall Sandvoss's conclusion that the limitations of the fan experience as a political phenomenon were determined by commodity relations. In the realm of new media, it is no accident that Henry Jenkins identifies 'convergence' as a phenomenon wherein transformations in media political economies demand that we rethink power beyond weak/strong audience binaries. That is, we have arrived at a third question. We began by illustrating the myopia of looking for what media do to children. We mentioned the importance of looking at what the young do with media. But to understand what this means, we also have to ask what media want young people to do with them.

## CONVERGENCE AND POLITICAL ECONOMY

**7.4** Writing about new media environments in 2002, Jenkins used his work on fans to argue that ideas about subversion and opposition are invalid ways of conceiving audience/media relations. This is not to say that power is irrelevant – many new industries in fact demand interactivity as a precondition for their success; but it is to suggest that under some circumstances it is more profitable to replace audience/media categories with the more fluid idea of interactive 'knowledge communities', defined as 'voluntary, temporary and tactical affiliations defined through common intellectual enterprises and emotional investments' (2002: 158). I found this a very rich statement, containing many ideas that helped me grasp how media related to my fire research, and indeed the role they played in formulating the relationships with the people I was researching. But to get to this, we need to understand that Jenkins's comments do not preclude the consideration of economic developments that determine how people are invited into knowledge communities.

The gaming industry provides an excellent example. Alvisi, Narduzzo and Zamarian's explanation of the massive success of the Sony Playstation (2003) affected a rapprochement between technological and cultural determinism in locating the Japanese corporation's power in its ability to react to unexpected market developments. As the authors state; 'by 1999, thirty-eight per cent of Sony's profits came from Playstation related business' (2003: 609). But how could this be, given that the console was not significantly superior to platforms offered by Nintendo and Sega, companies with far more gaming experience? One possible answer to this question is found in the relations between hardware and software; console sales benefited from mod chip developments producing a tide of pirated games. But more importantly, in the author's view, Sony quickly realized that the general industry tactic of marketing new consoles as home entertainment centres first and gaming devices second confused many customers. Thus Sony marketing framed the Playstation as a gaming tool, not a new version of a 'digital hearth' that would usurp domestic life as it was known. Industrial power, then, is a sort of accidental design.

Staying with Sony, Rehak (2003) showed the genealogy of new media ecologies and the framing of fan audiences as producers in his consideration of the industrial power of Lara Croft. While Croft's semiotic status renders her open to appropriation by amateur games 'modders', responsible for delights such as the self-explanatory *Nude Raider*, this does nothing to detract from her industrial status. Present not only in games, but also film and advertizing, 'Croft's transit across their public face serves as a kind of industrial signposting for consumers, a means of orientation within apparently competing forms of textuality and commerce' (Rehak, 2003: 482). In this context, Rehak replaced polysemy with the idea of 'transcoding', representing 'new media's endless translation between diverse technological frameworks and cultural hierarchies' (2003: 479).

It remains to relate these ideas to the notion of the knowledge community, sympathetic to Foucauldian power models where all actors in a social setting are potent in different ways. Sony's reactive marketing strategy indicates that this is an appropriate metaphor to describe gamers. The fit becomes snugger when we add that by some estimates, over seventy-seven per cent of gamers are aged over eighteen (Postigo, 2003), thus diminishing polar qualms over the exploitation of children. Additionally, it would seem that the gaming revolution is driven my 'modders'; unpaid gaming experts who alter the software provided by the industry. Although its toleration of moderation apparently signals a position of economic equivalence, seen another way the gaming companies enjoy massive comparative advantages due to the presence of a vast and able army of free labour:

> Paradoxically, the hobbyist status of game modders works against them ... since commercial video-game companies are able to circumvent initial investments and maintenance costs for hired programmers, and can simply choose from the most successful of the already developed mods. (Postigo, 2003: 597)

Returning to Jenkins's comments on convergence, the argument is not that audiences are only exploited by forces beyond their influence or comprehension, or that media industries have to accept 'poaching' as an inevitable business cost; it is that often there is no necessary antagonism between industrial strategy, use and pleasure.

## THERE'S NO PLACE LIKE HOME: MEDIA TECHNOLOGIES AND PLACE 150

**7.5** Convergence is worth exploring as it demonstrates the near impossibility of finding a metanarrative solution to the social impact that technologies wield. Empirically, what we can do is map how structural tendencies interact with specific users and their practices. To do this, we need to consider how media devices play a role in developing space and place as cultural phenomena. In many ways, this requires us to revisit the limitations of a focus on textual meaning. While it is certainly possible to explore the preferred readings of role playing video game narratives, for example, this ignores the argument that the main pleasure of such texts lies in opportunities to discover and rediscover new landscapes; gamers keep playing as, although the final narrative conclusion remains largely the same, the virtual/physical route one takes to the end is traversable in various ways (Consalvo, 2003).

The idea that media play a role in the way that we make sense of space, and what this sense making means for the way we live and understand our lives, is explored by Shaun Moores in his 2006 critique of phenomenologist geography (PG). PG begins from the useful assumption that human agency shapes geographical formation; although spatial arrangements appear natural, they are the product of expressive human labour. Where the paradigm errs, however, is in conceiving media as inauthentic intrusions into this process. Moores argues that it is wrong to see media as complicit in the fabrication of a series of placeless places that are nowhere because they could be anywhere. In doing so, he explores the limitations of technological determinism, offering an autethnographic note as evidence. Speaking of his own migration from the UK to Australia, Moores found no comfort in the presence of internet borne British radio in his new locale. Although technology creates the theoretical possibility for the expansion of the BBC's institutional power, Moores had no use for it in this new context; if anything, where media pleasure is often located in feelings of comfort (Noble, 2002), hearing a familiar show in an alien climate had the opposite effect, reminding Moores just how far he was from home. Contrary to utopian technological visions, the internet's physical conquest of space and time creates a yawning chasm in *feeling*.

This is not to say that Moores was, in this estranged moment, placeless; more that he was experiencing a 'doubling of place'. In her analysis of teenagers' use of mobile telephones, Caronia (2005) explores this multiplication in analysing how young people invest apparently 'nowhere' times and places with their own social significance. Placelessness infuses worries around youth and control; in my ASB survey, it was notable how empty spaces such as street corners, parks and bus shelters dripped with menace as notorious sites of disorder. Caronia argues that since young people live lives that are often denied autonomous spaces, they are well versed in projecting their own personalities onto 'in-between' times and places. Observing teens at work and play, Caronia noticed how mobile phones were often used as territorial markers, especially in claiming school time as social. Cumulatively, the technology's potential is realized in making teens always social; regardless of the way that the school and the home tries to isolate teens from peer sociality, mobiles offer means to prevail over these restrictions. Sociality is often tied to the project of the individual that fan scholars discuss. Caronia felt that the frequent use of mobiles in 'meaningless' public places is a strategy to display peer leadership.

In his analysis of the associations between meaningful material objects and the sense of comfort and home among Australians, Greg Noble (2002) demonstrated how the project of building a unique sense of place is nevertheless coloured by wider structural forces, in this case a sense of the national. Noble understood comfort as both a physical and mental thing, ultimately defined by a feeling of belonging reliant on the ability to integrate objects into a self-narrative that materially confirms one's place in the world.

Using qualitative interviews, he highlighted a woman's emotional invest-ment in a cup her father had made from a tin as an 8-year-old boy. The object had been a gift for his dying sister. At first blush, this would appear as an intensely personal story. As the narrative developed, however, it became clear that one of the things that made it important was that it drew on a national myth of Australian know-how; it was not simply a tale of what a kind person the woman's father was, but also confirmed that he was a great Australian. Noble further argued that these stories were important precisely because possibilities for 'comfort' seemed to be receding on a national scale, as economic uncertainties made the birthright of the good life less attainable for many.

Comfort thus appears as an ironic category, made even more so by the great amount of work that goes in to making the home a place of rest. Referencing media, Noble pointed to the labour that goes in to naturalizing the position of televisions, music systems and the like by hiding cables and arranging furniture. This tells us that conflicts around media do not simply occur in the interface between the domestic and the outside world, but are internalized within the home. The spatial arrangement of domestic media experiences has been defined as expressing gender-based and age-based struggles within a sphere that must be viewed as a social and cultural space.

The idea that television was a key agent in shaping post-World War Two domestic spaces, and the relationships that happened in them, has been explored by scholars such as Morley (1989), Lull (1990), Gray (1992) and Gauntlett and Hill (1999). As an independent variable, Wartella and Jennings (2001) trace teen bedroom culture to the television industry's efforts to overcome market saturation by marketing the idea of the multi-set home. This promotion had a markedly gendered flavour; boys and men could watch sports in the living room while women could watch something else in the kitchen. In offering a means of being 'alone together', television also furnished a tool of parental control. As cultural appliances, then, media technologies have the potential to amplify rather than ameliorate social inequalities, an apprehension presently voiced in the idea of the 'digital divide' (Wartella & Jennings, 2001).

However, this is to suggest neither that each domestic epoch is dominated by a single medium, nor that new media are neatly inserted into existing hierarchies. Keightley (2003) sees the post-World War Two period as properly conceived via tensions between audio and visual technologies, colouring and coloured by gender struggles. Radio, in her thesis, had been regarded ambiguously; while capable of delivering valued cultural artefacts, in the form of classical music, it was also allied to despised mass cultural forms. The arrival of television and hi-fi in the immediate post-war period bifurcated these fears, where television steered mass culture in a feminine direction, while hi-fi allowed men to construe themselves as cultural connoisseurs. Where the former technology was deemed to be foisted onto a largely female audience by slick and inexorable advertising, building hi-fis from components, and selecting the music to play on the new home built devices, was seen as a more skilled hobby. Yet beneath this apparently simple assertion of male power was the recognition that men's location in the home was a point of crisis. The post-war domicile threatened to pacify the male; the hi-fi was his way to reclaim it as a leisure space.

Both Morley (1989) and Gray (1992) would indeed agree that in 1980s and 1990s Britain, television and video were complicit in defining the home as an ambiguous site of leisure and work for women, a friction that men often avoided. But again, relations between media and gender are less straightforward than they might appear. Referencing new media, Fung writes 'media can be seen as having the potential to become decentralizing instruments for marginalized groups to break away from the normalizing process of society, and foster more autonomous means of collective identity' (2002: 191). In studying their relations with domestic technologies, Gray had argued that although their use often concretized men's apparently 'natural' technical competence, women used this to serve their own purposes. If the women she studied tended not to know how to programme video recorders, it was equally true that many did not wish to learn; to do so would simply be to extend the scope of their household chores.

Considering computers and internet use, Singh (2001) proposed a similar thesis in presenting evidence that differences in technical competence are products of language, not practice. Interviewing thirty-three Australian women, Singh found a tendency to disdain computer-mediated communication; email was regarded as a masculine form, since it lacks the markers of emotion characterizing face-to-face communication (a contestable conclusion, as we shall see). However, this common narrational device conflicts with the fact that Australian women and men use the internet equally. Furthermore, in farming locations, women are more likely than men to use computers for business purposes. Singh explained this apparent contradiction in the following way. When women master the internet, they understand their activity in terms of achieving a social goal, not the mastering of a technology per se. Technical incompetence is a linguistic thing; its roots lie in the way we narrate our relations with devices. Tufte (2003) saw the same theme at play in the realization of mobile phone cultures; as much as men and boys are deemed to be naturally inquisitive about technologies, multiplied by initial visions of mobile telephony as business tools, the reality is that cell phones are most frequently used for intimate forms of communication that are more stereotypically feminine.

So while media are central in the organization and definitions of social spaces, influencing the identities forged in them, the cultural forms emerging from this combustible mix are unpredictable. And, echoing Livingstone's introductory comments, new technologies do not simply replace older devices and the forms of communication associated with them. Perhaps most importantly, research on computer use sees the influence of oral and face-to-face communication. Fernback's research on orality and urban legends (2003) refines the internet as a medium owing much to the temporality and hierarchies of speech. The appeal of urban legends lies partly in their immediacy; old stories are constantly written into the present, where we know they are true since they happen to a friend of a friend. For example, speaking with students a few days after 9/11, it was striking that many had heard the tale of a terrorist warning an urban shopper of a pending attack. This story had been heard in Manchester, Liverpool and Birmingham. Later, an American colleague told me that the same story had circulated throughout the US via the internet. The instantaneous nature of internet communication, the impossibility of tracing a message's origins, and the difficulties of establishing and discerning hierarchies of trust render the medium closer to oral rumour than centralized electronic communication. According to research by O'Sullivan and Flanagin (2003), far from smoothing organizational waters by making for swifter, to the point communication, email has created an unexpected world of insults due to the fact that we make sense of them through ideas of tone and manners derived from oral and scribal cultures. The medium's capacity for speed and brevity often hampers rather than improves lines of communication.

To conclude this section, media take on a cultural life insofar as they influence the relationships between individuals, groups and institutions, expressed in formations of time and space that represent and determine values and power relationships. These times, places and associations are relatively fluid. Grasping this idea is fundamental to understanding current debates about children and media, especially as they touch on relations between education and leisure, public and private and the commodification of learning. All of these concerns affect the communicative dimensions of the 'Lantern' project.

## MEDIA AND EDUCATION: FUN AND LEARNING

**7.6** In the last chapter, we encountered the argument that institutions do not exist without culture; the nature of our encounters with them has a reflective capacity. Next, I have introduced the idea that media and communication do not simply occupy, but create space. Taken in combination, these views address current confusion over the nature and place of effective education and the role that media should or do have within it.

Returning to Seiter's research on computer provision in the California educational system, her conclusion is that money is better spent on teachers rather than technology. Her apparently Luddite disposition is based not only on the disruptive force that she observed computers playing, but also by deeper concerns that since the internet has already been colonized by commercial interests, it is ill suited as an educational tool. This is all the more the case as money has been spent on ICTs at the expense of teachers who can help students put the machines into practice.

On the other hand, the argument that computers do not work in the classroom opens a wider discussion on the location of learning between work and play. Buckingham and Sefton-Green (2003) identify this tripartism as fundamental to understandings of child audiences that in turn influence how we understand media power in more general terms. Taking the *Pokemon* phenomenon as an example, a study of how children actually interact with its various textual incarnations enable both 'good' and 'bad' readings of childhood play cultures. On the bad side, *Pokemon*'s popularity across a range of age groups is a reflex of a marketing strategy that targets different parts of the child audience. The lack of attention to aesthetic quality displays conspicuous contempt for audiences who keep consuming anyway. Positively, the practices that children build around *Pokemon* are clearly related to forms of learning that would be valued if applied to other objects. Buckingham and Sefton-Green liken the sort of knowledge that players must have about characters to a chemist's mastery of the periodic table.

The authors asked, however, what is the point of divining between good and bad? Adult wrath poured on *Pokemon* is prompted in part, in the author's view, by the belief that children should be doing something better with their time – i.e. proper learning. There are two problems with this position. First, children are people with the right to leisure. Second, if proper education pales in comparison with the delights of *Pokemon*, it is at least worth asking what it is about the structure of the latter experience that makes it so attractive. Schooling begins in the close association of work and play. As the child progresses, so the experiences are separated, and play is banished to the realm of the extra-curricular (Potter, 2005). Perhaps this should be rethought. Initially, if common sense associates video gaming with social withdrawal, in practice it forms the basis for community and information in social networks that achieve the sort of peer education that schools can only hope for (Williamson & Facer, 2004).

The integration of media studies into the national curriculum, no matter how grudging, makes young people's leisure pursuits even more pedagogically pertinent. Concluding '*Pokemon* is something you do, not just something you read, watch or consume', Buckingham and Sefton-Green (2003: 379) presage Sara Bragg's criticism of teaching around media literacy (2002).

In her view, media literacy courses often embark on the wrong foot by creating the impression that, since there is a gap between what media say and what they actually mean, the goal is to unmask their true meaning. Media literacy is thus established as an oppositional force to media itself. As a result, courses do not allow children to mobilize resources from their own experiences and pleasures.

Bragg based her thought on evidence collected in observation of a media studies module comprising a practical film-making project with a piece of analytical writing which asked students to use media theory to reflect on what they had made. In Bragg's view, the architecture of the course established an opposition between these tasks, where the essay became a privileged site where the students could display 'proper'– that is planned and theoretically structured – knowledge.

The error of this opposition was explored through the case of a student who produced what was deemed to be a poor account of the horror film he had made. If we liken film-making to grammar, it is possible that one can be cinematically skilled without being able to explain why you have this talent. Looking at the student's 'failed' analysis Bragg noticed a pattern, where the weakest parts of the essay were those where he struggled with a theory that clearly had little to do with the way he went about his project, and the strongest were those where he spoke of how he managed unexpected problems encountered as a student with limited resources. The argument is not that theory is unimportant, or that reflexive writing is a waste of time. It is simply that syllabi should make room for practical reasoning which, since it is reactive, does not fit into the planned linearity of orthodox academic practice. 'Literacy' she concluded 'is about enabling participation in media culture rather than learning hostility to it'. (2002: 42)

## BACK TO 'LANTERN': FRAMING AND CREATIVE RESEARCH METHODS

**7.7** The lesson of these studies is that the distinction we draw between work and play can sap young people of their creative energy and potential in educational environments. This has been an important lesson that has influenced how I have had to use my own 'practical reasoning' in a project that almost immediately diverted from plan.

It was agreed, in collaboration with the fire service, that the project should effect a 'thick description' (Geertz, 1973) by combining participant observation and media writing exercises with the interviewing of students and key personnel. The net effect of this was that I was going to spend a lot of time getting to know the young people and staff taking part in Lantern.

Inevitably, then, the project was to hinge in large part on my ability to establish rapport. This rapport, if it were to happen, would be found in the nexus between personalities and institutional roles. The immediate challenge I faced was in how to present myself and my activities to staff and students alike. Staff, for example, were prone to describe the study as an evaluation. I was not comfortable with this description as it implied that I knew how the programme should work, and had been sent to assess if it was 'reaching the bar'. Using the ethnographic idea of grounded theory, the reverse was true; Lantern was a mystery to me. The goal was less to evaluate and more to understand and explain how the course worked.

Put another way, one of the means that I tried to establish rapport was in abandoning expert status. However, the fact that I felt the need to abandon it spoke to a certain arrogance on my own part. Recall the idea that institutions do not exist in isolation. As I drafted the project plan, I had assumed that media and communication theory existed primarily within the institution of media studies. I equally assumed that one of my major tasks would be to persuade the fire service of the need to think beyond the quick fix; that there was little point in setting out to prove that Lantern was a panacea for the social problems that young people face. Neither of these assumptions proved to be the case.

To begin, the service and the team were very aware of framing issues. Fire officers had themselves raised the idea of the moral panic in discussing how Lantern was often confronted with suspicion by media and public convinced of 'youth-gone-wild' narratives. This was quite extraordinary given the problem of violence at work faced by firefighters. Despite the fact that they were subject to frequent attacks by young people in the course of their duties, staff associated with Lantern were convinced that a key strategy in combating this problem was to frame themselves as a community resource, rather than an alien, uniformed service. This relied on a communication strategy that drew a distinction between young people who have problems and young people who *are* problems.

An early interview with Sarah, Lantern co-ordinator, established the association between the project and the previous discussion on the integration of work and play in education. The 'fire ambassador' notion established one of Lantern's goals as the establishment of peer information networks. This could only be achieved, however, if students managed to reintegrate with school. Sarah was aware that this presented something of a problem if Lantern, which involved spending one day a week at a fire training station over twelve weeks, was understood as a 'jolly', simply a day off school which was also a day away from the idea of learning.

Despite my concerns that staff would expect me to produce hard-and-fast proof of the programme's success, in fact they could not have been more catholic in their attitude to valid data. The team routinely collected end of course evaluations from students, teachers and/or youth workers and parents. However, staff also maintained a 'soft data' file which logged any other sorts of feedback they received, whether it be reports from the local press, or letters from participants, their families or their schools. The team noted that there was a certain reticence in completing the evaluation surveys. These contained a combination of closed-ended questions, asking respondents to rate the course and its success on a scale of one to five, and open-ended questions giving the opportunity to expand on answers. Answers to the latter tended to be very short. The team were open to any method that would provide more expansive feedback.

Despite these reservations, the surveys did provide a useful tool in establishing basic expectations and benefits participants and the people who cared for and educated them expected and perceived. Quantifying the closed-ended questions, it became apparent that students and parents viewed Lantern slightly more positively than educational professionals. While the latter were positive about the course, improvements in educational application were often felt to be difficult to sustain. But what also emerged was that the positive feelings students had toward the course were often premised on a distinction made between it and school that was also related to a preference for 'doing' rather than 'learning'. Lantern involved classroom work on fire safety issues, and it was these parts of the course that the students tended to rate the least positively. As an opening exercise, I had designed a news writing workshop. Here, photographs provided by the fire service's own public relations department were to be shown to the students. I would then ask them to imagine they were journalists, and put together a story to fit the picture or pictures. The idea was to identify the sorts of ideas that they had about the fire service, and possibly how these ideas might draw on media narratives. The photographs featured a number of 'normal' fire fighting images, such as house fires, together with less high-profile activities, such as home fire safety demonstrations. Survey responses made me concerned that the students would see this as being too much like schoolwork.

Kevin, who was responsible for managing the daily exercises for the students, agreed that my workshop would feel too much like a homework assignment. Instead, he suggested showing individual images to the students and have them discuss what they thought was going on as a group. In the course of this exercise, two things became clear; my outsider status, and how little mainstream media mattered in shaping perceptions of fire-risk and the fire service. The former was highlighted in a discussion on an image of a car blaze. In narrating the image, the students agreed that a joyrider had deliberately set the fire. Knowing that car theft is a frequent feature of reality crime shows, I asked the students from where they got their information.

The ensuing conversation bespoke linguistic differences confirming the cultural gap between the students and myself:

Andy: Where have you learned about this?

Group: (laughs) From Lemmy.

Andy: From what?

Karen: From Lemmy.

Andy: Who's Lemmy?

Child Care Professional: Lemton ... it's where they're from.

Andy: Oh, oh, right. You'll have to excuse me – you might have guessed I'm not from round here!

I mention the laugh here as I felt it signalled the students' opinion that the answer to the question should be painfully obvious to anyone who had the first clue about where they were from. In discussions of an image of the aftermath of a gas explosion, the idea that the outside world knew little about Lemton was raised again.

Karen: There was a bomb set off in my street.

Andy: A bomb?

Karen: People don't believe me, but there was.

Youth Worker: Yeah, yeah there was.

The news writing exercise had activated personal experiences rather than media based ideas. The irrelevance of mainstream media was further under-lined the next week. Serendipitously, the BBC's *Newsround*, a news show for young people, had broadcast a twenty-five minute special on arson at school. Asking the fourteen students if anyone had watched, only one had bothered to tune in, and had rapidly changed channels as '*Friends* was on the other side'.

All of this left me feeling more than a little deflated. Media didn't seem that important to the students. The exercises I had designed were at odds with a programme based on learning by doing, where classroom sessions were tied to field activities. It was difficult to talk to the students, due largely to my unfamiliarity with their language. And the course staff had a better view of what would work with them than did I as the professional researcher.

I had also decided to interview Lantern graduates. This was to achieve a longitudinal dimension to the project. It was generally agreed that the long-term effect of Lantern should be to contribute to young people's ability to become as socially productive as they could be. It followed that students taking part would not be in a position to say how the course contributed to their general outlook on themselves, their education and their futures. Those who had graduated one, two or three years before would be better placed to comment. It was with this goal in mind that I interviewed Steve. Steve had come to Lantern having been excluded from school for fighting. He could not have been a better advertisement for the course. Two years down the line, Steve was doing well in college, had been offered a place in university, and had the ambition of becoming a firefighter. He was adamant that the course had helped him in a very specific way. Aside from giving him the confidence to achieve difficult goals, and equipping him with tools to handle frustrating educational situations, Lantern staff had also been instrumental in winning him a college place. Steve explained that once a young person has been excluded for an act of violence, it is very difficult to gain readmission to an educational establishment. He had been able to win over an academic counsellor with the help of a video made by the Lantern team that had documented his training, achievements and general ability to apply himself to a structured learning programme.

Steve's comments were an early 'eureka' moment in my study. The mistake I had made in the project design was to position media as an extrinsic force. The 'young arsonist' news story, and the lack of interest showed in the *Newsround* special diverted my attention from the way that other sorts of media were used throughout the programme. Kevin took digital photographs of the students on a weekly basis, to create a positive record of their achievements. The fire service itself had produced a series of instructional videos. One simply featured a match being dropped onto a sofa in a living room. Within three minutes, the room is engulfed in smoke. The video was shown to the students accompanied by a commentary from Geoff, a member of the Lantern team and former firefighter. In his narrative, Geoff fused information on how to deal with house fires with tales from his own experiences. The team would have liked to produce videos for the students, but the cost of doing so had proved prohibitive.

At this point, having access to video making resources, I arrived at the idea of helping the students to make their own video diary. By shifting the emphasis to what the team and the students could do with media in terms of production rather than reception, I hoped to make the project, and myself, a more natural fit within the course. On reflection, it made little sense to ask students what they would do if they had the chance to produce a media text when we had the resources to actually do it. To explain my thinking, it is necessary to review the emergence of creative techniques in audience research.

David Gauntlett has been a key figure in developing creative media techniques, beginning with a project where young people were encouraged to make videos on environmental issues (1996). His techniques are directly related to his well-known critique of effects researchers and their quest for what media do to people (1998). Reviewing knowledge surveys as measure of news comprehension, I mentioned the flaw that such methods assess people for what they do not know, not what they do. Gauntlett perceived the same error not only in effects research, but also qualitative methods such as focus group interviews that tend to demand an instant reaction to media fare. This makes it very difficult for audiences to present themselves as knowing cultural actors. This is also true because often researchers seek a written or oral reaction to a visual experience; like Bragg's comments on the grammar of film, Gauntlett argues that because knowledge is orally inexpressible does not mean it is not there (Gauntlett & Holzwarth, 2006). Getting to how people make sense of media by having them produce their own texts takes us, in his view, closer to actual media experiences, where audiences fuse and revise media experiences and images of the self. In making this argument, Gauntlett moves away from the term audience toward the more accurate 'cultural actor'.

This is neither to say that reception has ceased to matter, nor that creative methods are of no use to researchers who remain interested in what people make of mainstream media. Buckingham and Bragg (2004) used a 'media scrap book' exercise, in combination with interviewing, to look at how young people made sense of media representations of sex and sexuality. While not wishing to dismiss adult concerns that children are being pushed into precocious sexual identities by television, magazines and advertising, the authors were critical of the stance that this was a linear process emanating exclusively from a media centre. Although sexual depictions did cause discomfort – some of the boys in the study worried that the presentation of the male body might 'turn them gay', girls deemed the similar representation of female flesh as improper and families blanched at communal viewing of sex scenes – at the same time the young people in the study saw themselves as having a critical relationship to the media. 'Preachy' safe sex lessons from teen dramas that set a clear preferred meaning around sexuality were disliked. So the association between media representation and sexual identity is, according to Buckingham and Bragg, more properly understood as unstable. The scrapbook exercise, where the sample kept images and notes about the mediated representations of sexuality they encountered, provided a means to reflect upon not only things seen, read and heard, but also how this data could be used in the evolution of identity.

As a data gathering tool it also stood closer to the actuality of new media experiences. Although the content of fears adults profess about young people and new media environments are cyclical in nature, they are also motivated by the fact that young people are increasingly using media in self-exploration.

If Eric Klebold and Dylan Harris misinterpreted goth's passive heart, they perhaps did so by using internet home pages to combine a variety of ideas into the personae that motivated their actions; we cannot know if this really was the case, as America Online removed their pages immediately (Stern, 2004). These fears blinker the consideration of how personal web pages can serve as an important source of sociality rather than alienation. Stern (2004), in a content analysis of adolescents' home pages, concludes that these places are important resources in the definition of the self in an acknowledged transitional period (although one might ask what period of life is *not* transitional?). Stern also concluded, however, that adolescents often appeared to be maintaining the pages as much for their audience as themselves, meaning that they played an important role in forming respect for the self and others.

The idea of using media to mark and make sense of transitions while creating social bonds with others was a central impetus in the decision to pursue the video diary. Potter (2005) used a similar technique to encourage young people to reflect on who they are and where they are going. Addressing tensions between play, work and education, Potter analysed a video made by two UK-based 11-year-olds to mark their transition from middle to high school. The video was made in a unique hiatus in the boys' lives, produced in the eight week space between the SATS (nationally administered exams that determine secondary school streaming) and the end of the school year. SATS in many ways mark the apogee of the work/play distinction; most of the year is spent preparing for them. Potter felt the post-SATS video project made an insightful intervention into the work/play dilemma. If the distinction is maintained, how, he asked, are creative elements to be introduced into the curriculum? And what hurdles does this raise for the acknowledged need for media education? The video that was produced, in which two boys scripted and acted out what it meant to be moving into adolescence, enabled them to mobilize their cultural knowledge in a way that affected a connection between their 'public' educational experiences and their personalities; the sorts of people they thought they were, the things they liked to do, the people they hoped to be. Potter cautioned that none of this can be seen as innocent of external forces. The project is only possible because of the market forces making video technologies affordable for small-scale productions. Moreover, the argument that computers are at their most educationally valuable when they are placed in the home (Vryzas & Tsitouridou, 2002) complements a worrying trend where education is being commercialized and privatized, representing a shifting burden from state to family (Buckingham & Sefton-Green, 2003). Nonetheless the possibility remains that the current technological climate does present opportunities for including the voices of young people in conversations on what education and media should look like.

So, the Lantern video diary was intended to perform a number of functions. Many were pragmatically connected to the idea of comfort. In the first few weeks, despite the fact that I wore staff uniform and joined in with exercises, I was still markedly different from students and staff alike. My presence was ultimately observational, in that it was helping neither staff nor students achieve their goals. Steve had mentioned that one of the reasons why Lantern had worked for him was that it felt like home. Staff had given him the impression that they were interested in him, not the wage, and he had felt welcome to return after graduation. This seemed a significant point, given the concerns raised by youth professionals about the longevity of Lantern's positive effects. It was important that Lantern felt like a place that Steve could return to after graduation.

I was therefore concerned that my observational presence might make Lantern feel like a place where the young people were being tested. The fact was that this was exactly what was happening; each week presented a series of physical activities that were mentally challenging. The infamous 'rat run', for example, was a split-level $10\,m \times 2\,m$ enclosed metal cage through which students had to crawl, in the dark, in fire kit, to simulate a house rescue. Not for the claustrophobic. Generally, though, these sorts of exercises were seen as fun and helpful in boosting self-confidence. In the midst of this, I was the boring bloke from the university who made them talk about things they found irrelevant. I was worried that the feelings of frustration this created might spill over into the other activities organized by the team.

The main initial benefit of the video diary project was that it gave me a natural reason for being there, and a natural reason to ask the young people about their media habits. Introducing the project, I explained that the idea was to make a video that they would be able to show other people as proof of their achievements. They would also become peer educators for the students that would follow. I explained that what we would do was film activities each week, and then decide how the footage should be edited together to say what the students wanted to say about themselves and the course. Discussing the project, the young people were able to draw on a number of experiences; some had used camcorders with their families. As luck would have it, the UK's seventh series of *Big Brother* was about to commence. The students keenly anticipated this, and we were able to draw on what they liked or did not like about reality television to begin to map out how they might like the video to look.

The first filming session centred on students preparing and using fire hoses in teams of three. We agreed that it would be good to have young people explaining the exercise, with the teams in action in the background. Gill, John and Jen were chosen to narrate the scene. We came up with three sentences to be delivered to camera that would describe the action.

However, the students were not sure who should speak on camera; they were equally concerned about delivering all three sentences flawlessly. It was John who solved the problem: Each would deliver one sentence, height arranged on shot so that the exercise was clearly visible over the shoulder of the shortest person. We got it in one take. Afterwards I explained that we would need a number of general cutaway shots of staff and students in action and at rest for editing purposes. I suggested that Gill, John and Jen might like to take some time gathering these sorts of shots with the camera. We did this for the next half an hour, chatting about how the camera worked, and about the documentary form. In this, I stressed that the job at hand was not to present Lantern as it occurred naturally, but to organize footage in a way that said something about themselves and their experiences. As the exercise ended John, who had not spoken to me before, asked if I needed a hand with the equipment.

Much as I would like to end on this touching little *Goodbye Mr Chips* vignette, I cannot really do this in good conscience. Logistically, it is going to be very difficult to include all staff and students in the editing process. I am also concerned that, given the general public misapprehension that the discipline of media studies is production based, they are going to expect a broadcast quality documentary as a product. The project and the editing confront me with some stark choices in the question of 'whose side am I on?'. The truth is, I'm Lantern's side; both the staff who run the course, and the young people who take part. I have to be for the sake of the project; why would they talk to somebody they do not like? But I like them, staff and students. On an outward-bound trip, one of the students gave me a ham sandwich because I'd forgotten my lunch. What's not to like? So, we arrive back at the question of I. Does this mean that the final project will be nothing more than a flattering portrait of people I like, where the data says only things that I want it to say? That I am going to replace negative images of children with positive opposites, neither of which pays much attention to what real young people think and do in real situations?

I would argue that this is a simplification. The purpose of detailing stories about ham sandwiches is not to curry personal empathy, or to replace scholarly commentary with user-friendly trivia, but to point to the fact that research dilemmas are always experienced personally – just as Ball-Rokeach's research into media violence (2001), using 'proper' methods of experiments and surveys, was beset by threats and risk. Equally, the tactics I have adopted are not haphazardly selected, but grow from the intersection of data, or in this case lack of data, political and theoretical issues in the social positioning of young people, and the role media play. If youth are the hub of the ASB issue, it is agreed that it is less clear whether they should be viewed as victim or villain. Hearing what they have to say can help clarify the picture. The wider availability of production opportunities, the apparent irrelevance of mainstream media in influencing the young people's views on fire related disorder and the move toward creative research techniques that recognize the 'everyday-ness' of media production, make the video diary exercise a logical option. It will be messy. It might not work. But it will relate the broad issue of media and cultural power (Why am I there as an academic? Why are the students there, as people defined in specific ways by education and society? How come we have access to this technology? Can the technology help the programme and the young people frame themselves in socially productive ways?) to the question of how people relate to themselves and each other in a particular place and time. And it is in these sorts of situations that we can speak with confidence about what communication does.

Have I, however, unravelled the idea of 'audience' to the point where it no longer exists? Considering the fire and drinking research I am doing, isn't the real question what it is like to be a drinker or a young person in Liverpool in 2005–6? Of course the answer is 'yes'. So in a sense, these projects are really about how people emerge as actors in cultural settings, sometimes using media resources, sometimes feeling used by them, and often responding to other things in the environment. So what happens not just to 'audience', but to media studies?

What happens is, as I suggested in Chapter 2, we relocate both into the wider field of communication. We cannot dismiss 'audience' for two reasons. First, as scholars such as Butsch (2003) and Livingstone (2004) argue, audience has ever been a mutable concept. Second, the idea of audience remains of supreme importance to public institutions; in my work, health authorities and the fire service are anxious to know how their messages are received by the public.

The shift to communication also makes sense in that recent work by scholars such as Kitzinger (2004) and Philo and Berry (2004) position audience research as a tool to generate rather than measure or analyse discourse on matters of public concern (building on the need to recognize that the researcher is *there*). The point is to use media and reception as a foundation for exploring how different ways of framing and communicating social issues influence the way we feel and what we do about them. In the view of Roxanne Parrot (2004), this overcomes the behaviourist dilemma; although in the final instance what matters is how people act toward themselves and others, it is near impossible to establish persuasive causal relations between the messages audiences receive and the things that they do. For Parrot, this question is not the domain of a communication discipline grounded on the a priori assumption that some aspects of human behaviour are determined by the way we understand our place in the world. Phrasing things in another way, Parrot argues that communication is itself a form of behaviour;

looking at how the framing of issues influences how we discuss them is a form of effect.

These ideas combine with my earlier discomfort with macroexplanations of media power to indicate empirical projects that engage with discrete institutional issues. In the case of my alcohol research, the issue of how intertextual representations of drinking fuel UK binge culture is too big and complicated an issue. However, it is possible to ask how the sense that young drinkers in Liverpool make of their actions, and media representations of the alcohol problem, can be used to inform local initiatives that try to build awareness campaigns premised on the things that the target audience cares about. In this, those responsible for creating awareness messages are not conceived as automatons working in one big media machine, hostile to any form of external critique. Quite the reverse; in my experience, people involved in public health and safety campaigns are consciously caught in the dilemma of delivering strategies that work in a field where no-one really knows what *does* work and why. Consequently, public institutions are often open to new ways of conceiving communication. In my view, what this means is that if we place audience studies in communication, we see that there are many opportunities to engage with matters of public policy. Unravelling audiences makes them more relevant than ever.

# References

Abercrombie, N. and Longhurst, B. (1998) *Audiences*. London: Sage.

Ahmed, M. (2004) Pressure on police to deal with youth offending weakens preventive work. *Community Care*, 1546: 16.

Akass, K. and McCabe, J. (2004) Carried away in Manhattan. In K. Akass and J. McCabe (eds), *Reading Sex and the City*. London: I. B. Taurus. pp. 234–6.

Allor, M. (1988) Relocating the site of the audience. *Critical Studies in Mass Communication*, 5: 139–51.

Althusser, L. (1972) Ideology and iédeological state apparatuses. In L. Althusser (ed.), *Lenin, Philosophy and Other Essays*. London: New Left Books. pp. 119–73.

Alvisi, A, Narduzzo, A. and Zamarian, M. (2003) Playstation and the power of unexpected consequences. *Information, Communication and Society*, 6: 608–27.

Anderson, B. (1995) *Imagined Communities*. London: Verso.

Anderson, C. and Murphy, C. (2003) Violent video games and aggressive behavior in young women. *Aggressive Behavior*, 29: 423–9.

Anderson, J. A. and Baym, G. (2004) Philosophies and philosophic issues in communication, 1995–2004. *Journal of Communication*, 54: 589–615.

Andrejevic, M. (2002) The kinder, gentler gaze of *Big Brother*: reality TV in the era of digital capitalism. *New Media and Society*, 4: 251–70.

Ang, I. (1985) *Watching Dallas*. London: Routledge.

Angus, I. (2005) Media, expression and new politics: eight theses. www.inaangus.ca/media.htm. Accessed 15 February 2006.

Apel, K. O. (1977) The a priori of communication and the foundation of the humanities. In F. Dallmayr and T. McCarthy (eds), *Understanding and Social Inquiry*. Notre Dame, IN: University of Notre Dame Press. pp. 292–315.

Austin, T. (1999) Desperate to see it: straight men watching *Basic Instinct*. In M. Stokes and R. Maltby (eds), *Identifying Hollywood Audiences*. London: BFI. pp. 147–61.

Austin, T. (2007, forthcoming) *Watching the World: Screen Documentary and Audiences*. Manchester: Manchester University Press.

Babcock, W. and Whitehouse, V. (2005) Celebrity as postmodern phenomenon, ethical crisis for democracy and media nightmare. *Journal of Mass Media Ethics*, 20: 176–91.

Bacon-Smith, C. (1992) *Enterprising Women: Television Fandom and the Creation of Popular Myth*. Philadelphia: University of Pennsylvania Press.

Ball-Rokeach, S. (2001) The politics of studying media violence: reflections 30 years after the violence commission. *Mass Communication and Society*, 4: 3–18.

Banks, S. and Banks, A. (2000) Reading 'The Critical Life': autoethnography as pedagogy. *Communication Education*, 49: 233–8.

Banning, S. (2001) Do you see what I see? Third-person effects on public communication through self-esteem, social stigma and product use. *Mass Communication
and Society*, 4: 127–47.

Barker, M. (1997) Taking the extreme case: understanding a fascist fan of *Judge
Dredd*. In D. Cartmell, H. Kaye, I. Hunter and I. Whelehan (eds), *Trash
Aesthetics*. London: Pluto. pp. 14–30.

Barker, M. (2001) The problem of being a 'trendy travesty'. In M. Barker and
J. Petley (eds), *Ill Effects: The Media Violence Debate*. London: Routledge.
pp. 202–24.

Barker, M. (2003) Assessing the quality in qualitative research. *European Journal of
Communication*, 18: 315–35.

Barker, M. (2005a) '*The Lord of the Rings* international audience project: some key
findings', paper presented to the MECCSA/AMPE Joint Annual Conference,
University of Lincoln, 6 January.

Barker, M. (2005b) Loving and hating *Straw Dogs*: the meanings of audience
responses to a controversial film. *Particip@tions*, 2. www.participations.org/
volume%202/2_02_barker.htm

Barker, M. and Brooks, K. (1999) *Knowing Audiences: Judge Dredd, his Fans,
Friends and Foes*. Luton: University of Luton Press.

Barnhurst, K. (2000) Political engagement and the audience for news: lessons from
Spain. *Journalism and Communication Monographs*, 2: 5–60.

Barthes, R. (1975) *The Pleasure of the Text*. New York: Hill and Wang.

Bartholow, B. and Anderson, C. (2002) Effects of violent video games on aggressive
behavior: potential sex differences. *Journal of Experimental Social Psychology*,
38: 283–90.

Biltereyst, D. (2004) Media audiences and the game of controversy: on reality TV,
moral panic and controversial media stories. *Jounal of Media Practice*, 5: 7–24.

Bird, S. E. (1992) Travels in nowhere land: ethnography and the 'impossible
audience'. *Critical Studies in Mass Communication*, 9: 250–60.

Bird, S. E. (2003) News we can use: an audience perspective on the tabloidisation of
news in the United States. In V. Nightingale and K. Ross (eds), *Critical Readings:
Audiences and Media*. Maidenhead: OU Press. pp 65–86.

Bishop, P. (2000) Caught in the cross-fire: Tibet, media and promotional culture.
*Media, Culture and Society*, 22: 645–64.

Bjarkman, K. (2004) To have and to hold: the video collector's relationship with an
ethereal medium. *Television and New Media*, 5: 217–46.

Boden, S. (2006) Dedicated followers of fashion? The influence of popular culture
on children's social identities. *Media, Culture and Society*, 28: 289–98.

Bogaert, A. (2001) Personality, individual differences and preferences for the sexual
media. *Archives of Sexual Behavior*, 30: 29–53.

Bourdon, J. (2000) Live television is still alive: on television as an unfulfilled promise.
*Media, Culture and Society*, 22: 531–56.

Boyd, R. (1999) Compromising positions: or the unhappy transformations of a
'transformative intellectual'. *Communication Theory*, 9: 377–401.

Boyle, K. (2005) *Media and Violence*. London: Sage.

Bragg, S. (2002) Wrestling in woolly gloves: not just being critically media literate.
*Journal of Film and Popular Television*, 30: 41–52.

Brewer, J. (2000) *Ethnography*. Bucks: OU Press.

Brooker, W. (2002). *Using the Force: Creativity, Community, and* Star Wars *fans*.
New York, NY: Continuum.

Brooker, W. and Jermyn, D. (2002) *The Audience Studies Reader*. London: Routledge.

Brown, W., Basil, M. and Bocarnea, M. (2003) Social influence of an international celebrity: responses to the death of Princess Diana. *Journal of Communication*, 53: 587–605.

Browne, K. and Hamilton-Giachritsis, C. (2005) The influence of violent media on children and adolescents: a public health approach. *The Lancet*, 365: 702–10.

Bryant, J. and Miron, D. (2004) Theory and research in mass communication. *Journal of Communication*, 54: 662–704.

Bucholtz, M. (1999) You da man: narrating the racial other in the production of white masculinity. *Journal of Sociolinguistics*, 3: 443–60.

Buckingham, D. and Bragg, S. (2004) *Young People, Sex and the Media: The Facts of Life?* London: Palgrave.

Buckingham, D. and Sefton-Green, J. (2003) Gotta catch 'em all: structure, agency and pedagogy in children's media. *Media, Culture and Society*, 25: 379–99.

Burnett, R. and Appleton, C. (2004) Joined up services to tackle youth crime. *British Journal of Criminology*, 44: 34–54.

Burrows, J. (2004) Penny pleasures ii: indecency, anarchy and junk films in London's 'nickelodeons', 1906–1914. *Film History*, 16: 172–97.

Bury, R. (2003) Stories for boys girls: female fans read the *X-Files*. *Popular Communication*, 4: 217–42.

Butsch, R. (2003) Popular communication audiences: a historical research agenda. *Popular Communication*, 2: 15–21.

Calavita, M. (2003) Within the context of many contests: family, news media engagement, and the ecology of individual political engagement among generation Xers. *The Communication Review*, 6: 23–43.

Calhoun, L. (2005) Will the real Slim Shady please stand up? *Howard Journal of Communication*, 16: 267–94.

Camauer, L. (2003) Ethnic minorities and their media in Sweden. *NORDICOM Review*, 24: 108–118.

Cameron, D. (1996) Language: the accents of politics. *Critical Quarterly*, 38: 93–7.

Campbell, M. (2004) 'Go white girl!' Hip hop booty dancing and the white female body. *Continuum: Journal of Media and Cultural Studies*, 18: 597–608.

Capella, J. (2002) Cynicism and social trust in the new media environment. *Journal of Communication*, 52: 229–41.

Carey, J. (1989) *Communication as Culture*. Boston: Unwin Hyman.

Carey, J. and Kreiling, A. (1974) Popular culture and uses and gratifications: notes toward an accommodation. In J.G. Blumler and E. Katz (eds) *The Uses of Mass Communications: Current Perspectives on Gratifications Research*. Beverly Hills, CA: Sage. pp. 225–48.

Caronia, L. (2005) Mobile culture: an ethnography of cellular phone uses in teenagers' everyday life. *Convergence*, 11: 96–103.

Carragee, K. and Roefs, W. (2004) The neglect of power in recent framing research. *Journal of Communication*, 54: 214–33.

Carter, C. and Weaver, K. (2003) *Violence and the Media*. Buckingham: OU Press.

Casey, M., Allen, M., Emmers-Sommer, T. et al. (2003) When a celebrity contracts a disease: the example of Earvin 'Magic' Johnson's announcement that he was HIV positive. *Journal of Health Communication*, 8: 249–65.

Chada, K. and Kavoori, A. (2000) Media imperialism revisited: some findings from the Asian case study. *Media, Culture and Society*, 22: 415–32.

Chaffee, S. (1975) The diffusion of political information. In S. Chaffee (ed.), *Political Communication: Issues and Strategies for Research*. London: Sage. pp. 85–128.

Chaffee, S. (2001) Studying the new communication of politics. *Political Communication*, 18: 237–44.

Cherry, B. (2001) Refusing to refuse to look: female viewers of the horror film. In M. Jancovich (ed.), *The Horror Film Reader*. London: Routledge. pp. 169–78.

Chin, B, and Gray, J. (2001) One ring to rule them all: pre-viewers and pre-texts of the *Lord of the Rings*. *Intensities: Journal of Cult Media*, 2. davidlavery.net/Intensities/Intensities_2.htm

Chung, G. and Grimes, S. (2005) Data mining the kids: surveillance and market research strategies in children's online games. *Canadian Journal of Communication*, 30: 527–48.

Ciclitira, K. (2004) Pornography, women and feminism: between pleasure and politics [electronic version]. *Sexualities*, 7: 281–302.

Clifford, R. (2005) Engaging the audience: the social imaginary of the telenovella. *Television and New Media*, 6: 360–69.

Consalvo, M. (2003) *Zelda 64* and video game fans: a walkthrough of games, intertextuality and narrative. *Television and New Media*, 4: 321–44.

Converse, P. (1975) The nature of belief systems in mass publics. In S.Welch and J. Comer (eds), *Public Opinion*. Palo Alto, CA: Mayfield Press. pp. 92–106.

Couldry, N. (2000) *The Place of Media Power: Pilgrims and Witnesses of the Media Age*. London: Routledge.

Couldry, N. (2002) Playing for celebrity: *Big Brother* as ritual event. *Television and New Media*, 3: 283–93.

Couldry, N. (2003) *Media Rituals: A Critical Approach*. London: Routledge.

Couldry, N. (2004) Theorising media as practice. *Social Semiotics*, 14: 115–32.

Curran, J. (2002) *Media and Power*. London: Routledge.

Dahlgren, P. (2005) The internet, public spheres and political communication: dispersion and deliberation. *Political Communication*, 22: 147–62.

Davison, W. P. (1983) The third person effect in communication. *Public Opinion Quarterly*, 47: 1–15.

Denzin, N. and Lincoln, Y. (1994) Introduction: entering the field of qualitative research. In N. Denzin and Y. Lincoln (eds), *Handbook of Qualitative Research*. London: Sage. pp. 1–18.

DeSantis, A. (2002) Smoke screen: an ethnographic study of a cigar shop's collective rationalization. *Health Communication*, 14: 167–98.

Durham, M. (2004) Constructing the 'new ethnicities': media, sexuality, and diaspora identity in the lives of South Asian immigrant girls. *Critical Studies in Media Communication*, 2: 140–61.

Dyer, R. (1997) *White*. London: Routledge.

Eatwell, R. (2002) The rebirth of right-wing charisma? The cases of Jean-Marie Le Pen and Vladimir Zhirinovsky. *Totalitarian Movements and Political Religions*, 3: 1–23.

Eck, B. (2001) Nudity and framing: classifying art, pornography, information and ambiguity. *Sociological Forum*, 16: 603–32.

Ekstrom, M. (2002) Epistemologies of TV journalism. *Journalism*, 3: 259–82.

Eliasoph, N. (2004) Can we theorize the press without theorizing the public? *Political Communication*, 21: 297–303.

Ellis, J. (1999) Television as working through. In J. Gripsrud (ed.), *Television and Common Knowledge*. London: BFI. pp. 55–70.

Ericson, C. (2003) Football, foundry communities and the Swedish model. *Soccer and Society*, 4: 20–40.

Evans-DeCicco, J. and Cowan, G. (2001) Attitudes toward pornography and the characteristics attributed to pornography actors. *Sex Roles*, 44: 351–61.

Fairclough, K. (2004) Women's work? *Wife Swap* and the reality problem. *Feminist Media Studies*, 4: 344–47.

Farrad, G. (2002) Long distance love: growing up a Liverpool Football Club fan. *Journal of Sport and Social Issues*, 26: 6–24.

Fernback, J. (2003) Legends on the net: an examination of computer-mediated communication as a locus of oral culture. *New Media and Society*, 5: 29–45.

Ferris, K. O. (2003) Seeing and being seen: the moral order of celebrity. *Journal of Contemporary Ethnography*, 33: 236–64.

Festinger, L. (1963) The theory of cognitive dissonance. In W. Schramm (ed.), *The Science of Human Communication*. New York: Basic Books. pp. 17–27.

Fieschi, C. and Heywood, P. (2004) Trust, cynicism and populist anti-politics. *Journal of Political Ideologies*, 9: 289–309.

Fiske, J. (1982) *Introduction to Media Studies*. London: Routledge.

Fiske, J. (1987) *Television Culture*. London: Routledge.

Fitzpatrick, S. and Jones, A. (2005) Pursuing social justice or social cohesion? Coercion in street homelessness policies in England. *Journal of Social Policy*, 34: 389–406.

Flint, J. (2004) The responsible tenant: housing governance and the politics of behaviour. *Housing Studies*, 19: 893–909.

Fraser, B. and Brown, J. (2002) Media celebrities and social influence: identification with Elvis Presley. *Mass Communication and Society*, 5: 183–206.

Freeland, C. (2002) *But is it Art?* Oxford: Oxford University Press.

Fung, A. Y. H. (2002) Identity politics, resistance and new media technologies: a Foucauldian approach to the study of the hknet. *New Media and Society*, 4 (2): 185–204.

Gabriel, J. (1996) What do you do when minority means you? *Falling Down* and the construction of whiteness. *Screen*, 37: 129–51.

Gauntlett, D. (1996) *Video Critical*. Luton: John Libbey.

Gauntlett, D. (1998) Ten things wrong with the effects tradition. In R. Dickinson, R. Harindranath and O. Linne (eds), *Approaches to Audiences*. London: Arnold. pp. 120–30.

Gauntlett, D. (2002) *Media, Gender and Identity: An Introduction*. London: Routledge.

Gauntlett, D. and Hill, A. (1999) *TV Living*. London: BFI.

Gauntlett, D. and Holzwarth, P. (2006) Creative and visual methods for exploring identities. *Visual Studies*, 21: 82–91.

Geertz, C. (1973) *The Interpretation of Cultures*. New York: Basic Books.

Gerbner, G. (1998) Cultivation analysis: an overview. *Mass Communication and Society*, 1: 175–94.

Gerbner, G., Gross, L., Eleey, M. et al. (1978) Cultural indicators: violence profile number 9. *Journal of Communication*, 28: 176–207.

Giddens, A. (1971) *Capitalism and Modern Social Theory*. Cambridge: Cambridge University Press.

Giles, D. (2002) Parasocial interaction: a review of the literature and a model for future research. *Mediapsychology*, 4: 279–305.

Gillespie, M. (2002) *After September 11: TV News and Transnational Audiences*. afterseptember11.tv/download/11%20September%20Research.pdf

Gillespie, M. (2003) Transnational communications and diaspora communities. In V. Nightingale and K. Ross (eds), *Critical Readings: Media And Audiences*. Maidenhead: OU Press. pp. 145–62.

Gitlin, T. (1978) Sociology: the dominant paradigm. *Theory and Society*, 6: 205–253.

Giulianotti, R. (2002) Supporters, followers, fans and flaneurs: a taxonomy of spectator identities in football. *Journal of Sport and Social Issues*, 26: 25–46.

Giulianotti, R. (2005) Sports spectators and the social consequences of commodification. *Journal of Sport and Social Issues*, 29: 386–410.

Glascock, J. (2005) Degrading content and character sex: accounting for men and women's differential reactions to pornography. *Communication Reports*, 18: 43–53.

Glaser, B. and Strauss, A. (1967) *The Discovery of Grounded Theory*. Chicago: Aldine.

Glover, J. (2005) Killed over the price of a ciggie. *Liverpool Echo*, 23 December icliverpool.icnetwork.co.uk/0100news/0100regionalnews/tm_method=full%26 objectid=16516789%26siteid=50061-name_page.html. Downloaded 23 January 2006.

Golde, J., Strassberg, D., Turner, C. and Lowe, K. (2000) Attitudinal effects of degrading themes and sexual explicitness in video materials. *Sexual Abuse: A Journal of Research and Treatment*, 12: 223–32.

Goldson, B. (2000) Children in need or young offenders? Hardening ideology, organizational change and new challenges of social work with children in trouble. *Child and Family Social Work*, 5: 255–65.

Graber, D. (2005) Political communication faces the 21st century. *Journal of Communication*, 55: 479–507.

Graham-Bertolini, A. (2004) Joe Millionaire as fairy tale: a feminist critique. *Feminist Media Studies*, 4: 341–44.

Grana, J. L., Cruzado, J. A., Andreu, J. M., Munoz-Rivas, M. J., Pena, M. E. and Brain, P. F. (2004) Effects of viewing videos of bullfights on Spanish children. *Aggressive Behavior*, 30: 16–28.

Gray, A. (1992) *Video Playtime*. London: Routledge.

Gray, A. (2003) *Research Practice for Cultural Studies*. London: Sage.

Gray, J. (2003) New audiences, new textualities: anti-fans and non-fans. *International Journal of Cultural Studies*, 6: 64–81.

Gray, J. (2005) Antifandom and the moral text: television without pity and textual dislike. *American Behavioral Scientist*, 48: 840–58.

Green, S. Jenkins, C. and Jenkins, H. (1998) Normal female interest in men bonking: selections from *The Terra Nostra Underground* and *Strange Bedfellows*. In C. Harris and A. Alexander (eds), Theorizing Fandom: Fans, Subculture and Identity. Cresskill, NJ: Hampton Press. pp. 9–38.

Greene, K. and Krcmar, M. (2005) Predicting exposure to and liking of media violence: a uses and gratifications approach. *Communication Studies*, 56: 71–93.

Griffiths, M. (2000) Excessive internet use: implications for sexual behaviour. *Cyberpsychology and Behavior*, 3: 537–52.

Grimes, T., Bergen, L., Nichols, K. and Vernberg, E. (2004) Is psychopathology the key to understanding why some children become aggressive when they are exposed to violent television programming? *Human Communication Research*, 30: 153–81.

Gross, L. (1989) Out of the mainstream: sexual minorities and the mass media. In E. Seiter, H. Borcher, G. Kreutzner and E. Warth (eds) Remote Control: Television, Audiences and Cultural Power. London: Routledge. pp. 130–49.

Gunther, A. C. and Storey, J. D. (2003) The influence of presumed influence. *Journal of Communication*, 53: 199–215.

Hagan, I. (1997) Communicating to an ideal audiences: news and the notion of the 'informed citizen'. *Political Communication*, 14: 405–19.

Hall, S. (1980) Encoding/decoding. In S. Hall, D. Hobson, A. Lowe and P. Willis (eds), *Culture, Media, Language*. London: Hutchinson. pp. 128–38.

Hall, S. (1982)The rediscovery of 'ideology': the return of the repressed in media studies. In M. Gurevitch, T. Bennett, J. Curran, and J. Woollacott (eds), *Culture, Society, and the Media*. New York: Methuen. pp. 56–90.

Hall, S. (1996) New Ethnicities. In D. Morley and K.-H. Chen *Stuart Hall – Critical Dialogues in Cultural Studies*. London and New York: Routledge. pp. 441–49.

Hall, A. (2003) Reading realism: audiences' evaluations of the reality of media texts. *Journal of Communication*, 53: 624–41.

Hall, S., Crichter, C., Jefferson, T., Clarke, J. and Roberts, B. (1978) *Policing the Crisis*. New York: Holmes and Meier.

Hallett, T. and Fine, G. (2000) Ethnography 1900: learning from the filed research of an old century. *Journal of Contemporary Ethnography*, 5: 593–617.

Hardy, S. (2004) Reading pornography. *Sex Education*, 4: 3–18.

Harindranath, R. (2005) Ethnicity and cultural difference: some thematic and political issues on global audience research. *Particip@tions*, 2. www.participations.org/volume%202/issue%202/2_02_harindranath.htm

Harrington, C. L. and Bielby, D. (1995) *Soap Fans: Pursuing Pleasure and Meaning in Everyday Life*. Philadelphia: Temple University Press.

Harris, C. (1998) A sociology of television fandom. In C. Harris (ed.), *Theorizing Fandom: Fans, Subculture and Identity*. Cresskill, NJ: Hampton Press. pp. 41–53.

Healey, T. and Ross, K. (2002) Growing old invisibly: older viewers talk television. *Media, Culture and Society*, 25: 105–20.

Hebdige, D. (1979) *Subculture: The Meaning of Style*. London: Methuen.

Henning, B. and Vorderer, P. (2001) Psychological escapism: predicting the amount of television viewing by need for cognition. *Journal of Communication*, 51: 100–20.

Hermes, J. (1995) *Reading Women's Magazines*. Cambridge: Polity.

Hermes, J. (2005) Burnt orange: television, football and the representation of ethnicity. *Television and New Media*, 6: 49–69.

Hess, M. (2005) Hip hop realness and the white performer. *Critical Studies in Media Communication*, 5: 372–89.

Hill, A. (1997) *Shocking Entertainment: Viewer Response to Violence Movies*. Luton: University of Luton Press.

Hill, A. (2000) The language of complaint. *Media, Culture and Society*, 22: 233–36.

Hill, A. (2002) *Big Brother*: the real audience. *Television and New Media*, 3: 323–40.

Hill, A. (2005) *Reality TV: Audiences and Popular Factual Television*. London: Routledge.

Hills, M. (2002) *Fan Cultures*. London: Routledge.

Hills, M. (2004) Strategies, tactics and the question of un lieu propre: what/where is media theory. *Social Semiotics*, 14: 133–49.

Hills, M. (2005) Patterns of surprise: the 'aleatory object' in psychoanalytic ethnography and cyclical fandom. *American Behavioral Scientist*, 48: 801–21.

Hills, M. and Jenkins, H. (2001) Interview with Henry Jenkins. *Intensities: Journal of Cult Media*, 2.www.cult-media.com/issue2/CMRjenk.htm. Accessed 15 February 2006.

Holbert, R., Pillion, O., Tschida, D. et al. (2003) The *West Wing* as endorsement of the US presidency: expanding the bounds of priming in political communication. *Journal of Communication*, 53: 427–43.

Holmes, S. (2004a) But this time you choose! Approaching the interactive audience in reality TV. *International Journal of Cultural Studies*, 7: 213–31.

Holmes, S. (2004b) Reality goes pop!: reality, popular music and narratives of stardom in *Pop Idol*. *Television and New Media*, 5: 147–72.

Hovland, C. (1959) Reconciling conflicting results derived from experimental and survey studies of attitude change. *American Psychologist*, 14: 8–17.

Jackson, N. A. and Lilleker, D. G. (2004) Just public relations or an attempt at interaction? British MPs in the press, on the web and 'in your face'. *European Journal of Communication*, 19: 507–33.

Jacobs, K. (2004) Pornography in small places and other spaces. *Cultural Studies*, 18: 67–83.

Jago, B. (2002) Chronicling an academic depression. *Journal of Contemporary Ethnography*, 31: 729–57.

Jancovich, M. (2002) Cult fictions: cult movies, subcultural capital and the production of cultural distinctions. *Cultural Studies*, 16: 306–22.

Jarman, N. (2005) Teenage kicks: young women and their involvement in violence and disorderly behaviour. *Child Care in Practice,* 11: 341–56.

Jenkins, H. (1992) *Textual Poaching*. London: Routledge.

Jenkins, H. (1999) Congressional testimony on media violence. *MIT Communications Forum*. Web.mit.edu/comm_forum/papers/jenkins-ct.html. Accessed 10 January 2006.

Jenkins, H. (2002) Interactive audiences? In D. Harries (ed.), *The New Media Book*. London: BFI. pp. 157–70.

Jermyn, D. (2004) In love with Sarah Jessica Parker: celebrating female fandom and friendship in *Sex and the City*. In K. Akass and J. McCabe (eds), *Reading Sex and the City*. London: I. B. Taurus. pp. 201–18.

Jewkes, Y. (2002a) *Captive Audiences: Media, Masculinity and Power in Prisons*. London: Willan.

Jewkes, Y. (2002b) The use of media in constructing identities in the masculine environment of men's prisons. *European Journal of Communication*, 17: 205–25.

Jhally, S. (1994) Intersections of discourse: MTV, sexual politics and *Dreamworlds*. In J. Cruz and J. Lewis (eds), *Viewing, Reading, Listening*. CA: Westview Press. pp. 151–68.

Jhally, S. and Lewis, J. (1993) *Enlightened Racism*. London: Routledge.

Johnson, B. (2004). *Apologetic in Liverpool. Boris Johnson MP*. www.boris-johnson.com/archives/2004/10/apologetic_in_l.html

Jones, J. M. (2003) Show your real face. *New Media and Society*, 5: 400–21.

Juluri, V. (2002) Music television and the invention of youth culture in India. *Television and New Media*, 3: 367–86.

Katz, E. (2001) Lazarsfeld's map of media effects. *International Journal of Public Opinion Research*, 13: 270–79.

Katz, E. and Liebes, T. (1990) *The Export of Meaning*. New York: Oxford University Press.

Keightley, K. (2003) Low television, high fidelity: taste and the gendering of home entertainment technologies. *Journal of Broadcasting and Electronic Media*, 47: 236–59.

Kellner, P. (2004) Britain's culture of detachment. *Parliamentary Affairs*, 4: 830–43.

King, P., Sawyer, C. and Behnke, R. (1998) A case study of the Weberian leadership of Joseph Smith. *The Journal of Communication and Religion*, 21: 1–21.

Kitzinger, J. (2004) *Framing Sex Abuse*. London: Pluto Press.

Korth, B. (2002) Critical qualitative research as consciousness raising: the dialogic text of researcher/researchee interactions. *Qualitative Inquiry*, 8: 381–403.

Kuhn, T. (1974) Logic of discovery or psychology of research? In P. Schilp (ed.), *The Philosophy of Karl Popper*. La Salle, ILL: Library of Living Philosophers. pp. 798–819.

Lasswell, H. D. (1953/1975) Democracy through public opinion. In B. Berelson and M. Janowitz (eds), *Reader in Public Opinion and Communication*. Glencoe, ILL: Free Press. pp. 469–82.

Lazarsfeld, P., Berelson, B., and Gaudet, H. (1948) *The People's Choice*. New York: Columbia University Press.

Lee, C. (2004) Korean immigrants' viewing patterns of Korean satellite television and its role in their lives. *Asian Journal of Communication*, 14: 68–80.

Lemert, J. (1989) *Criticising the Media: Empirical Approaches*. Thousand Oaks: Sage.

Lemish, D. (2004) 'My kind of campfire': the Eurovision Song Contest and Israeli Gay Men. *Popular Communication*, 2: 41–63.

Lewis, J. (1997) What counts in cultural studies. *Media, Culture and Society*, 19: 83–97.

Lewis, J., Wahl-Jorgensen, K. and Inthorn, S. (2004) Images of citizens on television news: constructing a passive public. *Journalism Studies*, 5: 153–64.

Lisle, D. (2004) Gazing at Ground Zero: tourism, voyeurism and spectacle. *Journal for Cultural Research*, 8: 3–22.

Livingstone, S. (2003) Children's use of the internet: reflections on the emerging research agenda. *New Media and Society*, 5: 147–66.

Livingstone, S. (2004) The challenge of changing audiences. *European Journal of Communication*, 19: 75–86.

Livingstone, S. (2005) Mediating the public/private boundary at home: children's use of the internet for privacy and participation. *Journal of Media Practice*, 6: 41–51.

Livingstone, S., Allen, J. and Reiner, R. (2001) Audiences for crime media 1946–91: a historical approach to reception studies. *Communication Review*, 4: 165–92.

Lo, V. and Paddon, A. (2000) Third person perception and support for pornography restrictions: some methodological problems. *International Journal of Public Opinion Research*, 12: 80–89.

Luff, D. (2001) 'The downright torture of women': moral lobby women, feminists and pornography. *The Sociological Review*, 49: 78–99.

Lull, J. (1988) Critical response; the audience as nuisance. *Critical Studies in Mass Communication*, 7: 239–43.

Lull, J. (1990) *Inside Family Viewing*. London: Routledge.

Lynxwiler, G. (2000) Moral boundaries and deviant music: public attitudes toward heavy metal and rap. *Deviant Behavior*, 21: 63–85.

Machin, D. (2002) *Ethnographic Research For Media Studies*. London: Arnold.

Macias, W., Stavchansky Lewis, L. and Smith, T. (2005) Health-related message boards/chat rooms on the web: discussion content and implications for pharmaceutical sponsorships. *Journal of Health Communication*, 10: 209–23.

Madell, D. and Muncer, S. (2005) Are internet and mobile phone communication complementary activities amongst young people? A study from a rational actor perspective. *Information, Communication and Society*, 8: 64–80.

Mahan-Hays, S. E. and Aden, R. C. (2003) Kenneth Burke's 'attitude' at the crossroads of rhetorical and cultural studies: a proposal and case study illustration. *Western Journal of Communication*, 67: 32–55.

Mai, N. (2004) 'Looking for a more modern life ...' the role of Italian television in the Albanian migration to Italy. *Westminster Papers in Communication and Culture*, 1: 3–22.

Malamuth, N., Addison, T. and Koss, M. (2000) Pornography and sexual aggression: are there reliable effects and can we understand them? *Annual Review of Sex Research*, 11: 26–91.

McAra, L. and McVie, S. (2005) The usual suspects? *Criminal Justice: International Journal of Policy and Practice*, 5: 5–36.

McCombs, M. (2005) A look at agenda-setting: past, present and future. *Journalism Studies*, 6: 543–57.

McCracken, G. (2006) Ethnography at the MSI meetings. www.cultureby.com/trilogy/2006/05/_the_marketing_.html. Accessed 9 May 2006.

McDevitt, M., Kiousis, S. and Wahl-Jorgensen, K. (2003) Spiral of moderation; opinion expression in computer mediated discussions. *International Journal of Public Opinion Research*, 15: 454–70.

McDonald, D. and Kim, H. (2001) When I die I feel small: electronic game characters and the social self. *Journal of Broadcasting and Electronic Media*, 45: 241–58.

McKee, A. (2002) Fandom (*Buffy the Vampire Slayer*). In T. Miller (ed.), Television Studies. London: BFI. pp. 66–9.

McKee, A. (2004) Is *Dr Who* political? *European Journal of Cultural Studies*, 7: 201–17.

McKee, A. (2006) Censorship of sexually explicit materials in Australia: what do consumers of pornography have to say about it? *Media International Australia Incorporating Culture and Policy*, 120: 35–50.

McLeod, D., Detenber, B. and Evelans, P. (2001) Behind the third person effect: differentiating perceptual processes for self and other. *Journal of Communication*, 51: 678–95.

McQuail, D. (1998) With the benefits of hindsight: reflections on the uses and gratification paradigm. In R. Dickinson, R. Harindranath and O. Linne (eds), *Approaches to Audiences*. London: Arnold. pp. 151–65.

McVeigh, C., Hughes, K., Lushey, C. and Bellis, M. A. (2005) *Preventing Violence: From Global Perspectives to National Action*. Centre for Public Health: Liverpool John Moores University.

Mendible, M. (2004) Humiliation, subjectivity, and reality TV. *Feminist Media Studies*, 4: 335–8.

Metzger, M. (2000) When no news is good news: inferring closure for news issues. *Journalism and Mass Communication Quarterly*, 4: 760–87.

Meyer, G. (2004) Diffusion methodology: time to innovate? *Journal of Health Communication*, 9: 59–69.

Miller, D. (2002) Opinion polls and the misrepresentation of public opinion on the war with Afghanistan. *Television and New Media*, 2: 153–61.

Mitchell, K., Finkelhor, D. and Wolak, J. (2003) *Youth and Society*, 34: 330–58.

Mohammed, S. and Thombre, A. (2005) HIV/AIDS stories on the world wide web and transformation perspective. *Journal of Health Communication*, 10: 347–60.

Montgomery, M. (2001) The uses of authenticity: speaking from experience in a UK election broadcast. *The Communication Review*, 4: 447–62.

Moores, S. (2006). Media uses and everyday environmental experiences: a positive critique of phenomenological geography. *Particip@tions*, 3. www.participations.org/volume%203/issue%202%20-%20special/3_02_moores.htm

Morgan, M. (1989) Television and democracy. In I. Angus and S. Jhally (eds), *Cultural Politics in Contemporary America*. New York: Routledge. pp. 240–53.

Morgan, M. and Shanahan, J. (1996) Two decades of cultivation research: an appraisal and meta-analysis. *Communication Yearbook*, 20: 1–45.

Morley, D. (1980) *The Nationwide Audience*. London: BFI.

Morley, D. (1989). *Family Television*. London: BFI.

Morrish, L. and O'Mara, K. (2004) *Queer Eye for the Straight Guy*: confirming and confounding masculinity. *Feminist Media Studies*, 4: 350–52.

Murray, J., Liotti, M., Ingmundsen, P. et al. (2006) Children's brain activations while viewing television violence revealed by fMRI. *Media Psychology*, 8: 25–37.

Nash, M. and Lahti, M. (1999) 'almost ashamed to say I am one of those girls': *Titanic*, Leonardo DiCaprio and the paradoxes of girls' fandom. In K. Sandler and G. Studlar (eds), *Titanic*: Anatomy of a Blockbuster. New Brunswick: Rutgers University Press. pp. 64–88.

Nightingale, V. (1996) *Studying Audiences: the Shock of the Real*. London: Routledge.

Noble, G. (2002) Comfortable and relaxed: furnishing the home and nation. *Continuum: Journal of Media and Cultural Studies*, 16: 53–66.

Noelle-Neumann, E. (2001) Collections and recollections: my friend Paul Lazarsfeld. *International Journal of Public Opinion Research*, 13: 315–21.

Nowotny, H. (2003) Democratising expertise and socially robust knowledge. *Science and Public Policy*, 30: 151–56.

O'Connor, B. and Klaus, E. (2000) Pleasure and meaningful discourse: an overview of research issues. *International Journal of Cultural Studies*, 3: 369–87.

Oppenhuisen, J. and van Zoonen, L. (2006) Supporters or customers? Fandom, marketing and the political economy of Dutch football. *Soccer and Society*, 7: 62–75.

O'Sullivan, P. B. and Flanagin, A. J. (2003) Reconceptualizing 'flaming' and other problematic messages [electronic version]. *New Media and Society*, 5: 69–94.

Ozerov, M. (2002) Tony Blair: a labourite with Hollywood charisma. *International Affairs*, 48: 172–8.

Park, S. (2005) The impact of media use and cultural exposure on the mutual perception of Koreans and Japanese. *Asian Journal of Communication*, 2: 173–87.

Parrott, R. (2004) Emphasizing 'communication' in health communication. *Journal of Communication*, 54: 751–87.

Paul, B., Salwen., M. and Dupagne, M. (2000) The third person effect: a meta-analysis of the perceptual hypothesis. *Mass Communication and Society*, 3: 57–85.

Payne, L. (2003) Anti-social behaviour. *Children and Society*, 17: 321–4.

Pelias, R. J. (2000) The critical life. *Communication Education*, 49: 220–28.

Perloff, R. M. (1999) The third person effect: a critical review and synthesis. *Media Psychology*, 1: 353–78.

Peters, J. D. (1996a) Tangled legacies. *Journal of Communication*, 46: 85–7.

Peters, J. D. (1996b) The uncanniness of mass communication in interwar social thought. *Journal of Communication*, 46: 108–23.

Peters, J. D. (2001) Witnessing. *Media, Culture and Society*, 23: 707–23.

Philo, G. and Berry, M. (2004) *Bad News From Israel*. London: Pluto Press.

Pillsbury, B. and Mayer, D. (2005) Women connect!: strengthening communications to meet sexual and reproductive health challenges. *Journal of Health Communication*, 10: 361–71.

Porter, T. (2004) *Alcohol Harm Reduction Strategy: Qualitative Research to Inform Development of Communication*. London: Craig Ross Dawson.

Porto, M. (2005) Political controversies in Brazilian TV fiction. *Television and New Media*, 6: 342–59.

Postigo, H. (2003) From pong to Planet Quake: post-industrial transitions from leisure to work. *Information, Communication and Society*, 6: 593–607.

Potter, J. (2005) 'This brings back a lot of memories': a case study in the analysis of digital video production by young learners. *Education, Communication and Information*, 5: 5–23.

Potter, J. M. and Tomasello, T. K. (2003) Building upon the experimental design in media violence research: the importance of including receiver interpretations. *Journal of Communication*, 53: 315–29.

Potter, W. J. (2004) *The Eleven Myths of Media Violence*. London: Sage.

Press, A. (1991) *Women Watching Television*. Philadelphia: University of Philadelphia Press.

Quayle, E. and Taylor, M. (2003) Model of problematic internet use in people with a sexual interest in children. *Cyberpsychology and Behaviour*, 6: 93–106.

Radway, J. (1983) *Reading the Romance*. Chapel Hill, NC: University of North Carolina Press.

Ragan, S. (2000) 'The critical life': an exercise in applying inapplicable critical standards. *Communication Education*, 49: 229–32.

Rasolofondraosolo, Z. and Meinhof, U. (2003) Popular Malagasay music and the contruction of cultural identities. *AILA Review*, 16: 127–48.

Reading, A. (2005) Professing porn or obscene browsing? On proper distance in the university classroom. *Media, Culture and Society*, 27: 123–30.

Rehak, B. (2003) Mapping the bit girl: Lara Croft and new media fandom. *Information, Communication and Society*, 6: 477–96.

Reiss, S. and Wiltz, J. (2003) Why people watch reality TV. *Media Psychology*, 6: 363–78.

Richards, B. (2004) The emotional deficit in political communication. *Political Communication*, 29: 339–52.

Richards, B. (2006) 'Political journalism: challenging the bias against hope', paper presented to the Political Studies Association Annual Conference, University of Reading, 4 April.

Richardson, K. (2001) Broadcast political talk-a discourse of licensed inauthenticity. *The Communication Review*, 4: 481–9.

Riordan, J. (2003) The match of death: Kiev, 9 August 1942. Soccer and Society, 4: 87–93.

Rios, D. (2003) US Latino audiences of telenovellas. *Journal of Latinos and Education*, 2: 59–65.

Roccor, B. (2000) Heavy metal: forces of unification and fragmentation within a musical subculture. *The World of Music*, 42: 83–94.

Rockler, N. (2002) Race, whiteness, lightness and relevance: African American and European American interpretations of *Jump Start* and *The Boondocks*. *Critical Studies in Media Communication*, 4: 398–14.

Rogala, C. and Tyden, T. (2003) Does pornography influence young women's sexual behavior? *Women's Health Issues*, 13: 39–43.

Rogers, E. (2000) Reflections on news event diffusion research. *Journalism and Mass Communication Quarterly*, 3: 561–76.

Romer, D., Hall Jamieson, K. and Aday, S. (2003) Television news and the cultivation of fear of crime. *Journal of Communication*, 53: 88–104.

Ross, K. and Nightingale, V. (2003) *Media and Audiences: New Perspectives*. Maidenhead: OU Press.

Ruddock, A. (1997) It just doesn't matter: *The Simpsons* and resistive audiences. *Metro Education*, 11: 16–21.

Ruddock, A. (2001) *Understanding Audiences*. London: Sage.

Ruddock, A. (2002). Uses and gratifications research. In T. Miller (ed.), *Television Studies*. London: BFI. pp. 70–73.

Ruddock, A. (2005) Let's kick racism out of football – and the lefties too!: responses to Lee Bowyer on a West Ham website. *Journal of Sport and Social Issues*, 29: 269–85.

Ruddock, A. (2006a) Invisible centers: Boris Johnson, authenticity, cultural citizenship and a centrifugal model of media power. *Social Semiotics*; 16: 263–82.

Ruddock, A. (2006b) 'Does Boris Johnson have fans?' paper presented to the MECCSA Annual Conference, Leeds Metropolitan University, 14 January.

Ruddock, A. (2006c) *Communicating about Anti-Social Behaviour*. Liverpool City Council Anti-Social Behaviour Unit.

Russell, D. (1998) *Dangerous Relationships: Pornography, Misogyny and Rape*. London: Sage.

Ryfe, D. (2001) From media audience to media public: a study of letters written in reaction to FDR's fireside chats. *Media, Culture and Society*, 23: 767–81.

The St. Louis Court Brief (2003). Debating audience effects in public. www.participations.org/volume%201/issue%201/1_01_amici_contents.htm

Sandvoss, C. (2003) *A Game of Two Halves: Football, Television and Globalization*. London: Routledge.

Sandvoss, C. (2005a) *Fans: The Mirror of Consumption*. Cambridge: Polity Press.

Sandvoss, C. (2005b). One-dimensional fan. *American Behavioral Scientist*, 48: 822–39.

Scannell, P. (2002) *Big Brother* as a television event. *Television and New Media*, 3: 271–82.

Scheufle, D. and Moy, P. (2000) Twenty-five years of the spiral of silence: a conceptual review and empirical outlook. *International Journal of Public Opinion Research*, 12: 3–28.

Schlesinger, P., Dobash, R. E., Dobash, R. P. and Weaver, C. (1992) *Women Viewing Violence*. London: BFI.

Schneider, E., Lang, A., Shin, M. and Bradley, S. (2004) Death with a story: how story impacts emotional, motivational, and physiological responses to first-person shooter video games. *Human Communication Research*, 30: 361–75.

Schoenbach, K. (2001) Myths of media and audiences. *European Journal of Communication*, 16: 361–76.

Schroder, K., Drotner, K., Kline, S. and Murray, C. (2003) *Researching Audiences*. London: Arnold.

Scodari, C. (2003) Resistance re-examined: gender, fan practices and science fiction television. *Popular Communication*, 1: 111–30.

Seale, C. (2003) Health and media: an overview. *Sociology of Health and Illness*, 25: 513–31.

Seiter, E. (1999) *Television and New Media Audiences*. Oxford: Clarendon Press.

Seiter, E. (2004) Children reporting online: the cultural politics of the computer lab. *Television and New Media*, 5: 87–107.

Selwyn, N. (2003) Doing IT for the kids: re-examining children, computers and the information society. *Media, Culture and Society*, 25: 351–78.

Shade, L., Porter, N. and Sanchez, W. (2005) 'You can see anything on the internet, you can do anything on the internet!': young Canadians talk about the internet. *Canadian Journal of Communication*, 30: 503–26.

Shaffer, T. (2004) Performing backpacking: constructing authenticity every step of the way. *Text and Performance Quarterly*, 24: 139–60.

Sherry, J. (2001) Toward an etiology of media use motivations: the role of temperament in media use. *Communication Monographs*, 68: 274–88.

Shi, Y. (2005) Identity construction of the Chinese diaspora, ethnic media use, community formation and the possibility of social activism. *Continuum: Journal of Media and Cultural Studies*, 19: 55–72.

Shields, D. C. (2000) Symbolic convergence and special communication theories: sensing and examining dis/enchantment with the theoretical robustness of critical autoethnography. *Communication Monographs*, 67: 392–421.

Simpson, N. (2004) Coming attractions: a comparative history of the Hollywood studio system and the porn business. *Historical Journal of Film, Radio and Television*, 24: 635–52.

Sinclair, J. and Harrison, M. (2004) Globalization, nation and television in Asia: the cases of India and China. *Television and New Media*, 5: 41–54.

Singh, S. (2001) Gender and the use of the internet at home. *New Media and Society*, 3: 395–416.

Skuse, A. (2002) Vagueness, familiarity and social realism: making meaning of radio soap opera in south-east Afghanistan. *Media, Culture and Society*, 24: 409–27.

Slater, M. (2003) Alienation, aggression and sensation seeking as predictors of adolescent use of violent film, computer and website content. *Journal of Communication*. 53: 105–21.

Slater, M., Henry, K., Swaim, R. and Anderson, L. (2003) Violent media content and aggressiveness in adolescents: a downward spiral model. *Communication Research*, 6: 713–36.

Smith, C. (2002) Strengthening the voice of supporters. *Soccer and Society*, 1: 13–16.

Squires, P. and Stephen, D. (2005) Rethinking ASBOs. *Critical Social Policy*, 25: 517–28.

Stack, S., Wasserman, I. and Kern, R. (2004) Adult social bonds and use of internet pornography. *Social Science Quarterly*, 85: 75–88.

Stanyer, J. (2002). Politics and the media: a loss of political appetite? Parliamentary Affairs, 55: 377–88.

Stern, S. (2004) Expressions of identity online: prominent features and gender differences in adolescents' www home pages. *Journal of Broadcasting and Electronic Media*, 48: 218–43.

Street, J. (2002) Bob, Bono and Tony B: the popular artist as politician. *Media, Culture and Society*, 24: 433–41.

Such, E. and Walker, R. (2005) Young citizens or policy objects? Children in the 'rights and responsibilities' debate. *Journal of Social Policy*, 34: 39–57.

Taylor, J. (2005) Iraqi torture photographs and documentary realism in the press. *Journalism Studies*, 6: 39–49.

Tewkesbury, D. (2003) What do Americans really want to know? Tracking the behavior of news readers on the internet. *Journal of Communication*, 53: 694–710.

Tewkesbury, D. Moy, P. and Weis, D. (2004) Preparations for Y2K: revisiting the behavioural component of the third person effect. *Journal of Communication*, 54: 138–55.

Tolson, A. (2001) 'Being yourself': the pursuit of authentic celebrity. *Discourse Studies*, 3: 443–58.

Tsagarousianou, R. (2004) Rethinking the concept of diaspora: mobility, connectivity and communication in a globalised world. *Westminster Papers in Communication and Culture*, 1: 52–66.

Ten Have, P. (2004) *Understanding Qualitative Ethnomethodology*. London: Sage.

Thomas, J. (2004) 'A cloak of apathy': political disengagement, popular politics and the *Daily Mirror* 1940–1945. *Journalism Studies*, 5: 469–82.

Tichenor, P., Donohue, G. and Olien, C. (1970) Mass media flow and differential growth in knowledge. *Public Opinion Quarterly*, 70: 159–70.

Tuchman, G. (1978) *Making News: a Study in the Construction of Reality*. New York: Free Press.

Tudor, A. (1999) *Decoding Culture*. London: Sage.

Tufte, B. (2003) Girls in the new media environment. *Nordicom Review*, 24: 71–8.

Tulloch, J. (1999) *Performing Culture*. London: Sage.

Tulloch, J. (2000) *Watching Television Audiences*. London: Arnold.

Usborne, D. (2005) After the flood: the hard truths. *The Independent*, 15 October: 28–9.

Vandebosch, H. (2000) Research note: a captive audience? The media use of prisoners. *European Journal of Communication*, 15: 529–44.

Vettehen, P., Schaap, G. and Schlosser, S. (2004) What men and women think while watching the news. *European Journal of Communication Research*, 29: 235–51.

Vidal, M. Clemente, M. and Espinosa, P. (2003) Types of media violence and degree of acceptance in under 18s. *Aggressive Behavior*, 29: 381–92.

Vryzas, K. and Tsitouridou, M. (2002) The home computer in children's everyday life: the case of Greece. *Journal of Educational Media*, 27: 9–17.

Wahl-Jorgensen, K. (2002) The construction of the public in letters to the editor. *Journalism*, 3: 183–204.

Wahl-Jorgensen, K. (2004) Playground of the pundits or voice of the people? Comparing British and Danish opinion pages. *Journalism Studies*, 5: 51–70.

Wakefield, S. (2001) Your sister in St Scully: an electronic community of female fans of the *X-Files*. *Journal of Film and Popular Television*, 29: 130–38.

Walma van der Molen, J. (2004). Violence and suffering in television news: toward a broader conception of harmful television content for children. *Pediatrics*, 113: 1771–5.

Warren, J. (2001) The social drama of a 'rice burner'; a (re)constitution of whiteness. *Western Journal of Communication*, 65: 184–205.

Wartella, E. and Jennings, N. (2001) New members of the family: the digital revolution in the home. *Journal of Family Communication*, 1: 59–69.

Watkins, T. (2002) Cherries in the black: AFC Bournemouth's journey from bankruptcy to rude health under supporter leadership. *Soccer and Society*, 1: 57–63.

Wertham, F. (1955) *Seduction of the Innocent*. New York: Museum Press.

Wiley, S. (2004) Rethinking nationality in the context of globalization. *Communication Theory*, 14: 78–96.

Wilkin, P. (2004) Pornography and rhetorical strategies: the politics of public policy. *Media Culture and Society*, 26: 337–58.

Williams, C. (2001) Does it really matter? Young people and popular music. *Popular Music*, 20: 223–42.

Williamson, B. and Facer, K. (2004) More than just a game: the implications for schools of children's computer games communities. *Education, Communication and Information*, 4: 255–70.

Williamson, T., Ashby, D. and Webber, R. (2005) Young offenders, schools and the neighbourhood. *Journal of Community and Applied Social Psychology*, 15: 5–36.

Willis, P. (1977) *Learning to Labor: How Working Class Kids Get Working Class Jobs*. New York: Columbia University Press.

Winston, B. (1990) How are media born? In J. Downing, A. Mohammadi and A. Sreberney-Mohammadi (eds), *Questioning the Media*. New York: Sage. pp. 54–74.

Wober, J. (1998) Cultural indicators: European reflections on a research paradigm. In R. Dickinson, O. Linne and R. Harindranath (eds), *Approaches to Audiences: A Reader*. London: Arnold. pp. 61–73.

Wood, H. (2005) Texting the subject: women, television and modern self reflexivity. *The Communication Review*, 8: 115–35.

Yang, C., Wu, H., Zhu, M. and Southwell, G. (2004) Tuning in to fit in? Acculturation and media use among Chinese students in the US. *Asian Journal of Communication*, 1: 81–94.

Yep, G. and Camacho, A. (2004) The normalization of heterogendered relations in *The Bachelor*. *Feminist Media Studies*, 4: 338–41.

# Index